The History of Macon County Illinois

from Its Organization to 1876

John W. Smith, Esq.
OF THE MACON COUNTY BAR

HERITAGE BOOKS
2024

HERITAGE BOOKS
AN IMPRINT OF HERITAGE BOOKS, INC.

Books, CDs, and more—Worldwide

For our listing of thousands of titles see our website
at
www.HeritageBooks.com

A Facsimile Reprint
Published 2024 by
HERITAGE BOOKS, INC.
Publishing Division
5810 Ruatan Street
Berwyn Heights, MD 20740

Originally published
Springfield:
Rokker's Printing House
1876

— Publisher's Notice —
In reprints such as this, it is often not possible to remove blemishes from the original. We feel the contents of this book warrant its reissue despite these blemishes and hope you will agree and read it with pleasure.

International Standard Book Number
Paperbound: 978-0-7884-2228-7

CONTENTS.

CHAPTER I.—*Illinois.*—The Indians; Discovery of Illinois; Its Settlements; Its Government under the French, English, Canadians, Virginians, United States Government, Northwestern Territory, Indiana Territory, Illinois Territory, and State Organization.

CHAPTER II.—*Macon County.*—Its Organization; Original and present boundaries; Location of County Seat; Comparative advantages of County in location, public sentiment, intelligence, business, etc.; Its settlement: where made, drawbacks, fencing, speculators, markets, ague, etc., etc.

CHAPTER III.—*County Officers.*—County Commissioners' Court; County Court; Board of Supervisors; Judges of Circuit Court; Judges of County Court; State's Attorneys; Masters in Chancery; Circuit Clerks; County Clerks; County Treasurers; Sheriffs; Circuit Courts; Character of first cases; Early Juries; Attorneys; Biographical sketches of all county officers from organization of the county, etc.

CHAPTER IV.—Record of the County in the Black Hawk war, Mexican war, and Late war; Principal engagements each Company and Regiment participated in; Names of all who enlisted from Macon County, dates of enlistment, discharge, and if killed or wounded, when and where, etc.

CHAPTER V.—Incidents connected with the Early History of the County; Deep Snow; Sudden Change; Hard trials and tribulations of pioneer life; Games; Amusements; Bee Hunting, Deer Hunting, etc., etc.

CHAPTER VI.—Churches of the County: Methodist, Presbyterian, etc.; When Organized; Respective Pastors; Present condition, statistics, etc.; Sunday Schools: when organized, statistics, etc.

CHAPTER VII.—Our Manufactures, Improvements, Railroads, Agriculture, and Present Status of Each.

CHAPTER VIII.—Our Cities, Towns and Villages: Decatur, Maroa, Macon, etc.; Officers of Each.

CHAPTER IX.—Our Educational Interests; Early Schools; Ye Olde Schoolmaster; Early Methods of Teaching; School-houses and furniture; Comparison of Past and Present Educational Facilities; School Statistics, etc.

CHAPTER X.—Biographical Sketches of Early Settlers who came here prior to 1836, and their families, up to the Present time; Births, Marriages, Deaths, etc.

PREFACE

In the presentation to the public of a History of Macon county, the author feels that it is incumbent on him to make a few statements, partly by way of apology, and partly by way of explanation. He admits, in the outstart, that the work is by no means perfect, for the expectations of a remuneration for the time and labor necessary to be employed in its preparation have not been such as to justify him in devoting the time requisite for a more perfect work. In fact, the time and labor actually expended have been such as the author could illy afford to take from the business of his profession, however much pleasure it might have afforded him in other situations in life. The necessity of an accurate and authentic History of Macon County, from the organization to the present time, no one will probably deny. Fifty years hence that demand will be much more keenly felt. This being the Centennial year of the nation's history, a somewhat general interest has pervaded the public mind in reference thereto, which has awakened a kindred feeling, to some extent, regarding our more local affairs. In the Eastern States many counties, cities, towns, and even families, have their histories in book form, which are kept complete, and to which the interested turn with pride and satisfaction. Though over half a century has passed since the earliest settlements were made within the present limits of the county, scarcely a page has ever been written and embodied in book form, by which might be preserved, to some extent at least, the trials and incidents connected with Macon county pioneer life. It is already too late to make a complete and authentic record of these events. Many of the early settlers have long since passed away. Many others have moved to other localities, and thence to still others, and all trace of them is lost. The first settler, now living within the county, and whose portrait forms the frontispiece of this work, is almost on the verge of the grave. His physical and mental organizations are enfeebled, insomuch that he is unable to give an accurate account of his own family. The second settler in order, who purchased the first tract of land in the present limits of the county, has just removed to Kansas, leaving but one male representative of his family behind him. On the county records are found names of persons who participated in the early affairs of the county, of whom, after diligent inquiry, absolutely nothing can be ascertained. In the preparation of the family history of many of the pioneers, much difficulty has been experienced. Much of the information obtained in this regard is inaccurate; and especially so in reference to dates. Many large and influential families have been met with that have no written family record of the births, deaths and marriages of their individual members. Many others who were here, and took part in the scenes and prominent incidents connected with the early development of the county, can give from memory no accurate information as to dates. They may remember that the particular object of inquiry took place a few years before, or a few years after, the "deep snow," but when that was, to save their lives they cannot tell.

Yet, with the materials at command, the author has endeavored, as near as possible, to be accurate. It is hoped that all matter herein contained, from the county and city records, will be found substantially correct. The record of those who participated in the Black Hawk and Mexican wars has been taken from the muster rolls, and, of course, is reliable. The history of the participants in the late war, in which an attempt has been made to give the dates of enlistment, death, discharge, mustering out, etc., of those who enlisted from Macon county, has been taken from the Adjutant General's reports, and verified, as far as possible, by the recollection of members of the different companies in the various regiments. Of course no effort has been made to include in this work anything relating to those who are now residents, who enlisted from other counties or States, or of those who were then residents of this county, but were accredited to other counties or States. The war record has been made as full, complete and accurate as possible, so as to place in the hands of each who desires it, the personal record of all who engaged in the suppression of the rebellion who are accredited to this county. No tangible record of this kind exists, except the Adjutant General's reports, and they constitute eight large volumes, and are not suitable or designed for general circulation.

That part of this book devoted to incidents connected with the early history of the county, such as the "Deep Snow," "Sudden Change," "Hardships and Trials of Pioneer Life," etc., etc., has been prepared from the recollection of those who were witnesses and participants, and it is believed, will be found, in the main, a faithful portrayal, though by no means as exhaustive as it might be.

The author acknowledges with gratitude the assistance rendered by many of the early settlers, without which he would have failed in many important particulars. No effort has been made, whatever, at rhetorical embellishment; but on the contrary, simplicity has been sought to be attained.

It is hoped, therefore, that the public will, to some extent, appreciate and lend their assistance to this, the first feeble effort made to place in a permanent form the early history of the county, and overlook what imperfections and deficiencies may be found herein.

MEMORIAL LINES.

Hallowed mem'ries cluster round
On the consecrated ground
    Where we tread;
Of the pioneers who came,
Battling for a home and name,
    All are dead.

Savage yell, nor howling storms,
Famine's pangs, nor war's alarms,
    Drove them hence.
Here the native log they hewed;
Here with strength and grace imbued;
    Men of sense

Gathered 'round the cheerful blaze,
Telling tales of childhood's days—
    Here they sat,
With contentment and hard "pokes,"
Here they told the old-time jokes,
    This and that.

Roughened hand and sunburned face
Mingled here with rustic grace,
    In the dance:
Gentle grew the manly tone,
While the eyes that youthful shone
    Looked askance;

And the eye of beauty fell
With the tale which all must tell,

Soon or late.
Since in Eden Adam loved,
Time has always fully proved
　　'Tis man's fate.

Here, with rev'rent feet they trod,
As the pioneer of God
　　Read the Word.
Simple was the style, and rude,
With the grace of being good—
　　So they heard.

In this quiet, lonely spot,
May have stood a home forgot
　　By all on earth.
Not a trace of it to-day—
Time has spirited away
　　All its mirth.

In those quiet, silent graves,
Yonder where the river laves,
　　With its breast
Laden with the wildwood's bloom—
Peaceful in each silent tomb,
　　Low they rest.

Solemn stillness reigns supreme,
And the clouds e'en silent seem
　　In the skies.
So we stand with bending head
In the presence of the dead,
　　With sad eyes.

As the breezes glide along,
Whispering an angel's song,
　　With hearts moved,
Here all silently we stand,
Clasping with our spirit hand
　　Those we loved.

　　　　　　　　　　　M. L. CAIN.
DECATUR, *December* 19, 1876.
—2

CHAPTER I.

ILLINOIS.

THE INDIANS.

No authentic history of the successive tribes of Indians occupying the limits of the present State of Illinois has ever been written. What we have on the subject is largely founded on tradition and conjecture. Perhaps the *Algonquins* were the first that occupied that portion of the country, as far back as we have any authentic account. The *Illinois Indians*, or *Illinois Confederacy*, which was of Algonquin lineage, about the middle of the seventeenth century occupied the country southwest of Lake Michigan, extending down the Illinois river, and to the mouth of the Ohio. They were known as the " Illini," or " Illinois," and it is to them we owe the name of our State and of our principal river. The original signification of the word Illini is " real men," or "superior men," and of course is attributable to the characteristics of the Indians bearing that name. This confederation was composed of five tribes: the Tamaroas, Michagamies, Kaskaskies, Cahokies, and Peorias. Towards the close of the seventeenth century the Illinois Confederation was driven southward by a more hostile tribe from the north, and the greater portion of their territory passed into the possession of the *Pottowotamies*. This nation is said to have been the greatest, most warlike and hostile of modern times, and extended throughout the greater portion of Illinois, Michigan, Wisconsin and Indiana. The *Piankashaws* were in possession of the entire portion of the State along the Wabash. The *Winnebagoes* — " Having an ancient, fishy smell," — were occupants of the Rock River country. From tradition we learn that this tribe came from the west, and had a language entirely dissimilar to all other tribes. In 1763 the *Kickapoos* occupied the country southwest of the southern extremity of Lake Michigan. At a later day they emigrated southward, and were in the possession of the territory along the Mackinaw and the Sangamon rivers. They were the immediate predecessors of the white man on the territory of the present Macon county, and are said to have been "more civilized, industrious, energetic, and cleanly" than their neighboring tribes, but were the most implacable and inveterate haters of the white people. It was this tribe that led in the fierce charges at Tippecanoe, and was conspicuous in many of the bloody hostilities of the northwest. When they were finally overcome, they refused longer to live within the limits of the United States, and removed to Texas, then a province of Mexico. The *Sacs and Foxes* lived in the northwest part of the State, in the vicinity of Rock Island. They were formerly from the neighborhood of Quebec, and were driven west by the Iroquois, and took a conspicuous part, with the Pottowotamies, in driving out, and almost exterminating, the Illinois Confederacy. It was this tribe, led by the great chief Black Hawk, that waged the war of 1831-2, known as the Black Hawk war.*

THE DISCOVERY OF ILLINOIS.

About the middle of May, 1673, Jacques Marquette,† a Jesuit missionary, in company with M. Joliett, a Quebec merchant, left the missionary station at Mackinaw for a two-fold purpose, as expressed by Marquette: " My friend," referring to Joliett, " is an envoy of France, to discover new countries; and I am an embassador of God, to enlighten them [the Indians] with the truths of the Gospel."‡ They proceeded to Green Bay, thence up the Fox river and Lake Winnebago to the Portage, where they trans-

---

*It is related upon the authority of a participant in this war, who still resides near Clinton, Ill., that there were three men who served in the war—two in the same regiment, and another in the same brigade—that afterwards became famous in the history of the country, viz: Col. Zachary Taylor, Lieut.-Col. Jefferson Davis, and Capt. Abraham Lincoln.

† James Marquette, as given by Reynold's.

‡ Monette's "Valley of the Mississippi."

§ Called by the Indians, "Peckitanoni."

ferred their canoes, a distance of three miles, across the Wisconsin, and thence down that river to the Mississippi, which they discovered on the 17th of June. Thence they sailed down the "Father of Waters," discovering the confluence of the Missouri and Mississippi, which Marquette called "the most beautiful confluence of rivers in the world." Journeying southward, they discovered the mouth of the Ohio, which they mistook for the Wabash, and then to the site of the present city of Memphis, where they were met by the hostile Arkansas Indians, and barely escaped destruction. On the 17th of July, of the same year, they commenced ascending the river, and on reaching the mouth of the Illinois, they were informed by the Indians that it was much nearer for their return by that river, and they changed their course, and by so doing, traversed for the first time, by white men, that region which Marquette described as follows: " Nowhere did we see such grounds, meadows, woods, stags, buffaloes, deer, wildcats, bustards, swans, ducks, paroquetts, and even beavers, as on the Illinois river." M. Joliett hastened on to Canada, to make his discoveries known there and in France. This discovery and report‖ in France and Canada resulted in its settlement.

The object of Marquette's voyage seems to have been two-fold: *First*, the christianization of the Indians; and *second*, the discovery of a northwest passage to the East Indies and China. The news of Marquette's discoveries soon reached Canada, and thence spread to France, through which, and in consequence of the interest awakened by these, and the subsequent discoveries by LaSalle and Hennepin, the early French settlements were made in Illinois, and the country passed under the national control of France. M. Joliett was mainly instrumental in bringing this newly discovered country to the attention of the world.

SETTLEMENT OF ILLINOIS.

Between 1680 and 1690,—perhaps about the year 1688*—the first settlements in Illinois were made—or commenced rather. The first military occupation of the country was at Fort Creve-Coeur, in February, 1680; but there is no reliable information that a settlement was attempted there until sometime afterward.† The first

---

‖ By the capsizing of Joliett's canoe in Lachine Rapids, he lost all his papers relating to the voyage and discovery.
*Reynolds. †Annals of the West.

settlement in Illinois, or in the Mississippi valley, was commenced by the building of Fort St. Louis, on the Illinois river, in 1682;‡ but it remained in existence but a few years, so that Kaskaskia is now regarded as the first permanent settlement in Illinois.‖

Settlements were also made at Peoria and Kaskaskia, about the same time. M. Tonti was commander-in-chief of all the territory embraced between Canada and the Gulf of Mexico, and extending east and west of the Mississippi as far as his imagination or ambition pleased to allow. He spent twenty-one years in establishing forts and organizing the first settlements of Illinois. On the 14th of September, 1712, the French government granted a monopoly of all the trade and commerce of the country to M. Crozat, a wealthy merchant of Paris, who established a trading company in Illinois, and it was by this means that the early settlements became permanent and others established. From the impetus thus given, the people began to turn their attention to agricultural and commercial pursuits. The marvelous development of the State in population, improvement and wealth would be a theme upon which we could dwell with pleasure, but space, in this connection, forbids further mention.

ITS GOVERNMENT.

In 1717, M. Crozat, heretofore mentioned, surrendered his charter, and the Company of the West was organized, to "aid and assist" the banking system of John Law. Under this company a commandant and secretary were sent to Illinois, which constituted its first organized government. A branch of this company, called the Company of St. Philip's, was soon afterwards organized for the express purpose of working the rich silver mines supposed to be in Illinois, and Philip Francis Renault was appointed as its agent. In 1719 he sailed from France with two hundred miners, laborers and mechanics, which was the greatest acquisition to Illinois yet made.§ During 1719 the Company of the West was, by royal order, united with the "Royal Company of the Indies," but the charter was not surrendered until 1732, when Illinois became a part

---

‡Bancroft. ‖Bancroft.
§Renault purchased in the West Indies, en route to Illinois, five hundred negro slaves to work in his expected mines. This was the introduction of slavery in Illinois.

of the Royal Government of Quebec, with D'Artaquette¶ as its local Governor. La Buissonierre was appointed his successor, who was succeeded by Chevalier McCarty, who remained Governor until a short time previous to the cession of New France to England, in 1763, at which time M. St. Ange de Belle Rive was appointed Governor, and remained until 1765, when Capt. Sterling took possession under the treaty of two years previous. Frazier, Reed, Wilkins, Rocheflave, and perhaps others, were successive Governors. On the 4th of July, 1778, Kaskaskia was captured by Col. Clark, in pursuance of a plan matured by Patrick Henry (then Governor of Virginia), Thomas Jefferson, George Wyth and George Mason, in January previous. In a short time thereafter the county of Illinois was created by the Legislature of Virginia. It included Ohio, Indiana, Wisconsin and Michigan. John Todd* was made commander of Illinois, and in 1779 he organized courts and established a government. Timothy De Mountebrun was his successor. In 1784 Illinois was ceded to the United States by Virginia, and in 1787 Congress passed an ordinance for the government of the new territory—called the Northwest Territory—and Arthur St. Clair was appointed Governor, who continued in office until 1802. In that year Indiana Territory was formed, which included the present terrritory of Illinois, and William H. Harrison was appointed Governor. In the General Assembly of the new territory, in 1808, Jesse B. Thomas was elected as a delegate to Congress, and was instructed to obtain a division of the territory; and on the 23d of February, 1809, the Territory of Illinois was established, which extended on the north to the British possessions. A territorial government was organized, and Ninian Edwards was appointed Governor (through the solicitation of Henry Clay), Nathaniel Pope, Secretary, and Jesse B. Thomas, William Sprigg, and Alexander Stuart, Judges, by President James Madison. The Governor appointed John J. Crittenden§ Attorney General, who

---

¶This gallant and fearless man was, on May 20, 1736, dangerously wounded in an engagement between the French and Chickasaw Indians, near the source of the Tallahatchie river, in Mississippi, and was taken prisoner, and afterwards tortured and burned at the stake.

*Killed at Blue Lick, Kentucky, August 18, 1782.

§He returned to Kentucky, and afterwards became famous in Kentucky and national history.

was in a short time succeeded by his brother, William P. Crittenden. In 1818 a petition was prepared by the territorial legislature, petitioning Congress for admission into the Union. On April 18th the Enabling Act was approved, and in July following the Constitution was signed, and Shadrach Bond was elected Govenor; and on the 3d of December, 1818, Illinois was admitted into the Union.

COLUMBIA'S REVIEW.

I see the nations gathering to my hundreth jubilee,
And hear their loud hosannahs on the welkin of the free.

Outspread before me lie the trophies of a hundred years,
By wisdom won, by toil, by sacrificial blood and tears.

Behold this magic enginery, which with all curious art,
Fills full the lap of luxury in every merchant mart.

Here are my sacred battle-flags, blood-reddened, rent and torn,
Amid the death and carnage on a hundred fields upborne.

The curse of slavery gone—its stain expunged by fiery flood,
And all its wounds healed in the balsam of the nation's blood.

And shall the nation live?—born of the struggling past in pain,
Yet mightly as Olympian Jove, or Neptune of the Main.

The glad fruition of all hope, the answer of all prayer,
The pledge of equal rights, and freedom's earnest everywhere.

Unyielding, stern, she yet shall stand—all time's assault defy;
And at her feet shall Treason quail, and Fraud, despairing, die.

The nation, from its perils passed, a stronger life shall draw,
And justice, undismayed, assert the majesty of law.

The rushing of each headlight, and the rocking of each fleet,
Are but the pulse of commerce beating strong beneath my feet.

Oh! how my spirit strengthens with the marching of the years,
As, promise-crowned, the future beckons, while the century disappears!

A. J. WALLACE.

DECATUR, Ill., *Dec. 15, 1876.*

CHAPTER II.

MACON COUNTY.

ITS ORGANIZATION.

Previous to the meeting of the Legislature, in 1829, Benjamin R. Austin, Andrew W. Smith, and John Ward, had been selected to go to Vandalia, then capital of the State, and procure the passage of an act dividing the county of Shelby, of which the present county of Macon then formed a part, and forming a new county of the territory thus detached. They were successful; and at that session the following act was approved establishing the county of Macon.*

---

*NOTE.—Macon county derived its name from Hon. NATHANIEL MACON, of North Carolina, whose fame, at the time of the formation of the county, extended throughout the nation. He was born in Warren county, N. C., in 1757, and died in the same county, June 29th, 1837. He was educated at Princeton, N. J., and was there at the opening of the War of the Revolution. In 1777 he left college, and served for a short time as a private in a company of volunteers. At the expiration of his term of service, he commenced the study of law, but soon re-enlisted in the army under his brother John. He continued in the service until peace was declared. He was present at the fall of Charleston. For all his arduous services in the war, he steadily refused compensation, nor would he accept a pension after the government had provided one. Before he left the army he had been elected to the State Senate, in which he served until 1785. When the Constitution of the United States was proposed, he, like Patrick Henry, thought it "squinted too much in the direction of monarchy," and therefore opposed its adoption. He thought the general government proposed was too independent of the States. Mr. Macon was elected to the lower house of Congress in 1791, where he continued to serve until 1815, serving as Speaker from 1801 to 1806. From the lower house he was transferred to the U. S. Senate, in 1816, where he remained until 1828,

"AN ACT TO ESTABLISH A NEW COUNTY TO BE CALLED THE COUNTY OF MACON.

"SECTION 1. *Be it enacted by the people of the State of Illinois, represented in the General Assembly*, That all that tract of country lying within the following bounderies, to-wit: beginning at the southwest corner of section numbered eighteen, in township numbered fourteen north, of range numbered one east of the third principal meridian; thence due north with the said third principal meridian line to the northwest corner of township numbered twenty north, of range numbered one east; thence due east with the line between townships numbered twenty and twenty-one north, to the northeast corner of township numbered twenty north, of range numbered six east; thence due south with the line between ranges numbered six and seven east, to the southeast corner of section numbered thirteen, in township number fourteen north, of range numbered six east; and from thence due west along through the middle of townships numbered fourteen north, to the place of beginning, shall constitute a county, to be called the county of Macon; and the seat of justice therein, when located, shall be called the town of Decatur.

" SEC. 2. For the purpose of locating the seat of justice of the said county of Macon, the following named persons are appointed Commissioners, to-wit: John Fleming, Jesse Rhodes and Easton Whitton, whose duty it shall be to meet at the house of James Ward, in said county, on the first Monday in April next, or within ten days thereafter, and after being duly sworn before some justice of the peace of this State, faithfully and impartially to discharge the duties imposed upon them by this act, shall proceed to determine upon a place for the location of the said seat of justice, having

---

and was President *pro tem.* of that body in 1825-7. He was thirty-seven years in Congress, uninterruptedly — the longest continuous service of any one man.* Twice during Jefferson's administration he declined the office of Postmaster General. He was a Democrat in politics, and had an earnest conviction in the ability of the people for self-government. Jefferson said he was "the last of the old Romans," and Randolph called him "the wisest man he ever knew." In his temperment he was a stoic, disregarding style and conventionalties, and in all things practiced the strictest economy.

*American Encyclopædia.

due regard to the situation of the settlements, the convenience of the people, and the future population of said county.

"SEC. 3. The said Commissioners are hereby authorized to locate the said seat of justice on the land of any person or persons, who may be the fee simple owners thereof, if the proprietor or proprietors of such land shall donate and convey, with covenants of general warranty, to the County Commissioners, for the use of said county, a quantity of land not less than twenty acres, in a square or oblong form, upon which to erect the public buildings; or otherwise, the said Commissioners may, in their discretion, locate the said seat of justice on any of the public lands in said county, as may seem to be the most advantageous to the future interest of said county.

"SEC. 4. As soon as said service shall be performed, the said Commissioners shall make a report of their proceedings, under their proper hands and seals, to the first County Commissioners' Court, to be held for and in said county, designating particularly the place selected, and a description of the same. And if the situation on the public lands shall be preferred, after examination as aforesaid, the half quarter or quarter section of land upon which the same may be located shall be stated in said report; and in that event, it shall be the duty of the said County Commissioners, as soon thereafter as they may be enabled, to enter and purchase the same, at the proper land office, in their respective names, as County Commissioners, for the use of the county of Macon; all of which said proceedings the County Commissioners' Court shall cause to be entered at large on their books of record.

"SEC. 5. As soon as a suitable site shall have been selected for the seat of justice, and a report made thereof, as aforesaid, it shall be the duty of the County Commissioners to cause such donation, or tract of land (if public land should be selected), or so much thereof as they may deem advisable, to be laid off into lots, and be sold upon such terms and conditions as may be considered most advantageous to the interests of the county, and the proceeds of such sales shall be applied to the erection of a court house and jail, and such other public works as may be necessary for the use of said county. And as often as any lots shall be sold as aforesaid, it shall be the further duty of said County Commissioners to make conveyances for the same to the purchasers thereof, in their own names, as Commissioners for and in behalf of said county.

"Sec. 6. Until public buildings shall be erected for the purpose, the courts shall be held at the house of James Ward, in said county.

"Sec. 7. An election shall be held at the house of James Ward, on the second Monday of April next, for one Sheriff, one Coroner and three County Commissioners, for said county, who shall hold their offices, respectively, until the next general election, and until their successors are qualified; which said election shall be conducted in all respects agreeably to the provisions of the law regulating elections: *Provided*, that the qualified voters present may elect from among their number three qualified voters to act as judges of said election, who shall appoint two qualified voters to act as clerks.

Sec. 8. It shall be the duty of the Clerk of the Circuit Court, who may be appointed for such county, to give public notice, at least fifteen days previous to said election, of the time and place, when and where the same will be held, and the officers to be elected thereat; and in case there should be no clerk, it shall be the duty of the recorder, or any justice of the peace residing within the limits of said county, to give notice of the time and place of holding the same as aforesaid.

"Sec. 9. The Commissioners appointed to locate the seat of justice, as aforesaid, shall receive the sum of one dollar and fifty cents per day for each day by them necessarily consumed in discharging the duties imposed upon them by this act, to be allowed by the County Commissioners' Court, and paid out of the treasury of said county.

"Sec. 10. Until the next apportionment of members of the General Assembly shall be made, said county of Macon shall vote with the counties of Fayette, Bond, Montgomery, Shelby and Tazewell; and the clerk of the said county of Macon shall meet the clerks of the said counties of Fayette, Bond, Montgomery, Shelby and Tazewell, at Vandalia, the seat of justice of Fayette county, to compare the number of votes given for Senator and Representatives to the General Assembly, and sign the necessary certificate of election, at Vandalia, and deliver the same to the person or persons entitled thereto.

"Sec. 11. The said county of Macon shall be and is hereby attached to the first judicial circuit.

"This Act to take effect from and after its passage."

Approved January 19, 1829.

It will be observed by the foregoing act that the county, so formed, was much larger than it is at present. It then included all of what is now DeWitt county, except the northern tier of townships; all of Piatt county, except one township, and about half of Moultrie county. On the first of March, 1839, DeWitt county was formed, establishing the northern line of this county where it now is. On the following day an act was passed adding to the county of Macon that portion now known as Niantic township. It may be remarked, in this connection, that the formation of DeWitt, and the losing of that much territory to this county, was a source of but little concern to our people. In fact, at the time it was urged that the southern line of DeWitt should be extended far enough south to include the present towns of Maroa, Austin and Friends Creek. This tract of land, now rich, highly productive, and as finely improved as any other portion of the county, was then considered a burden, and not desired by Macon, and not wanted by DeWitt. It was not thought possible to cultivate the soil, or that it would ever be inhabited; and the expense of keeping up roads through it was considered to be largely in excess of the income to be derived. At that day there were but few people who dreamed even of the large prairies becoming settled and put into cultivation. The most that was claimed was that the farms would extend but a short distance from the timber, and the prairies remain forever wild, and used for grazing purposes only. Many of the early settlers made "clearings," and started their little farms in the timber, as they had been accustomed to do in the States from which they came. It is not strange, however, that the opinion was entertained that much of the prairie land was absolutely useless and valueless, for at that period, for the greater portion of the year, they were almost submerged with water. Horses and cattle would mire on land now considered dry, and forming some of the best farms in the county. It is asserted by some of our then residents of the county, that the object of securing the addition to the county of the present Niantic township, was to prevent the removal of the county seat from Decatur to a little town then just commenced in the township of Friends Creek, called Murfreesboro. It will be remembered that Piatt county was then a part of Macon, and the proposed new county seat, being nearer the center of the county than Decatur, may have actuated Mr. Gouge, who was then our representative in the legislature, in procuring this addition to our western territory. The assertion, however, that any such notions were entertained as to the proposed change in the county seat, is denied by others who were residents at the time. It is very probable, however, that there was a change of the "seat of justice" anticipated, for the Niantic territory was considered worthless, except as so much ballast to counterbalance the eastern portion of the county. And the prospects of Murfreesboro, it seems, were blighted about that time, and it has long since ceased to be, except in the recollection of a very few of our oldest residents.

In January, 1841, Piatt county was formed from portions of DeWitt and Macon counties, and in February, 1843, the county of Moultrie was formed from portions of Shelby and Macon counties, each by acts of the legislature. Macon county now remains as left after the passage of the last act, forming Moultrie county. It now contains an area of five hundred and seventy-seven square miles, or 369,280 acres.

The Commissioners appointed by virtue of the foregoing act, met on the tenth day of April, 1829, and proceeded to view the several proposed locations for a "seat of justice;" and as a result of their deliberation, made the following report, as appears by the record of the County Commissioners' Court:

"We, the Commissioners appointed for the purpose of locating the seat of justice for Macon county, after being duly sworn before John Miller, an acting justice of the peace for said county of Macon, having carefully and impartially viewed and examined the situation and convenience, likewise the advantages, of the present and future population, have located the said seat on the fifteenth section in township sixteen north, in range two east, northeast quarter and east half of said quarter, the southeast corner of said above-named half quarter, in compliance to an act of the General Assembly requiring us so to act. Approved January 19, 1829. Whereunto we have set our hands and seals this tenth day of April, in the year of our Lord, 1829.

"JOHN FLEMING, [Seal.]
"JESSE RHODES, [Seal.]
"EASTON WHITTON." [Seal.]

When the site had been selected, as referred to in the above report, an order was made on the first day of June, 1829, by the County Commissioners, directing the "laying off" of the town of Decatur, as follows:

"*Ordered*, That Benjamin R. Austin, County Surveyor for the county of Macon, be and is hereby required to lay off the town of Decatur, in said county, after the form of Shelbyville, and make and return to one of the commissioners of this court, a complete plat of the same on or before the first day of July next."

Under the above order the "old town" of Decatur was laid out and platted, which contained twenty acres. Its boundaries were: Prairie street on the north, Water street on the east, Wood street on the south, and Church street on the west, and was divided by Main street, running east and west, and by North Main street, running north and south. The "old town" remains substantially as platted, "after the form of Shelbyville," with the exception that Merchant street has been formed since, and some of the lots are divided so as to run north and south instead of east and west, as laid out.

By the act creating this county, the land upon which the Commissioners located the "seat of justice" was to be donated to the county. The land on which the county seat was located had not, in fact, been entered from the government at the time, but was afterwards entered by Parmenius Smallwood, Easton Whitton and Charles Prentice, and a deed was by them made to the County Commissioners, on the eighth day of October, 1831.

A sale of town lots, however, had been made by the County Commissioners on the tenth day of July, 1829, and bonds given to the purchasers.

The order of the Commissioners, under which this sale was made, is as follows:

"*Ordered*, That a sale of lots take place in the town of Decatur, in this county, on the tenth day of July next, on the following terms, to-wit: A credit of twelve months will be given, and note with approved security will be required, and that the clerk of this court is required to advertise the sale in the paper printed in Vandalia, until the day of sale."

The following order was also made, which we insert, showing the rate of taxation and the articles of property to be assessed:

"*Ordered*, That for the purpose of raising a revenue to defray expenses of the county for the year 1829, that a tax of one-half per cent. be levied upon the following personal property, to-wit: On slaves and indentured or registered negro or mulatto servants; on pleasure carriages; on distilleries; on stock in trade; on all horses, mares, mules or asses, and neat cattle over three years old; and on watches, with their appendages, and on all other personal property except the lawful fire-arms of each individual."

This tax, when collected, amounted to the sum of $109.32½.

At the same term of Court, the tavern rates were also fixed as follows:

"*Ordered*, That the tavern rates for this county shall hereafter be as follows, to-wit: For breakfast and horse fed, 37½ cents; keeping man and horse each night (the man to have supper and lodging), 62½ cents; dinner and horse fed, 37½ cents; brandy, rum, gin, wine or cordial, 25 cents per half pint; whisky, or cider brandy, 12½ cents per half pint."

This was also for the purpose of defraying the county expenses: No person was allowed to go into any sort of merchandising business without a license "first had and obtained" from the County Commissioners, for which a fee of from three to five dollars was charged. Ferries were established on the river, and license granted, and the rates of ferriage fixed by the court.

In connection with the organization of the county, a few things may be said in reference to its location, character of population, and commanding influence with reference to neighboring counties, etc. It is the geographical centre of the State—east and west, north and south. Its entire area is within the great corn-growing belt of Illinois, and it possesses a soil unsurpassed in rich and productive qualities. There is not an acre of it, scarcely, that is not susceptible of cultivation. Its population, composed, as it is, of emigrants from the east and south, in about an equal proportion, is a modification of the temperaments and sentiments of the two sections, possessing the extremes of neither. Politically, it has been Whig, Democratic and Republican, and never either way by a large majority. A just estimate of the political sentiment of Macon county has always been, almost without an exception, a true criterion of the sentiment of the State. As it has been in politics, so it has been in religion, in morality, in business. In the latter, we have never had the wealth of some other counties, nor the wild, reckless, speculating spirit of some others; but our business men have always been of the safe, conservative sort, that make gradual progress, and with that are satisfied, reference, of course, being here made to the general mass. We have never launched out into a system of public expenditures for this public improvement or that, not consistent with our actual wants and our ability to pay. We have no public city or county debt hanging over us and weighing us down to such an extent as to cripple our industries, and drive away our population. Our taxes are, and have always been medium, as compared with other counties in the State. Our improvements have been, for both county and city, just such as the public demands suggested. We have no court house at the present, it is true, but we have what satisfies the public in both economy and convenience, and have no one, two or three million dollar court house debt eating out the material prosperity of the people. Our school houses are ample in size, well built, and constructed usually with a view to health, comfort and convenience, rather than show and splendor. We have kept on straight forward, as the crow flies, and have met with no reverses, such as have overtaken other counties. In peace we have been peaceful, maintained order, and had but little or no outlawry. In war we have been actuated by the dictates of true and genuine patriotism, and have done our whole duty. In the Black Hawk war we furnished 50 men; in the Mexican war, 79; in the late war, a reference to Chapter IV of this work will satisfy everyone that Macon county was "in the fray." In the ranks we were not behind. Our Tuppers, Pughs, Oglesbys, Moores, Smiths, and a host of others were there. In education, with but 18 persons in the county, between the ages of 12 and 21, who can neither read nor write, we have nothing to be ashamed of, In crimes and misdemeanors our position is not unenviable. Smaller counties, with one-fourth our population, furnish more penitentiary convicts than we do.

Hence we say, for these reasons, and many others that might be mentioned in this connection, that while we are not boastful, and " have none of that other spirit that would drag angels down," yet we, as a county, can claim our share of whatever glory there may be in making Illinois one of the first States in the Union, in prosperity, wealth and commanding influence. We arrogate to ourselves nothing but what justly belongs to us, but if it were possible to blot our State from existence, the shock would affect the commercial world from center to circumference.

ITS SETTLEMENT.

The first house erected within the present limits of Macon county was the "trading house," about eight miles north-east of Decatur, on premises belonging to Wm. C. Johns, Esq., which was a log structure, built by Lortons for the purpose of trading with the Indians. A thriving business was carried on by these men until 1825 or '6, when the Indians ceased to visit this part of the country, except in very small companies. Prior to that, from 200 to 500 Indians would sometimes be camped in the vicinity at once. The men were principally engaged in hunting, and would bring to Lortons whatever furs or other articles they had for exchange, and purchase powder, whisky, blankets, etc. The trading house was erected about the year 1816. The Lortons were from St. Joe, Michigan, and returned to that place when the Indians left this part of Illinois. The second house erected in the present limits of Macon county was built by William Downing, near the present residence of Capt. D. L. Allin, on the south side of the Sangamon river. This was in fact the first residence, for the one built by Lortons was not intended as a permanent residence, but only for the purpose of trafficking with the Indians so long as they remained in the vicinity. Downing is said to have come into this vicinity for the purpose of trapping and gathering honey. He left the neighborhood of Vandalia in the spring of 1820, and built his cabin some time in the fall of that year. Downing remained here but a short time, and sold his "improvements" to John Ward, upon the latter's arrival in this vicinity. He then removed to Bond county, Illinois, where he lived a great many years. It is regretted that a more extended sketch of Downing cannot be given in this connection, but he was here but a few years, and there is, perhaps, but one man now living in the county who was here any portion of the time that Downing was; and it being over half a century since, he remembers but little of the old trapper and bee hunter.

The next house built was by Buel Stevens, in 1822, near what is now known as Stevens' creek, about three miles northwest of

Decatur. This became the nucleus of what was afterwards known as the Stevens' Settlement, which, with the Ward Settlement, on the south side of the river, were the only settlements within the present line of Macon county until about the year 1828, when people began to come into the county, and settle both up and down the river.

For an account of the early settlements made within what was then Macon, but which now constitutes Piatt county, we make the following extracts from a historical sketch of the latter county, read at Monticello on the Fourth of July, 1876, prepared by a committee consisting of William H. Piatt, Ezra Marquis and C. D. Moore, old and respected citizens of that county:

"Settlements commenced as early as 1823—over half a century ago. The first known settler in the territory comprising Piatt county was George Hayworth, a Quaker from Tennessee, who, in 1823, located on a piece of land included in the present city limits of Monticello, and built the first cabin. This historic structure is still standing in Monticello, and is used for a stable. He was joined during the same year by a Mr. Daggett, who erected a cabin on a spot just north of Monticello, where N. E. Rhodes' barn now stands. On the following March, 1824, Abraham Haneline, of Green county, Ohio, moved here with his sons, including Nathan, who is the oldest resident now living in the county. They located in the Sangamon timber, about four miles northeast of Monticello, at Coon's Spring. About the same time James and John Martin, from Virginia, built on Furnes' run, about a mile above the spring. The next year brought another settler by the name of York, who stopped near the mouth of Goose Creek. In 1828 James A. Piatt, Sen.,* formerly of Ohio, but later of Indianapolis, Indiana, purchased the claim of Hayworth, and in April, 1829, moved upon the claim with his family. In the autumn of the same year, Jeremiah Terry settled on what is now the Piatt county fair grounds. In 1831, Peter Souders, of Lee

---

*NOTE.—The James A. Piatt mentioned in the above extract, was for years a member of the County Commissioners' Court of Macon county, and was a very efficient and valuable officer. The records show that he was seldom absent from the meetings of the court, though he was compelled to ride a distance of over twenty miles over roads that must have been almost impassable at times.

county, Virginia, moved his family to the northeast part of the county, in the Sangamon timber. Settlers now began to increase more rapidly, but the rich, rolling prairie, with all its fertility and beauty, seemed to have few charms as a dwelling place for these early settlers. Instead, they invariably selected some spot in the timber for their abiding place, and it was not long before the first settlers had neighbors in all the belts of timber that line the banks of the Sangamon, Okaw, Camp Creek, Goose Creek, Willow Branch and Madden's Run. Among the early settlers that followed close upon the heels of those already mentioned, were Abraham and Ezra Marquiss, of Ohio; George Widick, a Mr. Dillow, James Chambers of Kentucky; John Madden, John Argo, William Wright, Peter Croninger, I. V. Williams, Joseph Mallory, George Boyer, Samuel and Jacob Cline, Thomas Welch, John Bailey, George Evans, A. Rizor, Samuel Suver, John Hughes, A. J. Wiley, Luther and Joe Moore, William Monroe, Simon Shonkwiler, Daniel Stickel, and others."

We are also permitted to make the following extract from the history of DeWitt county, by Mr. W. L. Glessner, of Clinton, which was prepared for the Fourth of July celebration of the present year, and published in the Clinton *Register* of the 7th of July, 1876. It will be remembered that the portions of DeWitt county referred to, constituted a part of Macon until 1839, so that all the settlements referred to were made in what was then Macon county, and are interesting as a part of Macon county history:

" The first settlers of DeWitt county, as near as I have been able to ascertain, were a party consisting of six persons: Zion Shugart, Edom Shugart, their mother, Elisha Butler and his wife, and John Coppenbarger, of whom the only living member is Edom Shugart, who now resides at Marysville, Nebraska. This party arrived in what is now section seven, Tunbridge township (on what is known as the Emily Hayes farm), on the 29th day of October, 1824. They put up a hastily constructed log cabin, and made ready for the winter. During the winter of 1824, Nathan Vestal, with a large family, moved in and settled a short distance from the Shugarts, and in the following spring John Coppenbarger removed his family into the neighborhood, and thus was commenced the settlement of that portion of the territory of Illinois now known as DeWitt county. During the winter of 1824 a little girl of Nathan Vestal's died, and was buried on the hill near Emily Hayes' residence. As there was no lumber in the country, a coffin was made by splitting slabs out of trees and hewing them into shape. The nearest settlement to the Shugarts', at that time, was the residence of a man named Laughery, ten miles down Salt Creek, in what is now Logan county.

" Another settlement was made in what was called Fork Prairie, in the vicinity of the present town of Marion, in 1831 and '32, the first settlers being Thomas R. Davis, James Morris, John Morris, Benjamin Lisenby, Alexander Dale, Josian Harp, Charles McCord and Hugh Davenport.

" The first settlement about Clinton was made by Joseph (or Josiah) Clion, in 1830. He erected a cabin on what is now known as the Paschal Mills farm, about one mile west of Clinton."

There were also early settlements made in what was then this county, but which now forms a part of Moultrie, as early as 1829 and '30.

It is worthy of remark that the first who came here, as a general thing, commenced their improvements in the timber. But few, for a great many years, thought it advisable to attempt farming in the prairie. They at first were not satisfied that crops could be successfully cultivated there. It was almost the unanimous opinion that the large prairies never would be in a state of cultivation, but useful only for grazing purposes. Another obstacle was in the way for a good many years, and that was, there were no plows suitable for breaking the prairie land. The sod was very much tougher then than it was in after years when the stock had pastured the prairies and killed out the grass to some extent. It would be astonishing to many of our present residents to see the immense crops of prairie grass that in early days grew upon their present fields. It grew in places to the height of from six to twelve feet, and was " almost as thick," some of the old settlers say, " as the hair on a dog's back." It was these immense crops of grass that furnished the fuel for the terrible fires that swept over the prairies during the fall season of the year, and were so often productive of loss of life and property. And then, again, there was so much of the prairie land that was considered too wet to be ever suitable for cultivation. Thousands of acres that now constitute some of the best farms, in the highest state of cultivation, and possessing the very richest of soil, were condemned as swamp lands. The fact is that there is much of the land of Macon county that is now considered high and dry, or at least sufficiently so for all practical farming purposes, that was so wet that during a greater portion of the year it was absolutely dangerous to ride over it on horseback, for fear of miring. There was another drawback in the settlement of the prairies, and that was the great labor and cost of fencing. It is a well authenticated fact that the northern portion of Illinois might have been under a general state of improvement a great many years sooner than it was, but for the difficulty and great expense of fencing the farms. The Supreme Court of this State, at an early day, entertaining the idea generally prevailing, that our immense prairies would always remain commons, and used only for pasturing purposes, reversed the common law idea prevailing almost universally, in consequence of which every man was compelled to fence his entire farm so as to keep his neighbor's stock out, in order to protect his crop. It would have been much less expensive for each man to have protected himself against his own stock, than to have protected himself against the stock of the entire neighborhood. This decision of the Supreme Court, requiring stock to be fenced out instead of in, has been the most expensive decision to the people of Illinois of any other, perhaps, ever made. It has cost the farmers of Macon county, who entered their land of the government, more to build these fences and keep them in repair, by far, than the land cost, and all the necessary implements of husbandry. Our prairies would have been in a splendid state of cultivation long before they were, but for the inability of the people to build the necessary fences to protect their crops from destruction by the few cattle that were permitted to run at large and feed on the commons or speculator's land. One-tenth of the land that might have been in cultivation but for the expense of fencing, would have produced more than sufficient corn to have fattened all the hogs running at large merely for the sake of the fall masts. Another thing retarded the early settlement of the county to some extent, which was the fact of speculators and capitalists from the east coming into the county and buying up large tracts of the best and most available lands, and holding them for an advance in price occasioned by the development and improvement of the surrounding lands. Every person who came into the county to make it his home was welcomed. He was assisted in every possible way to induce him to become a resident. But the speculator, who brought nothing into the county, and did nothing whatever to develop the growth of the country by building or improvements of any kind, was not held in very high esteem by the residents generally. He bought his lands and paid the small annual assessments thereon, and waited for other people's labor and money to enhance the value of his investments. It should be mentioned, however, in this connection, that Philo Hale, who owned as much if not more land in Macon county than any one else, was an exception to the rule just stated. He owned large bodies of land in the county, but he came here and made this his home. He was one of the people. He induced others to come, and did all in his power to advance the material prosperity of the county. He published in the eastern papers flaming accounts of our rolling prairies, rich soil, etc., etc. The people of the county were often astonished at reading in the newspapers published in the eastern States, glowing accounts of large and enthusiastic mass meetings, at which Judge so and so presided, and Captain so and so acted as secretary, when and where resolutions were passed endorsing this or that local improvement, and expressing the gratitude of the people for the rapid progress in the construction of a railroad from Chicago to St. Louis or Chicago to New Orleans, or Vincennes to Nauvoo! Of course the meetings and the resolutions passed only existed in the mind of Mr. Hale, and, of course, the result to be accomplished was commendable, whether some of the means he resorted to were justifiable or not. Had he lived to old age, Mr. H. would have been instrumental in aiding immensely in the material advancement and improvement of the county.*

Another obstacle was also in the way of the rapid advancement of the country, and that was, the lack of markets for the produce raised, which continued until railroad facilities were offered by the opening of the great Western Railroad (now T., W. & W. R. R.), and the Illinois Central—the former in 1852, and the latter in 1854. The hogs and cattle sold had to be driven overland to St. Louis, Chicago and other markets. There was no sale, of course, for

---

*NOTE.—He died about 1836, and was buried on the "Hale farm," in Mt. Zion township. His grave is said to be unmarked and neglected, although at the time of his death he owned thousands of acres of land in this county which has since become valuable!

corn—or comparatively none—and wheat, when hauled to Springfield, but very seldom realized over thirty-three cents per bushel, so that there was no impetus given to the raising of grain of any sort, except for home consumption. But upon the construction of the railroads above mentioned, dividing the county into four quarters, a new era commenced in the history of Macon county. The fact is, that the day that the first train of cars ran into Decatur, is the day from which the material advancement of Macon county dates. That was the beginning of our improvements; that was the beginning of our settlement proper; that was the beginning of our agricultural development. It was the commencement of our manufacturing institutions; it was the commencement of the city of Decatur. According to the United States census for 1850, the entire population of Macon county at that time was but 3,998. From 1850 to 1870—a period of twenty years—the population had increased to 26,481. In 1830, the year after the organization of the county, our population was but 1,122, so that the increase in population for the twenty years preceding the construction of our two leading railroads was but 2,876, and for the twenty years following was 22,483. In 1850 but a small portion of our prairies were in cultivation, but now they are a solid mass of farms, and many of them are in a splendid state of cultivation. There were in cultivation during the year 1876, 258,315 acres of land. But it must be remembered that this vast body of land now in cultivation, does not produce as much by one-half as it is capable of under a judicious and systematic treatment, such as we find in some of the older states.

Another influence also operated in retarding the rapid settlement of the county during its early history, and that was what was variously styled the "ague," "chills and fever," and "Illinois shakes." It was a terror to newcomers. In the fall season of the year, like Brady's bitters, everybody took it. It was no respecter of persons; everybody shook with it, and it was in everybody's system. They all looked pale and yellow, as though they were frost-bitten. It was not contagious, but was a kind of miasmi that floated around the atmosphere and was absorbed in the system. It kept on absorbing and accumulating from day to day, until the whole body corporate became charged with it as with electricity, and then the shock came; and the shock was a regular shake, with a fixed beginning and an ending, coming on each day, or each alternate day, with a regularity that was surprising. And after the shake, then came the fever, and this "last estate was worse than the first." It was a burning hot fever, and one that lasted for hours. When you had the chill you couldn't get warm, and when you had the fever you couldn't get cool. It was awkward in this respect. It was, indeed. It would not stop, either, for any sort of contingency. Not even a wedding in the family would stop it. It was imperative and exacting. When the appointed hour came around, everything else had to be stopped to attend to its demands. It didn't have any Sundays or holidays. After the fever went down, you didn't still feel much better. You felt as though you had gone through some sort of a collision, and came out not killed, but badly demoralized. You felt weak, as though you had run too far after something, and then didn't catch it. You felt languid, stupid and sore, and was down in the mouth and heel and partially raveled out, so to speak. Your back was out of fix, and your appetite was in a worse fix than that. Your eyes had more white in them than usual, and altogether, you felt poor, disconsolate and sad. You didn't think much of yourself, and didn't believe other people did either. Your didn't care whether there was any school or not. You didn't think much of suicide, but at the same time you almost made up your mind that under certain circumstances it was justifiable. You imagined that even the dogs looked at you with a kind of self-complacency. You thought the sun had a kind of sickly shine about it. About this time you came to the conclusion that you would not take the whole State of Illinois as a gift, and picked up Hannah and the baby and your traps, and went back "yander" to Injeany, Ohio, or old Kaintuck.

The above is no picture of the imagination. It occurred in hundreds of cases. It put us in bad repute with our neighbors, and for that reason they refused to come and settle with us. Whole families would sometimes be sick at once, and not one member scarcely able to wait on the others. And when an emigrant happened to stop in a neighborhood affected with this disease, he did not stay long.

Persons emigrating to the county usually selected their locations and commenced their improvements on government land, and waited until they were able to amass from the scanty resources enough to purchase the forty or eighty acres—as the case might be —at the sales at the land office at Vandalia. In the earlier days the government price of land was fixed at $1.25 per acre. Amusing incidents are related in connection with the races that were sometimes made by different persons desiring to enter the same piece of land. It was not unfrequent that men who had about exhausted their means in reaching the country, and had labored hard and undergone all sorts of privations in securing a comfortable home and other necessary improvements, and had, perhaps, a few acres of ground in cultivation—when they had at last obtained, by the strictest economy, or perhaps borrowed enough money, to purchase from the government their little forty-acre home, found that some speculator had preceded them and entered their land. It is said, however, that in some instances the speculator did not retain the improvements; for, by some magical power or otherwise, in a remarkable short space of time almost, the identical improvements appeared at some other locality not far away, and having the same occupants.

The first piece of land ever entered in Macon county was the west half of the northeast quarter of section thirty-one, in township sixteen north, range two east of the third principal meridian. on the ninth day of November, 1827, by Lewis B. Ward. This was owned by Mr. Ward until the fall of 1876, when it was sold to Bartley G. Henry. There were about eight hundred acres of land entered during that year, and there is now probably not an acre of land in the county belonging to the government.

CHAPTER III.

COUNTY OFFICERS.

At the time of the formation of the county, all county affairs were transacted by the County Commissioners' Court, which was composed of three men, who were usually selected with reference to their qualifications for the peculiar and responsible duties of the office. This court assumed jurisdiction upon almost all manner of subjects, except the exercise of judicial functions, and the record shows that, even in this respect, upon one occasion at least, the court assumed to fine a man for an indignity to that honorable body, which supposed indignity the court characterised as "flouting," whatever that may mean.

COUNTY COMMISSIONERS' COURT.†

1829-30—Benjamin Wilson,
    Elisha Freeman,
    James Miller,
1831-32—James Miller,
    I. C. Pugh,
    David Davis,
1833-34—Elisha Freeman,
    Hugh Bolls,
    Philip D. Williams.
1835-36—James A. Piatt,
    Wm. Muirhead,
    Benj. Wilson.

1830-31—Elisha Freeman,
    James Miller,
    I. C. Pugh.
1832-33—James Miller,
    I. C. Pugh,
    David Davis.
1834-35—James A. Piatt,
    Wm. Muirhead,
    Benj. Wilson.
1836-37—James A. Piatt,
    Wm. Muirhead,
    Benj. Wilson.

---

†Established under act of March 22, 1819.

1837-38—James A. Piatt,
        Wm. Muirhead,
        Josiah Clifton.
1839-40—*Elisha Freeman, 3 yrs
        *Benj. Wilson, 2 yrs.,
        *Hiram Chapin, 1 yr.
1841-42—Elisha Freeman,
        John Rucker,
        Abraham H. Keller.
1843-44—John Rucker,
        Leonard Ashton,
        Andrew W. Smith.
1845-46—Andrew W. Smith,
        James D. Tait,
        Elisha Freeman.
1847-48—Elisha Freeman,
        Samuel Rea,
        James D. Campbell.

1838-39—Wm. Muirhead,
        James A. Piatt,
        Abram Chapin.
1840-41—Elisha Freeman,
        Benj. Wilson,
        John Rucker.
1842-43—John Rucker,
        Abraham H. Keller,
        Leonard Ashton.
1844-45—John Rucker,
        Andrew W. Smith,
        James D. Tait.
1846-47—Elisha Freeman,
        Samuel Rea,
        James D. Campbell.
1848-49—Elisha Freeman,
        Samuel Rea,
        James D. Campbell.

It will be noticed that there are but two members of the above court remaining in Macon county, viz: James D. Tait and Samuel Rea. The others are either dead or have ceased to be residents.

By an act of the Legislature, approved February 12, 1849, the County Commissioners' Court was abolished, and the COUNTY COURT established. This act provided for the election of a county judge and two additional justices of the peace, whose duty it should be "to sit with the county judge as members of the court, for the transaction of all county business." The County Court was in existence from 1850 to 1860. The following constituted our County Court during that period:

COUNTY COURT.

1850-51—William Prather, County Judge.
        Jacob Hostetler, Associate Justice.
        John Rucker, Associate Justice.

---

*These Commissioners were allotted to the respective terms opposite their names by the County Clerk, under an act approved March 1st, 1837. Under this act the term of service of the County Commissioners was fixed at three years, one to be elected each year.

HISTORY OF MACON COUNTY. 37

1851-52—William Prather, County Judge.
    Jacob Hostetler, Associate Justice.
    John Rucker, Associate Justice.
1852-53—William Prather, County Judge.
    Jacob Hostetler, Associate Justice.
    John Rucker, Associate Justice.
1853-54—William Prather, County Judge.
    Jacob Hostetler, Associate Justice.
    John Rucker, Associate Justice.
1854-55—William Prather, County Judge.
    Jacob Hostetler, Associate Justice.
    John Rucker, Associate Justice.
1855-56—William Prather, County Judge.
    Jocob Hostetler, Associate Justice.
    John Rucker, Associate Justice.
1856-57—John Rickets, County Jndge.
    Jacob Hostetler, Associate Justice.
    John Rucker, Associate Justice.
1857-58—John Rickets, County Judge.
    Jacob Spangler, Associate Justice.
    M. G. Camron, Associate Justice.
1858-59—John Rickets, County Judge.
    Jacob Spangler, Associate Justice.
    M. G. Camron, Associate Justice.
1869-70—John Rickets County Judge.
    Jacob Spangler, Associate Justice.
    M. G. Camron, Associate Justice.

There are but three members of the old County Court now living, viz: Judge John Rickets, and Associate Justices Jacob Spangler and M. G. Camron.

BOARD OF SUPERVISORS.*
1860.

Hickory Point, J. Y. Braden.   Oakly, G. W. Forest.
Austin, James Parker.   Long Creek, John Rucker.

NOTE.—On the 17th of February, 1851, an act was passed authorizing counties to adopt the system of "Township Organization" therein prescribed, upon the petition and vote of citizens of the county. At the September

Maroa, William Crawford.   Whitmore, Jas. Lichtenberger.
Friends Creek, D. K. Wilson,   Harristown, Abraham Eyman.
Decatur, H. B. Durfee.   Decatur, John W. Koehler, ast.
Niantic, J. H. Hughes.   Mt. Zion, W. C. Meyers.
S. Wneatland, I. S. Boardman.   South Macon, W. D. Hamilton.
Blue Mound, J. C. Armstrong.

1861.

Decatur, H. B. Durfee.   Decatur, John W. Koehler, ast.
Friends Creek, D. K. Wilson.   Blue Mound, W. T. Moffett.
Maroa, W. F. Crawford.   Mt. Zion, W. C. Meyers.
Hickory Point, J. Y. Braden,   S. Wheatland, I. S. Boardman.
Niantic, J. H. Hughes.   .Harristown, J. H. Pickrell.
Oakley, G. W. Forest.   South Macon, L. M. Clement.
Long Creek, J. C. Rucker.   Whitmore, Henry Rhodes.
Austin, J. S. Parker.

1862.

Harristown, J. B. Hanks.   Hickory Point, J. Y. Braden.
Whitmore, Jas. Lichtenberger.   Maroa, W. F. Crawford.
Long Creek, J. C. Rucker.   Mt. Zion, B. W. Davidson.
Niantic, J. A. Pritchett.   Friends Creek, Comely Lukens.
S. Wheatland, I. S. Boardman.   Blue Mound, F. A. Brown.
South Macon, A. H. Martin.   Decatur, H. B. Durfee.
Decatur, John W. Koehler.   Austin, A. Emery.
Oakley, Laban Chambers.

term, 1859, of the County Court, a vote of the county was authorized to be submitted to the legal voters at the November election ensuing. The proposition to go into township organization was carried, and at the December term following of the County Court, William Cantrill, David Garver and James Dingman, were appointed as commissioners to divide the county into townships, which they did, and reported to the court their action on the 14th of January, 1860. At that time the county was divided into fourteen townships, as follows: (1) Friends Creek (2) Maroa, (3) Montgomery (afterwards changed to Austin), (4) Bull Point (afterwards changed to Hickory, and then to Hickory Point), (5) Decatur, (6) Long Creek, (7) Whitmore, (8) Oakley, (9) Harris (afterwards changed to Harristown, (10) Wilson (afterwards changed to Mt. Zion), (11) South Wheatland, (12) South Macon, (13) Madison (afterwards changed to Blue Mound), (14) Niantic. Illini, Milam, and Pleasant View have been since formed of parts of other townships.

HISTORY OF MACON COUNTY. 39

1863.

Harristown, M. G. Camron.
Whitmore, John Gill.
Long Creek, John S. Kizer.
Niantic, J. W. Corbett.
S. Wheatland, I. S. Boardman.
South Macon, W. W. Dean.
Decatur, B. F. Dillehunt.

Hickory Point, J. Y. Braden.
Maroa, W. F. Crawford.
Mt. Zion, B. W. Davidson.
Friends Creek, Andrew Dickey.
Blue Mound, F. A. Brown.
Decatur, H. B. Durfee.
Austin, J. S. Parker.
Oakley, H. McCoy.

1864.

Hickory Point, J. Y. Braden,
Whitmore, Charles Wooster.
Niantic, J. W. Corbett.
Decatur, J. E. Roberts.
Maroa, W. F. Crawford.
South Macon, Frank Babcock.
Mt. Zion, John Scott.
Blue Mound, W. T. Moffett.

Illini, J. H. Pickrell.
Austin, J. S. Parker.
S. Wheatland, I. S. Boardman.
Decatur, David Morgan.
Oakley, H. McCoy.
Friends Creek, Comely Lukens.†
Long Creek, John W. Tyler.
Harristown, M. G. Camron.

1865.

Hickory Point, J. Y. Braden.
Whitmore, Joshua Green.
Niantic, J. W. Corbett.
Decatur, W. O. Jones.
Maroa, Anderson Franklin.
S. Macon, Frank Babcock.
Mt. Zion, Jehu Scott.
Blue Mound, W. T. Moffett.

Illini, John S. Childs.
Austin, J. S. Parker.
S. Wheatland, I. S. Boardman.
Decatur, David Morgan.
Oakley, O. J. Doyle.
Friends Creek, D. K. Wilson.
Long Creek, John W. Tyler.
Harristown, M. G. Camron.

1866.

H. Point, W. F. Montgomery.
Whitmore, Joshua Green.
Niantic, J. W. Corbett.
Decatur, H. B. Durfee.
Maroa, John Crocker.
South Macon, N. Failing.
Mt. Zion, John A. Henry.
Blue Mound, W. T. Moffett.

Illini, J. S. Childs.
Austin, C. F. Emery.
S. Wheatland, Jno. Montgomery.
Decatur, W. A. Barnes.
Oakley, O. J. Doyle.
Friends Creek, William Daves.
Long Creek, John W. Tyler.
Harristown, M. G. Camron.

†Resigned.

1867.

Decatur, H. B. Durfee.
Whitmore, Jas. Lichtenberger.
South Macon, R. Gray.
Niantic, A. W. Pritchett.
South Macon, N. Failing.
Mt. Zion, J. A. Henry.
Illini, J. S. Childs.
Harristown, M. G. Camron.

Decatur, W. A. Barnes.
Friends Creek, Wm. Daves.
Austin, C. F. Emery.
Blue Mound, W. T. Moffett.
S. Wheatland, I. S. Boardman.
Long Creek, J. S. Kizer.
Oakley, E. Rhodes.
H. Point, W. F. Montgomery.

1868.

Decatur, H. B. Durfee.
Whitmore, J. G. Harnesberger.
South Macon, Joel T. Walker.
Niantic, Sheldon Parks.
South Macon, John Lyon.
Mt. Zion. J. A. Henry.
Illini. J. C. Tucker.
Harristown, M. G. Camron.

Decatur, M. Forstmeyer.
Friends Creek, S. Payne.
Austin, T. B. Campbell.
Blue Mound, W. T. Moffett.
S. Wheatland, I. S. Boardman.
Long Creek, Joseph Spangler.
Oakley, E. Rhodes.
Hickory Point, H. S. Mannon.

1869.

Decatur, James Milliken.
Whitmore, J. G. Harnesberger.
Macon, Joel T. Walker.
Niantic, Shaw Pease.
Maroa, John T. Lyon.
Mt. Zion, R. M. Foster.
Illini, J. J. Bachelder.
Harristown, M. G. Camron.

Decatur, M. Forstmeyer.
Friends Cr'k, Payne & Swantes.
Austin, Robert T. Morris.
Blue Mound, W. T. Moffett.
S. Wheatland, I. S. Boardman.
Long Creek, Samuel Gillispie.
Oakley, Reed Spencer.
Hickory Point, A. McBride.

Pleasant View, D. Powles.

1870.

Decatur, Reuben Betzer.
Whitmore, Jas. Lichtenberger.
Macon, J. T. Walker.
Niantic, Thomas Acom.
Maroa, John T. Lyon.
Mt. Zion, R. M. Foster.

Decatur, M. Forstmeyer.
Friends Creek, F. Swantes.*
Austin, Peter Bennett.
Blue Mound, R. H. Hill.
Wheatland, I. S. Boardman.
Long Creek, J. Benson Myers.

*Resigned, and T. H. Barr appointed.

HISTORY OF MACON COUNTY.

Illini, J. J. Bachelder.
Hasristown, M. G. Camron.
Pleasant View, D. D. Powles.

Oakley, Reed Spencer.
Hickory Point, A. McBride.
Milam, J. B. Gleason.†

1871.

Milam, G. A. Bartlett.
Mt. Zion, William Davis.
Decatur, M. Forstmeyer.
Whitmore, Joshua Green.
Maroa, Samuel Lowe.
Long Creek, J. B. Myers.
Pleasant View, D. D. Powles.
Illini, J. C. Tucker.
South Macon, J. T. Walker.

Harristown, M. G. Camron.
Austin, C. F. Emery.
Decatur, Joseph Mills.
Blue Mound, R. H. Hill.
Friends Creek, John Marsh.
Hickory Point, A. McBride.
Oakley, E. Rhodes.
S. Wheatland, Hiram Ward.
Niantic, S. Parks.

1872.

Harristown, M. G. Camron.
Whitmore, Joshua Green.
Decatur, H. Hummell.
Hickory Point, A. McBride.
Mt. Zion, G. A. Smith.
Long Creek, A. T. Davis.
Austin, D. Patterson.
S. Wheatland, Hiram Ward.
Pleasant View, John Hatfield.

South Macon, N. Failing.
Niantic, John Gordy.
Decatur, Jacob Spangler.
Maroa, Jason Rogers.
Oakley, Read Spencer.
Niantic, S. Parks.
Illini, J. C. Tucker.
Milam, G. A. Bartlett.
Blue Mound, D. F. Barber.

1873.

Harristown, M. G. Camron.
Blue Mound, Frank Coleman.
Mt. Zion, Wm. Davis.
Macon, N. Failing.
Decatur, Jacob Spangler.
Hickory Point, H. Lehman.
Maroa, John Orr.
Friends Creek, R. H. Park.
Whitmore, J. C. Ruddock.

Oakley, Dr. S. Cooper.
Long Creek, A. T. Davis.
Niantic, James Dingman.
Decatur, David S. Hughes.
Pleasant View, E. House.
Illini, L. R. Morse.
Austin, D. Patterson.
Milam, J. W. Rogers.
S. Wheatland, H. Ward.

1874.

Harristown, M. G. Camron.

Oakley, Dr. S. Cooper.

†Organized in 1869.

Blue Mound, Frank Coleman.   Mt. Zion, Wm. Davis.
Niantic, James Dingman.   Oakley, Wm. Grason.
Macon, W. S. Gage.   Decatur, David Hughes.
Decatur, Jacob Spangler.   Decatur, H. Hummel.
Pleasant View, E. House.   Austin, Robert Morris.
Hickory Point, A. McBride.   Maroa, John Orr.
Friends Creek, J. Ruddock.   Maroa, Jason Rogers.
Wheatland, H. Ward.   Long Creek, Samuel Gillispie.

1875.

Blue Mound, F. M. Coleman.   Harristown, M. G. Camron.
Whitmore, J. C. Ruddock.   Decatur, M. Forstmeyer.
Decatur, H. B. Durfee.   Decatur, Jacob Spangler.
Oakley, William Grason.   South Macon, W. S. Gage.
Long Creek, Samuel Gillispie. Pleasant View, E. House.
Mt. Zion, J. A. Henry.   Milam, W. E. Kyker.
Austin, Robert Morris.   Hickory Point, A. McBride.
Illini, L. R. Morse.   Maroa, John Orr.
Friends Creek, Jas. W. Brown. South Wheatland, H. Ward.

1876.

Decatur, Samuel Powers.   Decatur, D. L. Hughes.
Decatur, M. Forstmeyer.   Milam, W. E. Kyker.
Pleasant View, E. House.   Maroa, John Longstreet.
Oakley, William Grason.   Wheatland, H. Ward.
Hickory Point, Henry Lehman. Whitmore, J. C. Ruddock.
Illini, L. R. Morse.   Long Creek, H. W. Davis.
Harristown, M. G. Camron.   Niantic, A. C. Edgar.
Mt. Zion, W. H. Wallace.   Friends Creek, J. W. Brown.
Blue Mound, W. T. Moffett.   Macon, R. H. Woodcock.
            Austin, A. Hackyard.

Y'r.	Circuit Judge.	Judge of Probate.	State's Atto
1830	S. D. Lockwood	D. McCall	John H. Pugh.
1831	"	"	"
1832	"	"	"
1833	"	"	"
1834	"	"	"
1835	*S. T. Logan	Chas. Emerson	"
1836	"	"	D. H. Campbell
1837	†Wm. Brown	"	"
		PROBATE JUSTICE.	
1838	Jesse B. Thomas	Kirby Benedict	"
1839	S. H. Treat	"	"
1840	"	"	Josiah Lamborr
1841	"	"	"
1842	"	"	"
1843	"	John G. Spear	"
1844	"	"	John A. McDou
1845	"	"	"
1846	"	Thomas H. Read	"
1847	"	"	"
1848	"	"	David Campbel
1849	David Davis	"	"
		COUNTY JUDGE.	
1850	"	William Prather	"
1851	§ "	"	"
1852	"	"	Elam Rust

*Thos. Ford held the September term of court for Logan. †Held the October ter held court at May term.

Y'r.	Circuit Judge.	Judge of Probate.	State's
1853	*David Davis	William Prather	Elam Rus
1854	Charles Emerson	"	"
1855	"	"	"
1856	"	John Rickets	J. R. Eder
1857	"	"	"
1858	"	"	"
1859	"	"	"
1860	"	"	†James P.
1861	"	S. F. Greer	"
1862	"	"	"
1863	"	"	"
1864	"	"	D. L. Bun
1865	"	"	"
1866	"	"	"
1867	A. J. Gallagher	"	"
1868	"	"	M. B. Th
1869	"	"	"
1870	"	"	"
1871	"	"	"
1872	"	"	C. C. McC
1873	C. B. Smith	"	"
1874	"	"	"
1875	"	"	"
1876	"	"	I. A. Buck

*May term held by Davis for Charles Emerson. †Resigned, and D. L. Bunn a

Y'r.	Circuit Clerk.	County Clerk.	County Trea...
1829	D. McCall............	D. McCall............	B. R. Austin ...
1830	"	"	John Miller....
1831	"	"	B. R. Austin ...
1832	"	"	James Johnson
1833	"	"	"
1834	*H. M. Gorin.........	"	Joseph Hostetler
1835	"	"	Joseph Stevens.
1836	"	"	"
1837	"	H. M. Gorin..........	§J. Renshaw—L
1838	"	"	"
1839	"	"	Henry Snyder.
1840	"	‖ "	"
1841	†N. W. Peddecord.....	N. W. Peddecord......	"
1842	"	"	"
1843	"	"	"
1844	"	"	
1845	"	"	¶Thomas H. Re
1846	"	" .. [by.	George W. Pov
1847	‡ "	E.B. Hall & W.W.Ogles-	"
1848	William Prather.......	"	S. C. Allen....
1849	"	"	"
1850	"	"	"
1851	"	W. W. Oglesby........	"

*McCall discharged, and H. M. Gorin appointed. †Appointed. ‖N. W. Peddecord White appointed. ¶Resigned March 2, '46. **Resigned in 1838.

Y'r.	Circuit Clerk.	County Clerk.	County
1852	William Prather......	W. W. Oglesby........	S. C. Alle›
1853	"	"	I. C. Pug›
1854	"	"	"
1855	"	"	"
1856	J. Q. A. Odor.........	"	"
1857	"	Samuel Rea..........	"
1858	"	"	William C
1859	"	"	"
1860	W. L. Hammer........	"	"
1861	"	"	"
1862	"	"	"
1863	"	"	Ira B. Cu›
1864	"	"	"
1865	"	I. C. Pugh............	"
1866	"	"	"
1867	"	"	"
1868	"	"	"
1869	E. McClellan	H. W. Waggoner......	William M
1870	"	"	"
1871	"	"	"
1872	"	"	"
1873	"	"	R. H. Par›
1874	"	"	"
1875	"	"	George M
1876	"	"	"

The first Circuit Court held in the county was in the town of Decatur, commencing on the eighth day of May, 1830, and was presided over by Judge Samuel D. Lockwood. Wm. Warnick was sheriff, and Daniel McCall clerk, and John H. Pugh was prosecuting attorney. There were on the docket for trial, at this term, the following cases: Thomas Cowan vs. Wm. King, appeal; John Hanks vs. John Henderson, slander; Wm. Webb vs. Hubbell Sprague, slander; Wm. Webb vs. Phillip D. Williams, appeal. The two appeal cases were dismissed at the cost of the defendants, and the first slander suit was dismissed at the cost of the plaintiff, and the second at the cost of the defendant. At the March term, 1830, of the County Commissioners' Court, the following order was made, and the persons therein named constituted the first grand and petit jurors:

"*Ordered*, That the following named persons appear before the Circuit Court, to be held at Decatur on the sixth day of May next, at the hour of eleven o'clock A. M., to serve as grand jurors, to-wit: Benjamin R. Austin, Francis G. Hill,* Robert Foster, William Freeman, Lambert G. Bearden, James Ward, Jeremiah Ward, William D. Baker*, Michael Myres, William Wheeler, Edmund McDaniel,* William Miller, John Miller, sr., James Hanks, Isaac Miller, David Miller (2d), Samuel Miller, William King, Thomas Cowan, Luther Stevens, John Miller (2d), John Hanks,* and Jonathan Miller; and that the following named persons appear at the Circuit Court, at the time and place above mentioned, to serve as petit jurors, to-wit: David Miller, Doras Stevens, Matthias Anderson, Parmenas Smallwood, James Owens, Winkfield Everett, William Ward, John Widick, Samuel Widick, James W. D. Taylor, James A. Ward, James Myres, John Mowry, Henry Ewing, James Finly, James McGinas, George Widick, Landy Harrell, Peter Walker, William Cox, Berry Rose, Randolph Rose, David Davis and John Warnick."

Substantially the same juries were selected at the August term, 1829, of the County Commissioners' Court, to serve at a fall term of the Circuit Court to have been held at the house of James Ward. The writs issued were returnable at a court to be held at James Wards also; but there is no record of a court held in the

---

*Four of this grand jury are still living; but none of the petit jury.

fall of 1829, and one of the jurors who served at the first term of court informs me that it was held in Decatur in 1830. There is an impression, however, in the minds of many, that the first court was held at Ward's, four miles south of Decatur.

The grand jury selected as above stated, were charged by John H. Pugh, after which they retired " to consider the presentments." On the same day they " returned into court, and having no business, nor the attorney for the people any for them," were discharged.

There appears to be no evidence as to what attorney attended this term of court, either from the record files or docket, excepting Mr. Pugh.

The second term of court was held on the second and third days of May, 1831. At this term there were six cases pending for trial, one of which was an indictment for cheating, on change of venue from Tazewell county, which was continued. Another was for " damages," which was dismissed by the plaintiff. The other four cases were for slander, two of which were continued by consent, one dismissed by the plaintiff, and one tried, in which the jury rendered a verdict of guilty, and assessed the plaintiff's damages at one cent.

The attorneys engaged in these cases were: George Forquer, John H. Pugh, W. L. D. Ewing, and Hon. John T. Stuart, all of Springfield.

The following persons constituted the grand jury: James Johnson, foreman; Benjamin Wilson, Thomas Ward, Ephraim Cox, Hiram Reavis, William Christopher, John Walker, William Muirheid, Richard Dauget, Benjamin Frazie, Jacob Coppenbarger, John Ballard, Moses Harrel, Christopher Miller, Joseph Stevens, John Taylor, David L. Allin, John Ingram, Reuben Beecher, Josiah Allen, James Bone, John Smith and Landy Harrell, who, on being sworn and charged, "retired to consult;" after which they brought into court one indictment charging the defendant with larceny.

The petit jury at this term was as follows: Emanuel Widick, Lewis B. Ward, Jacob Caulk, Elisha Freeman, John Rose, Lemuel Walker, Henry Traughber, Allen Travis, Kinian Ingram, Thomas S. Taylor, William Shepard, James Shepard, George Hawks, John Coppenbarger, Alexander Scott, James Miller, Jonathan Flory, Philip Ballard, Alfred Layman, Thomas Johnson, Daniel Shinkle, Abraham Shepard, Isaac Bigelow and Philip D. Williams.

But one of the grand jurors—David L. Allin—and four of the petit jurors are now living. At the close of the first day the court adjourned until *six* o'clock the next morning, at which time, it having no further business, adjourned until court in course.

There would be much of public interest connected with a detailed analysis of the early courts of this county, and a more extensive notice of the lawyers who engaged in the early practice; but our limits forbid. Many of the illustrious men of this country, who have since become famous in its politics, jurisprudence and national history, have practiced at the Macon county bar. Among them we mention: Abraham Lincoln, Stephen A. Douglas, David Davis, Edward D. Baker, John A. McDougall, Anthony Thornton, Horatio M. Vandeveer, Charles Emerson, Leonard Swett, John T. Stuart, U. F. Linder, Josiah Lamborn and Stephen T. Logan.

Mr. Emerson was the first resident attorney, and came here in the spring of 1834*; Kirby Benedict* was the second, who came here in 1836; and J. S. Post was the first attorney admitted to practice from the county.* George Powers* and Jerome R. Gorin* were admitted next in order.

BIOGRAPHIES OF COUNTY OFFICERS.

COUNTY JUDGES.

DANIEL McCALL, *First County Judge.*— Daniel McCall moved from Fayette county to Macon in the early part of 1829. He was then about thirty-six years of age. He was postmaster at the time of the organization of the county, and also held the offices of probate judge, circuit clerk and county clerk at the same time. But little is known of his early history prior to his coming to this county, or after he left here. He was educated, and had the ability to be a useful and influential member of the community, but, unfortunately, was very much dissipated. He left this county and emi-

---

*See sketch, chapter 10.

grated to Texas, and, as reported, died there; but at what period we have been unable to learn.

CHARLES EMERSON, *Second County Judge.*—[See sketch in chapter 10.]

KIRBY BENEDICT, *Third County Judge.*—[See sketch in chapter 10.]

Dr. JOHN G. SPEAR, *Fourth County Judge.*—[See sketch in chapter 10.]

THOMAS H. READ, *Fifth County Judge.*—[See sketch in chapter 10.]

WILLIAM PRATHER, *Sixth County Judge.*—Mr. P. was born in Maryland about the year 1806, and died on the twenty-ninth day of August, 1870. He was appointed circuit clerk in 1847, and elected to the same office in 1848, and re-elected in 1852. In 1850 he was elected county judge, and retained that position until 1856. He always had very infirm health.

JOHN RICKETS, *Seventh County Judge.*—Mr. R. was born in 1814, in Lynchburg, Campbell county, Va. In 1832 he moved with his father to Kentucky, and came to Illinois in 1834, and located at Bloomington, where he remained until 1839, when he came to Decatur. In 1841 he removed to Monticello, where he remained until 1847, and then returned to Decatur. Was a justice of the peace for a good many years, and was judge of the county court from 1856 to 1861.

SAMUEL F. GREER, *Eighth County Judge.*—Mr. G. was born in Fairfield county, Ohio, September 8, 1824, and removed to Macon county in 1854. He engaged in the sale of dry goods for about five years. He was elected judge of the county court in 1861, and has been re-elected at the expiration of each term since. Has also been a member of the board of education, and has held other offices of trust and responsibility.

CIRCUIT CLERKS.

D. MCCALL, *First Circuit Clerk.*—[See sketch above.]

H. M. GORIN, *Second Circuit Clerk.*—Mr. Gorin was born October 14, 1812, in Kentucky, and came to Macon county in 1831 or '32, and was clerk of the circuit court from 1834 or '40—having been appointed in the place of D. McCall, discharged—and was clerk of the county court from 1837 to 1840. He removed from Macon county, in 1840, to Scotland county, Mo., where he was afterwards elected clerk of the circuit court, and where he now resides. He married Mary Ann Love, and was a brother of Jerome R. Gorin, of Decatur.

N. W. PEDDICORD, *Third Circuit Clerk.*—Mr. Peddicord was born in Montgomery county, Maryland, and removed to Macon county in 1836, where he engaged as a clerk for Adamson & Prather, and afterwards formed a co-partnership with Joseph Stickel in merchandising. He was appointed clerk of the circuit court to succeed Mr. Gorin, in 1840, and served in that capacity until 1847, and was also clerk of the county court from 1840 to 1846. He removed from Macon county and became a resident of Missouri, California and Iowa. He died in the latter state about 1870.

WILLIAM PRATHER, *Fourth Circuit Clerk.*—[See above, as county judge.]

JOSEPH Q. A. ODOR, *Fifth Circuit Clerk.*—Mr. Odor was born May 30, 1827, in Garrard county, Kentucky, and came to Macon county in April, 1852, where he engaged in farming and teaching school until 1854, when he was appointed deputy sheriff under Stephen M. Whitehouse. He was elected clerk of the circuit court in 1856, and served four years. In 1861 he became a member of the firm of Milliken & Odor, in the banking business, and continued until 1863, when he went to Louisville, Kentucky, and again engaged in banking. In 1869 he returned to Macon county, and resumed business here as a member of the firm of Smiths, Hammer & Co., and afterwards, upon the dissolution of that firm, became a partner in the firm of Rucker, Hammer & Co., which position he now holds.

WILLIAM L. HAMMER, *Sixth Circuit Clerk.*—William L. Hammer, the sixth circuit clerk of Macon county, was born Nov. 2, 1817, in Winchester, Clark county, Kentucky, and came from Kentucky to Sangamon county, Illinois, in 1827. From there he removed to that part of Shelby county, now Christian county, in 1837, and thence to Macon county in 1854. In 1860 he was elected circuit clerk of Macon county, and was re-elected in 1864, serving two full terms with entire satisfaction to his constituents. On retiring from office he became a director, and subsequently president, of the First National Bank of Decatur, and on the liquidation of that institution he became senior member of the banking house of Rucker, Hammer & Co. He was mayor of the city of Decatur in 1869, and a member of the board of education of Decatur school district from 1865 to 1874, and was largely instrumental in the erection of the elegant and commodious school buildings that are a pride to the citizens of Decatur. Mr. H., in his business and official relations, has been gentlemanly and upright. In his social and domestic relations he is kind and indulgent.

E. McCLELLAN, *Seventh Circuit Clerk.*—Mr. McClellan was born October, 1818, in Franklin county, Pennsylvania, and came to Illinois in 1835. He was elected sheriff in 1856, and served two years. He was city marshal from 1863 to 1865. He was elected circuit clerk in 1868, and re-elected in 1872, and again in 1876, and also served as deputy clerk, under Mr. Hammer, for three years. He married Judith Snyder, who was born in Kentucky in 1825 or '6, and removed to Macon county in 1834.

COUNTY CLERKS.

D. McCALL, *First County Clerk.*—[See county judge above.]

H. M. GORIN, *Second County Clerk.*—[See circuit clerk above.]

N. W. PEDDICORD, *Third County Clerk.*—[See circuit clerk above.]

E. B. HALE, *Fourth County Clerk.*—Mr. Hale was a son of Philo Hale, elsewhere mentioned in this work. He is a resident of Cleveland, Ohio, and is the owner of a large amount of land in Macon county which was entered by his father, and is said to be wealthy. We have applied to Mr. H. for information regarding his father's and his own history, but have received no response.

WARNER W. OGLESBY, *Fifth County Clerk.*—Mr. O. was born October 1, 1817, in Kentucky. He held the office of county clerk from 1847 to 1856. He died on the twenty-second day of August, 1860. He held other positions of trust, and was loved and respected by all.

SAMUEL REA, *Sixth County Clerk.*—[See sketch in chapter 10.]

I. C. PUGH, *Seventh County Clerk.*—[See sketch in chapter 10.]

HISTORY OF MACON COUNTY. 53

H. W. Waggoner, *Eighth County Clerk.*—Mr. W. was born November 9, 1835, in Perry county, Pennsylvania. He removed to Chicago in 1855, and a short time afterwards to Macon county. He was deputy county clerk from 1855 to 1866, and in 1869 was elected clerk of that court, and was re-elected in 1873.

SHERIFFS.

William Warnick, *First Sheriff.*—[See sketch in chapter 10.]

John McMennamy, *Second Sheriff.*—[See sketch in chapter 10.]

James Stevens, *Third Sheriff.*—[See sketch in chapter 10.]

William Wheeler, *Fourth Sheriff.*—[See sketch in chapter 10.]

Samuel Rea, *Fifth Sheriff.*—[See sketch in chapter 10.]

Stephen M. Whitehouse, *Sixth Sheriff.*—Mr. W. was born February 8, 1821, in Washington county, Virginia, and came to Illinois in 1846, and located in this county. He married Mary E. Falconer, March 7, 1850, and was elected sheriff in the fall of 1854, and served two years. He removed to Kansas in 1869, where he died, December 6, 1875.

E. McClellan, *Seventh Sheriff.*—[See sketch as circuit clerk.]

George Goodman, *Eighth Sheriff.*—Mr. Goodman was born in Coles county, Indiana, in 1823, and came to this state in 1836, and located on the Okaw, in what is now Moultrie county, but then a part of Macon. He came to Decatur in 1837, was elected sheriff of Macon county in 1860, and served two years, and has been a justice of the peace for seventeen years. He says, in his early days he was a most excellent shoemaker.

John W. Bear, *Ninth Sheriff.*—Mr. B. was born about 1830, in Mechanicsburg, Pennsylvania, and came to Illinois in the spring of 1854. He was elected sheriff in 1862, and served two years, and also served as a member of the city council, and was a justice of the peace. He is now a resident of Wichita, Kansas.

A. A. Murray, *Tenth Sheriff.*—Mr. M. was born in 1822, in Jefferson county, New York. He removed to Illinois in 1847, and located in Springfield, Illinois, where he remained five years, and then went to Bloomington and remained four years, and came to Decatur, Illinois, in 1857. Was elected sheriff in 1864, since which time he has been engaged in the sale of agricultural implements.

JOHN E. JONES, *Eleventh Sheriff.*—Mr. Jones was born in Madison county, Ohio, and came to Macon county in 1854, and was in the army during the late war. After his return he engaged in merchandising for a short time, and was elected sheriff in 1867, and served one term. He died in Decatur in August, 1870.

JAMES TRAVIS, *Twelfth Sheriff.*—Was born in Kentucky about 1810. He removed to Tippecanoe county, Indiana, and thence to Macon county, where he was elected sheriff in 1868, and served for one term. In 1873 he removed to Grand Rapids, Michigan. His present residence unknown.

GEORGE M. WOOD, *Thirteenth Sheriff.*—Mr. W. was born in Hart county, Kentucky, in May, 1828, and came to Illinois in 1835, and settled in Greene county. He remained there until 1849, and went to Texas and staid two years. Thence he returned to Illinois and located in Springfield, and came to Macon county in 1854, and engaged in the sale of dry goods. He was elected sheriff in November, 1870, and served two years, and was then appointed deputy under Mr. Jennings, and served in that capacity until November, 1875, when he was elected county treasurer, which position he now holds.

I. D. JENNINGS, *Fourteenth Sheriff.*—Mr. J. was born July 10, 1825, in Somerset county, New Jersey, where the rocks are so thick that the noses of the sheep are compelled to be sharpened before they—the sheep—can subsist on the grass that grows between the rocks. He came to Illinois in 1850, and located at Jacksonville, where he remained until 1853, when he came to Decatur. He was elected sheriff in 1872, and served two years, and was reelected in 1874, and also served as deputy under Sheriff Wood. He was city marshal from 1867 to 1870.

MARTIN FORSTMEYER, *Fifteenth Sheriff.*—Was born in South Bavaria, March 21, 1830, and emigrated to America in 1852, and located in Decatur in 1854. With the exception of two years he has been a member of the board of supervisors since 1864, and was mayor of the city of Decatur in 1872, and was a member of the city council from 1862 to 1871. At the recent election he was elected sheriff by a large majority.

COUNTY TREASURERS.

B. R. AUSTIN, *First County Treasurer.*—[See sketch in chapter 10.]

JOHN MILLER, *Second County Treasurer.*—We have been unable to learn much of Mr. M. He was probably born in Virginia, and was about fifty years of age when he held the office of county treasurer.

JAMES JOHNSON, *Third County Treasurer.*—Came from Kentucky to Macon county at least as early as 1830. He was county treasurer in 1832 and '3, and was colonel in the Black Hawk war. He removed from Macon county to Pike county, Illinois, where he died—date unknown.

JOSEPH HOSTETLER, *Fourth County Treasurer.*—[See sketch in chapter 10.]

JOSEPH STEVENS, *Fifth County Treasurer.*—[See sketch in chapter 10.]

JAMES RENSHAW, *Sixth County Treasurer.*—[See sketch in chapter 10.]

DAVID DAVIS, *Seventh County Treasurer.*—[See sketch in chapter 10.]

HENRY SNYDER, *Eighth County Treasurer*—[See sketch in chapter 10.]

THOMAS H. READ, *Ninth County Treasurer.*—[See sketch in chapter 10.]

GEORGE POWERS, *Tenth County Treasurer.*—[See sketch in chapter 10.]

SAMUEL C. ALLEN, *Eleventh County Treasurer.*—[See sketch in chapter 10.]

I. C. PUGH, *Twelfth County Treasurer.*—[See sketch in chapter 10.]

WILLIAM CANTRILL, *Thirteenth County Treasurer.*—[See sketch in chapter 10.]

IRA B. CURTIS, *Fourteenth County Treasurer.*—[See sketch in chapter 10.]

WILLIAM M. BOYD, *Fifteenth County Treasurer.*—Mr. Boyd was born on the thirtieth of May, 1842, in Warren county, Vir ginia, and came to Decatur, Illinois, in the fall of 1860. He was elected county treasurer in the fall of 1869, and served two terms, and was elected as a member of the city council in 1875, and has been for several years occupying an important and responsible position in the banking house of Peddecord & Burrows.

R. H. PARK, *Sixteenth County Treasurer.*—Mr. Park was born November 11, 1833, in Madison county, Kentucky; came to Illinois, March, 1861; settled in Macon county; was elected treasurer in 1873, and served two years.

GEORGE M. WOOD, *Seventeenth County Treasurer.*—[See sketch as sheriff, above.]

STATE'S ATTORNEYS.*

D. L. BUNN, *Ninth State's Attorney.*—D. L. Bunn, " was born on the banks of the raging Okaw," as he strenuously insists, McLean county, Ill., on the 27th day of September, 1837, and came to Macon county in 1855. He was appointed prosecuting attorney by Gov. Yates, in 1862, to fill out the unexpired term of James P. Boyd, and was re-elected in 1864, and served four years, and then "retired in good order." Mr. B., in his official capacity, was regarded by all as a successful prosecutor, and faithfully discharged the duties of his office.

M. B. THOMPSON, *Tenth States Attorney.*—Mr. Thompson was born in 1833, in Vigo connty, Indiana, and came to Illinois in 1856, and settled in Urbana, Champaign county. He was elected state's attorney in 1868, for the seventeenth judicial circuit, of which Macon county formed a part at that time.

CHAS. C. MCCOMAS, *Eleventh State's Attorney.*—Mr. McComas was born in Jasper county, Illinois, August 10, 1844, and came to Macon county in 1861, where he enlisted and served for three years in the army. After his return he studied law, and was admitted to practice in 1869, and in 1872 was elected prosecuting attorney for Macon county, being the first elected for the county under the constitution of 1870.

I. A. BUCKINGHAM, *Twelfth State's Attorney.*—Mr. Buckingham was born in Hamilton county, Ohio, July 25, 1840. He studied

---

*NOTE.—We are enabled to give sketches of the state's attorneys from 1864 only.

law with Tilden & Caldwell in Cincinnati, Ohio, and was admitted to the bar in 1853, and came to Macon county in September, 1863, at which time he formed a co-partnership with Capt. J. S. Post in the practice of law, and has been in active practice ever since. He was appointed city attorney for the years 1873, '4, '5 and '6, respectively, and in Nov., 1876, was elected state's attorney for Macon county for the period of four years.

MASTERS IN CHANCERY.

I. C. PUGH, *First Master in Chancery.*—[See sketch in chapter 10.]

WM. A. BARNES, *Second Master in Chancery.*—Wm. A. Barnes was born in Claremont, Sullivan county, N. H., March 15, 1824, and came to this county in 1853. He now holds the positions of president of the board of education of Decatur, president of the public library board, and president of the Citizens' Association of Decatur. Was Master in Chancery from 18— to 1864.

R. H. MERRIWEATHER, *Third Master in Chancery.*— Was born in Howard county, Md., June 23, 1820, and came to Macon county in 1858. He was appointed Master in Chancery in May, 1864, and continued to hold the office until January, 1874. He was deputy circuit clerk for four years under Hammer, and most of the time under McClellan.

JOHN A. BROWN, *Fourth Master in Chancery.*—John A. Brown was born July 23, 1843, in Abington, Mass. Removed from that state, with his father, to Cincinnati, Ohio, and thence to Missouri in 1857, and thence to Illinois in 1860, and to Decatur, Ill., in 1865. Was connected with the newspapers at Decatur, Illinois, for three years. He then commenced the study of law, and after the usual course of study was admitted to the bar in 1876, and immediately entered into a co-partnership with F. B. Tait in the practice of law at Decatur. He was appointed by Judge C. B. Smith master in chancery of Macon county, in 1873, and has performed the duties pertaining to the office faithfully and efficiently.

—8

CHAPTER IV.

THE BLACK HAWK WAR.

In 1831 a treaty was made by which Black Hawk and his tribes of Indians were to remove to the west side of the Mississippi river, and release all claim upon the east side. Emissaries of the British government, from Canada, induced the Indians to disregard the treaty and return to their former homes in Illinois. On the sixth day of April, 1832, Black Hawk, with his followers, crossed the Mississippi, bringing with them their women, children and property. He announced that his mission was peaceful—but no doubt his object was to reclaim the territory he had released under the treaty of the year before. Governor Reynolds, learning of the movement of Black Hawk, called for volunteers to repel the invaders. Eighteen hundred volunteers, under Whiteside and Reynolds, were mustered into service, and General Atkinson dispatched them in pursuit of the Indians. On the twelfth of May they reached Dixon's ferry, where they were joined by Major Stillman with 275 men. Stillman considered his command independent of Whiteside, and declined to join Whiteside's brigade. Stillman, with Major Baily, received orders to go to "Old Man's creek," now Stillman's run, to ascertain the movements of the Indians. The two battalions camped about ten miles from the ferry on the evening of the thirteenth, and on the morning of the fourteenth Stillman took command of both battalions, and continued in pursuit until sunset, when they encamped in "front of a small creek" (Stillman's run) about thirty miles from Dixon. Black Hawk hearing of their approach, sent out three men to meet them and take them to his camp, that a council might be held; but the men were taken prisoners. Five others were sent out for the same purpose, but two of them were killed. This aroused Black Hawk, and with about forty men he met the assailants—the main body of his warriors being about ten miles away—and routed them completely, and in great confusion. Some of Stillman's men, it is said, did not stop until they reached Dixon. In the fight, Major Perkins, Capt. Adams, and nine men, were killed, one of whom, James Milton, was from Macon county. William Cox, and others from this county, had their horses shot.

The following is a complete copy of the muster roll of the company from Macon county engaged in the war, showing the names of the volunteers, date of enlistment, date of discharge, and status of company at the time of discharge:

" Muster roll of Captain Johnson's company of mounted volunteers, belonging to the Fifth regiment, commanded by James Johnson, of the brigade of mounted volunteers of Illinois militia, commanded by Brigadier General Samuel Whiteside. Mustered out of service of United States at mouth of Fox river, the state of Illinois, on the 27th day of May, 1832; distance, miles, 150 from place of enrollment.

[The date of enlistment of all was April 24, 1832; and the term was 35 days.]

1 Jas. Johnson, Captain, promoted to Colonel 16 May, 1832.
2 William Warnick, 1st Lieutenant, absent with leave.
3 I. C. Pugh, 2d Lieut., promoted to Captain 16 May, 1832.
4 J. D. Wright, 1st Sergeant, absent on extra duty.
5 James A. Ward, 2d Sergeant, promoted to 2d Lieutenant.
6 Walter Bowls, 3d Sergeant, absent with leave.
7 Joseph Hanks, 4th Sergeant.
8 Henry M. Gorin, 1st Corporal.
9 S. R. Shepard, 2d Corporal.
10 G. Coppenbarger, 3d Corporal, absent with leave.
11 James Milton, 4th Corporal, killed in battle.
12 Asher Simpson, private.
13 A. W. Bell, private.
14 Abram Black, private.
15 D. McCall, private.
16 D. H. Stewart, private, absent on extra duty.
17 Elisha Butler, private, absent with leave.
18 G. D. Smallwood, private.

19 John Hanks, private.
20 Jacob Lane, private, absent on extra duty.
21 John Henderson, private, absent with leave.
22 James Querry, private.
23 James Miller, private.
24 John Manly, private.
25 James Ennis, private, absent with leave.
26 John Clifton, private, absent with leave.
27 Jesse Dickey, private, wounded in battle.
28 John Williams, private, absent with leave.
29 John Murphy, private.
30 Jacob Black, absent with leave.
31 James Herrod, private, absent with leave.
32 Kinian Ingram, private, absent with leave.
33 C. Hooper, private, absent with leave.
34 Robert Smith, private.
35 S. B. Dewees, private, sick.
36 S. Miller, private.
37 S. Troxel, private, absent with leave.
38 Thos. Devanport, private, absent with leave.
39 William Hanks, private, absent with leave.
40 William Adams, private, absent with leave.
41 William Miller, private.
42 William Hooper, private, absent with leave.
43 William Cox, private, absent with leave.
44 Joseph Clifton, private, absent with leave.

I certify, on honor, that the muster roll exhibits the true state of the company of mounted volunteers under my command, of the Illinois militia, of the brigade of mounted volunteers under the command of Brigadier General Samuel Whiteside on this day, and that the remarks set opposite the names of the men, are accurate and just.

Signed Fox River, Ill., this the 27th day of May, 1832.

I. C. PUGH, Captain,
Commanding the Company."

There was also a company of Rangers organized during the summer of 1832, commanded by Captain William Warnick. This company was out in the vicinity of Kickapoo town near the head of the Big Vermilion, but found no Indians and soon returned.

THE MEXICAN WAR.

War was declared with Mexico in May, 1846, and Illinois, under the call for volunteers, was entitled to three regiments. The sheriff of Macon county, under the proclamation of Gov. Ford, called for the enlistment of volunteers. Under this call company C of what was afterwards the 4th regiment was raised, consisting of 78 men. When the company reached Springfield thirty companies had already reported, and the three regiments were full. E. D. Baker*, then a prominent man of Illinois, through the influence of Hon. O. B. Ficklin, our member in Congress, prevailed on President Polk to allow him to raise a 4th regiment from Illinois, and by this means the Macon county men entered the service. Mr. Baker was elected Colonel, Lieut. Gov. Moore was elected Lieutenant Colonel, and Thomas Harris† was elected Major of the regiment. The late Gen. I. C. Pugh was elected Captain of company C, and Senator R. J. Oglesby, 1st Lieutenant; Anderson Fromon, 2d Lieutenant; John P. Post, 3d Lieutenant; Stephen Osborn, 1st Sergeant; G. W. Galbreath, 2d Sergeant; B. F. Oglesby, 3d Sergaant; B. L. Martin, 1st Corporal; James Hollingsworth, 2d Corporal; W. J. Usrey, 3d Corporal; and G. W. Nelson, 4th Corporal.

The following is a list of the volunteers:

Madison Bradshaw,	G. M. Braden,	W. W. Chapman,
P. T. Bebee,	A. Botkin,	G. W. Church,
Laban Chambers,	George Carver,	J. B. Case,
J. M. Dickey,	G. W. Dillow,	W. Dean,
W. P. Davidson,	Daniel Davis,	A. Greenfield,
James Greenfield,	David Huffman,	Sterne Helm,
J. Horner,	D. Howell,	S. K. Harrell,
Wm. Hawks,	M. M. Henry,	W. D. B. Henry,
Levi Hite,	John Henry,	I. Inman,
T. Johnson,	J. A. Lowrie,	J. C. Leadbetter,
H. Lord,	Thomas Lord,	A. B. Lee,
J. C. Malson,	G. J. Malson,	Ben. Martin,
I. Martin,	H. Martin,	Wm. McDaniel,
Chris. Mayers,	Chas. Nelson,	Wm. Nesbitt,

*Afterwards Senator from Oregon, Major General in the late war, and who was killed at Ball's Bluff.

†After whom Harristown was afterwards named.

J. S. Post,	J. Perryman,	S. Rice,
James Rea,	Wm. Robinson,	E. Rice,
J. Sheppard,	Jason Sprague,	R. H. Stewart,
D. G. Stevens,	W. E. Lee,	Dan. Spangler,
J. A. Shepley,	T. Souther,	J. Saunders,
James Turner,	F. E. Travis,	J. B. Travis,
J. D. Travis,	T. D. Turney,	William Wheeler,
W. R. Wheeler,	Lewis Ward,	B. E. Wells,
W. E. Warnick,	J. W. White,	B. White,
Robert Warnick,	James Freeman,*	J. M. Arwood,
Richard Barnwell,	Miles Bosworth,	Jesse Butler,
	David Bailer.	

Company C marched from Decatur to Springfield about the middle of June, 1846, where the regiment was formed. After remaining at Springfield a short time, the regiment marched to Alton, where arms were in store, which the regiment procured by a little maneuvering on the part of Col. Baker and Capt. J. S. Post. Col. J. J. Hardin, believing that he was entitled to these arms, stoutly protested against their appropriation by Col. Baker, and a wordy warfare ensued which came near resulting in a duel. From Alton the regiment was transferred to Jefferson Barracks, and there placed under charge of Col. Churchill, commandant, under whom it received thorough discipline and drill. About the 20th of July the regiment was mustered into service by Col. Crogan, of Fort Meigs notoriety. In a few days the regiment received orders and embarked for New Orleans, and thence to Brazos, Santiago Bay, four miles north of the mouth of the Rio Grande, where it disembarked. After remaining at this point for about a week, orders were received to march up the Rio Grande eight miles, where occurred the first death in Co. C, viz: Second Sergeant George Galbreath. As Col. Baker and a squad of twelve men, all from Macon county, detailed to bury Mr G., were about to return to camp, they heard a disturbance on board of a steamboat near by, and on arriving at the scene, they learned that an Irish company, in a drunken melee, had driven from the boat the Kennesaw rangers. Baker ordered his handful of men on the boat to quell the disturbance; but no sooner had he done so, than a hand-

---

*Joined the company at Brazos.

to-hand encounter ensued, in which the colonel and his squad were soon overpowered and compelled to retire: but not without loss. Col. Baker received a rapier thrust, penetrating his mouth and extending through the back of his neck; Capt. J. S. Post was wounded in the breast, having a rib broken; Charles Dillow,* killed; R. H. Stewart, bayoneted in the thigh; and seven others of the squad more or less injured. At this point orders were received to move still further up the river to Matamoras, on the Mexican side, where they remained a few days, and then moved on to Camargo, where a great deal of sickness ensued. Returning to Matamoras, they then marched to Victoria—marching on Christmas day forty-five miles. About the first of January, 1847, orders were received to March to Tampico, two hundred miles distant, at which place preparations were made for an attack on Vera Cruz. Taking ship at Tampico about the first of February, Vera Cruz was reached in sixteen days, and Company C assisted in the construction of the batteries and the bombardment of the city, which surrendered March 29. After the taking of the city of Vera Cruz, Scott's army marched for the City of Mexico, and *en route* met Santa Anna, at the mountain pass of Cerro Gordo, on the eighteenth of April, where a battle was fought. Company C had but forty-eight men in this engagement, two of whom were killed and ten wounded. The killed were J. C. Malson and George Nelson.

At this battle Santa Anna came near being taken prisoner, and in his effort to escape left in his carriage $25,000 in silver and his cork leg, which were captured by Company C, it being at the head of the brigade. The next morning ensuing the battle, Gen. Scott followed on to Jalapa, where Company C remained about a month, when the time of enlistment expired, and the company returned via New Orleans and St. Louis, arriving at home about the first of June, 1847, bringing with them the banner received from the citizens on their departure. They were very enthusiastically received. A grand barbecue was prepared for the returning volunteers, and day of general rejoicing was had, still remembered with satisfaction by the participants.

---

*His last words were: "If I have got to go, the road to heaven is just as near from here as from Macon county."

THE LATE WAR.

It is unnecessary in this connection, and, in fact, would consume entirely too much space, to give any details as to the causes of the rebellion. It is our purpose, rather, to give Macon county's record, as complete as we can, in the suppression of that rebellion. The long list of names following, of those who were sacrificed on the altar of their country, will sufficiently attest the patriotic impulses that actuated our people, and convince the most casual observer that Macon county, when called, was at her post and performed her whole duty valiantly.

In the succeeding pages of this chapter we give a brief synopsis of the principal engagements of the various regiments, together with a regimental and company roster, and the names, date of enlistment, discharge, etc., of those only who enlisted from the county.

SEVENTH ILLINOIS CAVALRY.

The 7th Cavalry was organized at Camp Butler, Illinois, and mustered into service Oct. 13, 1861. The companies A, C, I and G were directly ordered to Bird's Point, Missouri, where the other eight companies arrived on the 25th of December. Some time in January, all, except companies B, C, I and L, moved to Cape Girardeau, Mo. Company I, to which most of the men from Macon county belonged, remained at Bird's Point, and were engaged in scouting during the winter. At New Madrid the regiment again united. Was at Island No. 10. After this moved to Hamburg Landing, Tennessee river, thence in the direction of Corinth. Was engaged in the battle of Iuka, and afterwards at Corinth, Oct 2d, 3d and 4th. Nov. 23, seven companies met Richardson near Somerville; Dec. 1, assigned to Col. Dickey's command of cavalry. At Holly Springs, Miss.; followed Price as far south as Coffeeville and retreated. In Western Tenneessee. On the 17th of April, started on "Grierson's Raid" to Baton Rouge. Dec. 26th, the regiment fought the entire force of Forrest. In an engagement at Moscow, Tenn. Moved to Decatur, Ala. Returned to Nashville, and was mustered out of service, and received its final pay and discharge at Camp Butler, Ill., Nov. 17, 1865. Its period of service was about four years and three months.

HISTORY OF MACON COUNTY.   65

ROSTER SEVENTH CAVALRY—COMPANY " I."

Name, and date of Rank.   *Remarks.*

COLONELS.

W. P. Kellogg, Sept. 8, 1861. Resigned June 1, 1862.
Edward Prince, June 1, '62.   Tm. exp'd Oct. 15,'64, was Lt. Col.
John M. Graham, Mar. 1,'65.   Must'd out Nov. 4, '65, was Maj.

LIEUTENANT COLONELS.

W D. Blackburn, Feb. 10, '63. Died of wounds May 17, '63.
Geo. W. Trafton, Mar. 17, '63. Dismissed Nov. 4, '64.
H. C. Forbes, Mar. 1, '65.   Must'd out Nov. 4, 65, was Maj.

MAJORS.

Cyrus Hall, Sept. 21, '61.   Res. for promotion Feb. 9, '62.
Jas. Rawalt, Sept. 21, '61.   Res. June 10, '62.
Z. Applington, Nov. 13, '61.   Killed in battle May 15, 62.
Henry Case, Feb. 1, '62.   Resigned Apr. 4, '62.
H. C. Nelson, April 24, '62.   Resigned June 22, '63.
A. P. Koehler, May. 15, '62.   Resigned May 14, '63.
A.W. MDconald, June 22, '63.   Mustered out Nov. 4, '65.
Geo. A. Root, May 10, '65.   Must'd out Nov. 4,'65, was Adjt.
M. G. Wiley, May 10, '65.   Mustered out Nov. 4, '65.

ADJUTANTS.

Henry Stockdale, Jan. 30 '62. Mustered out May 26,'62.
Allen W. Heald, May 10, '65.   Mustered out Nov. 4, '65.

BATTALION ADJUTANTS.

Geo. Bestor, Jan. 15.   Mustered out '62.
Chas. Wills, Jan. 15.   Mustered out '62.

QUARTERMASTERS.

W. A. Dickerson, Oct. 25,'61. Mustered out May 26, '62.
J.R.W. Hinchman,Oct. 28,'62.   Mustered out Nov. 4, '65.

BATTALION QUARTERMASTERS.

Jas. T. Myers, Dec. 25, '62.   Mustered out '62.
John W. Resor, Dec. 25, '61.   Mustered out May 26, '62.

Name, and date of Rank.   *Remarks.*

SURGEONS.

C. D. Rankin, Oct. 28, '61.   Resigned Jan. 1. '62.
Daniel Stahl, Sept. 9, '62.   Discharged Sept 9, '64.
Thos. J. Riggs, Sept. 16, '64.   Must. out Nov. 4, '65, was 1st Ast.

FIRST ASSISTANT SURGEON.

Chas. H. Novell, April 3, '65.   Mustered out Nov. 4, '65.

SECOND ASSISTANT SURGEON.

A. G. Gilbert, May 29, '63.   Discharged Sept. 5, '64.
M. W. Nesmith, Apr. 16, '65.   Mustered out Nov. 4, 65.

CHAPLAIN.

Simon G. Meinor, Oct. 3, '61.   Term expired Oct 15, '64.

COMMISSARIES.

H. F. Barker, Oct. 1, '62.   Term expired Oct 15, '64.
Daniel F. Robbins, Oct. 4, '64. Mustered out Nov. 4, '65.

CAPTAINS.

A. J. Gallagher, Aug. 16, '61.   Resigned June 20, '62.
Wm. Ashmead, Jnne 20, '62.   Term expired Oct. 15, '64; was 2d [Lieutenant.
Byron H. Tuller, Nov. 28, '65.   Mustered out Nov. 4, '65.

FIRST LIEUTENANTS.

Wm. H. Stratton, Aug. 19, '61.   Term expired Oct. 15, '65.
Horace K. Rice, May 28, '65.   Mustered out Nov. 4, '65.

SECOND LIEUTENANTS.

S. G. Washburn, June 20, '62.   Term expired Oct. 4, '64.
O. L. Kendall, June 28, '65.   Mustered out Nov. 4, '65.

FIRST SERGEANT.

Clark, Wm. F., Sept. 3, '61.   Killed in action Mar. 1, '62.

QUARTERMASTER SERGEANT.

Flattery, Geo., Sept. 3, '61.   Mustered out Oct. 15, '64.

SERGEANTS.

Haworth, Jno. W., Sept. 3, '61. Mustered out Oct. 15, '64.

Name, and date of Rank.	Remarks.
Ruby, Matthew, Sept. 3, '61.	Mustered out Oct. 15, '64.
Gardner, Geo. H., Sept. 3, '61.	Mustered out Oct. 15, '64.
Washburn, S, G., Sept. 3, '61.	Promoted 2d Lieut.

CORPORALS.

Dickson, Archb'ld, Sept. 3, '61.	Re-enlisted as veteran.
Dunbar, Daniel H., Sept. 3, '61.	Mustered out Oct. 15, '64.
Kaylor, Geo. W., Sept. 3, '61.	Killed in action May 1, '62.
Ashmead, Marion, Sept. 3, '61.	Killed in action May 30, '62.
McComas, W. D., Sept. 3, '61.	Discharged Dec. 1, '62.
Jordan, Abner H., Sept. 2, '61.	Killed in action May 30, '62.
Varney, Thad. P., Sept 3, '61.	Mustered out Sept. 8, '64.
Hilt, Wm, Sept. 3, '61.	Mustered out Oct. 15, '64.

BUGLERS.

King, Davis T., Sept 3, '61.	Promoted chief bugler.
Strong, Jos. J., Sept 3, '61.	Promoted Chief bugler.

FARRIER.

Furr, Argyle W., Sept. 3, '61.	Mustered out Oct. 15, '64.

BLACKSMITH.

Fornof, Geo., Sept. 3. '61.	Mustered out Oct. 15, '64.

WAGONER.

Deal, Wm., Sept. 3, '61.	Mustered out Oct. 15, '64.

PRIVATES.

Adams, John O., Sept. 3, '61.	Re-enlisted as veteran.
Bohrer, John, Sept. 3, '61.	Mustered out Oct. 15, '65.
Belknap, C. M., Sept. 3, '61.	Re-enlisted as veteran; mustered out Nov. 4, '65, as sergeant.
Bartlett, Robt., Sept, 3, '61.	
Beals, Luther, Sept. 3, '61.	Discharged Oct., '62.
Calhoun, Webster, Sept. 3, '61.	Mustered out Oct. 15, '64.
Calhoun, David, Sept. 3, '61.	
Cornwell, Isaac P., Sept. 3, '61.	Re-enlisted as veteran; mustered out Nov. 4, '65.
Clark, Geo., Sept. 3, '61.	Re-enlisted as veteran; mustered out Nov. 4, '65.

Name, and date of Rank.   *Remarks.*

Name, and date of Rank.	Remarks.
Dugan, Chas., Sept. 3, '61.	Re-enlisted as veteran; mustered [out Nov. 4, '65.
Dugger, Wm. A., Sept. 3, '61.	Mustered out Oct. 15, '64.
Doner, Wm. H., Sept. 3, '61.	Re-enlisted as veteran.
Dawson, Eb., Sept. 3, '61.	Must'd out Oct. 15, '64, as sergt.
Dickson, Geo., Sept. 3, '61.	Mustered out Oct. 15, '64.
Earles, Walter, Sept. 3, '61.	
Fletcher, Geo. W., Sept. 3, '61.	Discharged April 8, '63, as corp'l.
Gibbs, Ed. M., Sept., 3, '61.	Must'd out Oct. 15, '64, as sergt.
Goff, Chas., Sept. 3, '61.	Discharged March 4, '62.
Grove, Wm., Sept. 3, '61.	Re-enlisted as veteran; mustered [out Nov. 4, '65.
Grady, Henry, Sept. 3, '61.	Mustered out Oct. 15, '65.
Hartman, Jno. P., Sept. 3, '61.	Discharged July, '62.
Hopkins, Chas. P., Sept. 3, '61.	
Hays, John, Sept. 3, '61.	Mustered out Oct. 15, '64.
Haworth, Frank, Sept. 3, '61.	Died Andersonville, Aug. 10, '64.
Hafrau, Jas., Sept. 3, '61.	Died Andersonville, July 23, '64.
Jones, Jas. M., Sept. 3, '61.	Mustered out Oct. 15, '64.
Jones, John S., Sept. 3, '61.	Must'd out Oct. 15, '64, as serg't.
Kendall, O. L., Sept. 3, '61.	Re-enlisted as veteran, private, ser-[geant, then lieutenant.
Knipple, Henry, Sept. 3, '61.	Re-enlisted as veteran; mustered [out Nov. 4, '65, as corporal.
Ledbetter, Jas. C., Sept. 3, '61.	Discharged July, '62.
Martin, Wm., Sept. 3, '61.	Re-enlisted as vet.; mustered out [Nov. 4, '65.
Martin, Henry, Sept. 3, '61.	Discharged Oct., '62.
May, Marion, Sept. 3, '61.	Discharged Dec., '62.
Myers, Henry, Sept. 3, '61.	Transferred to Co. M.
McRay or McKay, Sept. 3, '61.	Must'd out Oct. 15, '64, as corpr'l.
Melville, Edward, Sept. 3, '61.	
Miller, Lawrence, Sept. 3, '61.	Re-enlisted as vet.; mustered out [Nov. 4, '65, as sergeant.
McElroy, Jas., Sept. 3, '61.	Died of wounds received in camp.
McDougal, J. R., Sept. 3, '61.	Discharged April 6, '63.
McCay, Thos., Sept. 3, '61.	

Name, and date of Rank.	Remarks.
Nicholson, Jas., Sept. 3, '61.	Re-enlisted as vet.; mustered out [Nov. 4, '65.
Nicholson, Jas. P., Sept. 3, '61.	Discharged May, '62.
Powers, John, Sept. 3, '61.	Died wounds received Dec. 5, '62.
Powers, Michael, Sept. 3, '61.	Re-enlisted as vet.; mustered out [Nov. 4, '65, as veteran.
Paine, Robert S., Sept. 3, '61.	Mustered out Oct. 4, '64.
Riley, Wm., Sept. 3, '61.	Mustered out Oct. 15, '64.
Ruby, Henry, Sept. 3, '61.	Re-enlisted as vet.; mustered out [Nov. 4, '65, as corporal.
Rice, Horace K., Sept. 3, '61.	Promoted serg't, then 1st lieut.
Sullivan, M., Sept. 3, '61.	Mustered out Nov. 4, '65, as corp.
Tuller, Byron H., Sept. 3, '61.	Promoted to captain.
Smith, Cyrus B., Sept. 3, '61.	Discharged Jan., '62.
Stookey, Jno. A., Sept. 3, '61.	Died Feb. 11, '62.
Smythe, Chas. E., Sept. 3, '61.	Mustered out Sept. 20, '65.
Temple, Pulaski L., Sept. 3, '61.	Discharged Sept., '62.
Tater, Henry, Sept. 3, '61.	Discharged April 16, '63.
Taber, Augustus A., Sept. 3, '61.	Private hospital steward, U. S. A.
Thomas, Jno. R., Sept. 3, '61.	Mustered out Aug. 29, '64.
Vancourt, Jno. D., Sept. 3, '61.	Disch'd April 30, '62, as corporal.
Weatherby, W. D., Sept. 3, '61.	Discharged July, '62.
Williams, Chas., Sept. 3, '61.	Discharged July, '62.
Wood, Geo. W., Sept. 3, '61.	Mustered out Oct. 15, '64.
Webb, Edward S., Sept. 3, '61.	Discharged Sept., '62.
Westfall, Chas., Sept. 3, '61.	Discharged May, '62.
Walters, Jas. L., Sept. 3, '61.	Discharged Mar. 4, '62.
Yopes, Simon, Sept. 3, '61.	Mustered out Sept. 8, '64.

RECRUITS.

Arbuckle, Jno. H., Aug. 6, '62.	Mustered out July 12, '65.
Adams, David, Dec. 22, '63.	Mustered out Nov. 4, '65.
Able, Dempsey, Dec. 15, '63.	Mustered out Nov. 4, '65.
Ater, Wm. H., Sept. 3, '61.	Died Nov. 14, '63.
Anderson, Jacob, Aug. 12, '62.	
Bradley, Worth R., Feb. 2, '64.	Mustered out Nov. 4, '65.
Rockway, D. S., Jan. 24, '64.	Mustered out Nov. 4, '65.
Boddy, Robert, Dec. 14, '63.	Mustered out Nov. 4, '65.
Carmean, Robt., Dec. 14, '63.	Mustered out Nov. 4, '65.

Name, and date of Rank.	Rrmarks.
Carmean, G. W., Dec. 18, '63.	Mustered out Nov. 4, '65.
Daniels, Jas. W., Jan. 29, '64.	Must'd out Nov. 4, '65, as sergt.
Dunston, J. O., Jan. 4, '64.	Mustered out Nov. 4, '65.
Daily, Jno., March 18, '64.	Mustered out Nov. 4, '65.
Dunston, Chas., Jan. 4, '64.	Died at LaGrange, Tenn., July 14, ['64, wounded.
Earles, Edward, Jan. 30, '64.	Mustered out Nov. 4, '65.
Emerson, Jerome, Feb. 7, '65.	Mustered out Nov. 4. '65.
Gregerty, John, Jan. 27, '64.	Mustered out Nov. 4, '65.
Gibbs, Jas. A., Jan, 15, '64.	Must'd out Nov. 4, '64, as corp.
Hall, Eugene, Dec. 10, '63.	Mustered out Nov. 4, '65.
Holman, Wm., Jan. 26, '64.	Mustered out Nov. 4, '65.
Hoffman, Peter, Jan. 10, '64.	Must'd out Nov. 4, '65, as corp.
Holman, And. J. Feb. 9, '64.	Died at Memphis, Tenn, June 9, [1864.
Lawson, Taylor, Jan. 16, '64.	Mustered out Nov. 4, '65.
Lehn, Wilson, April 25, '64.	Mustered out June 5, '65.
Martin, Henry, Dec. 15, '63.	Mustered out Nov. 4, '65.
McDougal, Jno. R., Jan. 4, '64.	Mustered out Nov. 4. '65.
McCune, Martin, Dec. 19, '63.	Mustered out Nov. 4, '65.
May, Theodore, Dec. 19, '63.	Mustered out Nov. 4. '65.
Pate, Robert, April, 7, '64.	Mustered out Nov. 4, '65.
Ruby, Horace S., Jan. 30, '64.	Mustered out Nov. 4, '65.
Rea, John T., Jan. 1, '64.	Mustered out Nov. 4, '65.
Reed, Elhannan, April 1, '64.	Mustered out Nov. 4, '65.
Reedy, Jas. A., Jan. 26, '64.	
Scott, Wm. F., Dec. 31, '63.	Must'd out Nov. 4, '65, as corp.
Shinneman, A. T., Feb. 13, '64.	Mustered out Nov. 4, '65.
Stookey, H. L., Jan. 30, '64.	Mustered out Nov. 4, '65.
Smith, Wm., Dec. 11, '63.	Absent, sick at mustering out of [regiment.
Stewart, Wm. C., Mar. 20, '64.	Absent, sick at mustering out of [regiment.
Wood, James, April 16, '64.	
Williams, Chas., Jan. 25, '64.	Vet.; mustered out Nov. 4, '65.
Webber Philip, Feb. 1, '64.	Discharged Dec. 8, '65.
Wood, Geo. W., Feb. 9, '65.	Mustered out Nov. 4, '65.
Young, Geo., Mar. 24, '64.	Mustered out Nov. 4, '65.

Name, and date of Rank.   *Remarks.*

UNASSIGNED RECRUITS.

Dorris, Jas., Jan. 26, '64.
Daniels, Jas., Feb. 12, '64.
Earles, Chas. W., April 7, '64. Rejected.
Glove, Alonzo M., Jan. 27, '64. Discharged May 10, '64.
Saunders, Forest, Jan. 23, '64. Discharged July 2, '64.
Scott, Wm. F., Dec. 21, '63.
Wilson, Wm. H., Mar. 9, '65. Discharged May 11, '65.
White, Wm. D., Mar. 7, '65.

EIGHTH ILLINOIS INFANTRY.

This regiment was organized on the 25th day of April, 1861, for the three months service, Col. R. J. Oglesby commanding. Stationed at Cairo until mustered out, at close of term. Re-organized for three years service; moved to Bird's Point, Mo., Feb. 2, 1862; embarked for Tennessee river; engaged enemy near Ft. Henry; attacked Ft. Donelson about middle of Feb., where most valuable service was rendered, and where serious loss was sustained. Maj. John P. Post was taken prisoner in this battle. Was engaged in the battle of Shiloh. Actively participated at the seige of Corinth, where Col. Oglesby was dangerously wounded and borne from the field in expectation of immediate death. Met enemy at Raymond. Sent to Camp Butler in '64, on veteran furlough. Afterwards the regiment was in Western Tennessee, Mississippi and Louisiana. Mustered out of service at Baton Rouge, May 4, 1866. Ordered to Springfield for final payment and discharge, where it arrived May 13, 1866.

ROSTER EIGHTH ILL. INFANTRY. (THREE MONTHS.)

COLONEL.

R. J. Oglesby, May 3, '61.   Re-enlisted 3 years service.

LIEUTENANT COLONEL.

Frank L. Rhodes, May 3, '61.   Re-enlisted 3 years service.

MAJORS.

John P. Post, May 3, '61.   Re-enlisted 3 years service.
Herman Leib, Oct. 7, '62.   Promoted Col. 9th Inf. (col.)

Name, and date of Rank.   *Remarks.*

CAPTAIN CO. "A."

I. C. Pugh, April 23, '61.   Re-enlisted 3 years service; Col. 41st regiment.

FIRST LIEUTENANT.

I. N. Martin, April 23, '61.

SECOND LIEUTENANT.

G. M. Bruce, April 23, '61.   Re-enlisted 3 years service.

CAPTAINS CO. "B."

H. P. Westerfield, Apr. 30, '61.
John P. Post.

FIRST LIEUTENANT.

John M. Lowry, Apr. 25, '61.   Resigned Sept. 3, '62.

SECOND LIEUTENANT.

Thos. Goodman, April 25, '61.   Resigned July 25, '61.

ROSTER EIGHTH REGIMENT INF. (THREE YEARS.)

COLONELS.

R. J. Oglesby, April 25, '61.   Promoted Brig.-Gen. April 1, '62; Major-Gen. Nov. 9, '62.
F. L. Rhodes, April 1, '62.   Resigned Oct. 7, '62.
John P. Post, Oct. 7, '62.   Resigned Sept. 28, '63.
Josiah A. Shietz, Sept. 23, '63.   Prom. to Brevet Brig.-Gen. Nov. 25, '65; resigned Feb. 9, '66.
Loyd Wheaton, Feb. 9, '64.   Mustered out May 4, '66.

LIEUTENANT COLONELS.

R. H. Sturges, Oct. 7, '62.   Resigned July 25, '63.
Noah Dennison, Nov. 8, '66.   Mustered out May 4, '66.

MAJORS.

H. Lieb, Oct. 7, '62.   Prom. Col. 9th Louisiana (col.)
Daniel Sayers, Mar. 8, '66.   Mustered out May 4, '66.

ADJUTANTS.

W. C. Clark, Jan. 25, '61.   Resigned June 25, '62.

| Name, and date of Rank. | Remarks. |

B. F. Monroe, June 25, '62.   Promoted Capt. Co. "I."
Fred. A. King, July 25, '64.   Resigned Oct. 9, '64.
Wm. W. Carver, Oct. 9, '64.
Leander A. Sheetz, Nov. 25, '65. Mustered out May 4, '6–.

QUARTERMASTERS.

Sam'l Rhodes, Jan. 25, '61.   Resigned Dec. 9, '61.
H. N. Pearse, Dec. 10, '61.   Resigned Aug. 1, '63.
R. T. Mercer, Aug. 1, '63.   Mustered out May 4, '66.

SURGEONS.

S. T. Trowbridge, Apr. 25, '61. Mustered out July 27, '64.
C. N. Dennison, July 27, '64.   Mustered out May 4, '66.

FIRST ASSISTANT SURGEONS.

John M. Phipps, April 25, '61. Resigned Feb. 16, '63.
W. F. Buck, Nov. 28, '63.   Mustered out May 4, 66.

SECOND ASSISTANT SURGEON.

C. M. Spalding, May 27, '65.   Mustered out May 4, '66.

CHAPLAIN.

Samuel Day, Jan. 28, '66.   Mustered out Jan. 29, '65.

CAPTAINS.

G. M. Price, July 25, '61.   Resigned Feb. 5, '62.
Frank Leeper, Feb. 5, '62.   Killed in battle.
Geo. D. Durfee, May 14, '63.   Mustered out May 4, '66.

FIRST LIEUTENANTS.

W. J. Taylor, Feb. 5, '62.   Resigned Jan. 28, '63.
W. A. Albert, May 14, '63.   Term expired Jan. 27, '64.
Sam'l Nicholson, Jan. 27, '64. Mustered out May 4, '66.

SECOND LIEUTENANT.

J. W. Reavis, Jan. 28, '64.   Mustered out May 4, '66.

SERGEANT.

D. W. Greenawalt, July 25, '61. Died at Bird's Point, Mo., Nov.
  [18, '61.

—10

74   HISTORY OF MACON COUNTY.

Name, and date of Rank.   Remarks.
                        CORPORALS.

James Dunbar, July 25, '61.   Re-enlisted as vet.; mustered out
                                  [May 4, '66.
Michael Matthews, July 25, '61. Killed at Ft. Donelson, Feb. 15,'62.
Wm. M. Bullard, July 25, '61.   Died at Cincinnati, O., Mar. 4, '62,
                                  [of wound rec'd at Donelson.
Robert E. Horey, Jnly 25, '61. Discharged July 24, '64.
Geo. S. Leach, July 25, '61.   Killed at Ft. Donelson, Feb, 15,'62.
John B. Lowell, July 25, '61.   Died Bird's Point, Mo., Nov. 1, '61.
Marcellus Warner, July 25, '61. Killed at Raymond, Miss., May
                                  [12, '63.

                        PRIVATES.

Baker, Abijah J. July 25, '61. Prom. sergeant; died June 4, '63,
                                  [of wounds rec'd at Vicksburg.
Bashford, G. D., July 25, '61. Promoted sergeant.
Bacon, John H., July 25, '61.   Mustered out May 4, '66.
Cochrane, Henry, July, 25, '61. Killed at Shiloh, April 6, '62.
Cook, Andrew E., July 25, '61. Re-enlisted as veteran.
Dunn, James W., July 25, '61.   Mustered out July 30, '64.
Denniston, Wm., July 25, '61.   Killed at Shiloh, April 6, '62.
Dudley, Jos. S., July 25, '61. Promoted corporal; mustered out
                                  [May 4, '66.
Florey, A. J., July 25, '61.   Disch'd Aug. 15, '62, of wounds
                                  [at Donelson.
Fouch, Jos., July 25, '61.   Prom. serg't; disch'd July 10, '65,
                                  [of wounds rec'd at Jackson.
Greer, B. F., July 25, '61.   Re enlisted.
Hagart A. H., July 25, '61.   Prom. corp.; M. O. May 4, '66.
Helm, L., July 25, '61.   Prom. sergeant; dis. Jan. 27, '62.
Hess, Joseph, July 25, '61.   Discharged June 22, '62, of wounds
                                  [received at Donelson.
Hudson, James, July 25, '61.   Killed at Raymond, Miss., May
                                  [May 12, '63.
Idell, Robert, July 25, '61.   Mustered out May 4, '66.
Jefferson, W. J., July 25, '61. Killed at Ft. Donelson, Feb. 15,'62.
James, Geo. W., July 25, '61.   Prom. corp.; killed at Champion
                                  [Hill, May 16, '63.

Name, and date of Rank.	Remarks.
Jones, Andrew, July 25, '61.	Killed at Ft. Donelson, Feb. 15, '62.
Livingston, M. C., July 25, '61.	Mustered out July 30, '64.
Leach, James, July 25, '61.	Mustered out July 30, '64.
Leland, Jas. H., July 25, '61.	
Muirhead, T. J., July, 25, '61.	Killed at Shiloh April 6, '62.
McDonald, J. C., July 25, '61.	
Moskell, Ellis, July 25, '61.	Mustered out May 28, '66.
Pope, Geo. S., July 25, '61.	Killed at Shiloh April 6, '62.
Reavis, Jas. W., July 25, '61.	Promoted to 2d lieut.
Rock, Jos. W., July 25, '61.	Mustered out May 4, '66.
Shively, H. C., July 25, '61.	" July 30, '64.
Smith, Jos. W., July 25, '61.	" "
Whitbeck, H., July 25, '61.	Killed at Fort Donelson Feb. 15, ['62.

RECRUITS.

Albert, Wm. A., Aug. 15. '61.	Promoted lieut.
Ault, Jos., Dec. 11, '63.	Promoted sergeant; mustered out [May 4, '66.
Bradbury, J. A., Aug. 15, '61.	Promoted sergeant; killed at Shi-[loh April 6, '62.
Craine, Robt. W., Aug. 5, '61.	Discharged Dec. 27, '61.
Dumman, J. W., Aug. 15, '61.	Discharged Aug. 15, '62, of wound [at Donelson.
Green, John H., Aug. 10, '61.	Killed at Raymond, Miss., May [12, '63.
Helpman, Irwin, Aug. 15, '61.	Re-enlisted as vet.
Holtz, Ernest, Aug. 15, '61.	Discharged July 22, '62, of wound [at Donelson.
Hatchett, Wm., Aug. 15, '62.	Discharged Aug 14, '64.
Haggard, Jas., Aug. 16, '61.	Died at Decatur, Ala., April 11, ['62.
James, B. F., Aug. 15, '61.	Killed at Donelson Feb. 15, '62.
Kunkleman, J. H., Aug. 10, '61.	
McCarty, Patrick, Aug. 5, '61.	Died at Carthage, La., of wounds [received on steamer Moderator.
Marsh, Peter, Dec. 15, '61.	Mustered out May 4, '66.

76   HISTORY OF MACON COUNTY.

Name, and date of Rank.	Remarks.
McKinly, W. A. Aug. 10, '61.	Died at Memphis, Tenn., Mar. 10, ['63.
Norris, John H., Aug. 5, '61.	Discharged Feb. 19, '63.
Nicholson, J. R., Aug. 15, '61.	Mustered out May 4, '66.
Nicholson, Jer., Aug. 15, '61.	Discharged Aug. 14, '64; tm. exp.
Paine, R. T., Aug. 5, '61.	Transferred to 9th regt. La. Inft. [May 5, '63.
Pearce, Irwin, Aug. 25, '61.	Discharged Dec. 25, '61.
Pope, Wm. F. Jan. 1, '62.	Promoted capt.; discharged Oct. [31, '65; disabled.
Rector, John W., Dec. 15, '62.	Died in hospital at Vicksburg, July [2, '63, disease.
Stevenson, W. B. Aug. 2, '61.	Transferred, and disch'd Feb. 2, ['66, of wounds at Jackson, Miss.
Squire, Geo. W., Aug. 15, '61.	Died at Memphis, Tenn., Sept. 12, ['63.
Steel, Jas. F., Aug. 15, '61.	Discharged Aug. 14, '64; tm. expd.

DRAFTS AND RECRUITS.

Bosworth, J. B., Sept. 26, '64.   Mustered out Sept. 26, '65.

COMPANY "B."

CAPTAINS.

H. Lieb, Jan. 25, '61.	Promoted major.
Peter Schlosser, Oct. 7, '62.	Term expired Jan. 27. '64.
H. A. Miller, Jan. 28, '64.	Mustered out May 4, '66.

FIRST LIEUTENANTS.

| B. Zick, Oct. 7, '62. | Term expired Jan. 28, '64. |
| Thos. McInery, Jan, 28, '64. | Mustered out May 4, '66. |

SECOND LIEUTENANTS.

| H. J. Marsh, Jan. 25, '61. | Killed at Ft. Donelson. |
| John Collmer, Oct. 7, '62. | Term expired Jan. 27, '64. |

FIRST SERGEANT.

H. C. Oglesby, July 25, '61.   Reduced to ranks; drummed out of service, Sept. 15, '63.

HISTORY OF MACON COUNTY. 77

Name, and date of Rank. *Remarks.*

SERGEANTS.

B. F. Snow, July 25, '61.   Disch'd Sept. 22, '62, of wounds [at Donelson.
W. F. Gardenhire, July 25, '61.   Discharged May 2, '62; disabled.
Chas. Albert, July 25, '61.   Mustered out July 30, '64.

CORPORALS.

John M. Collmer, July 25, '61.   Promoted 2d lieut.
C. P. A. Goddard, July 25, '61.   Died Oct. 31, '63.
Chas. Fechner, July 25, '61.   Killed at Shiloh April 6, '62.
John Smith, July 25, '61.   Mustered out July 30, '64.
Thos. Scantlin, July 25, '61.   Transferred to non-com. staff as [com. sergt.

PRIVATES.

Athons, W. H., July 25, '61.
Abin, Geo., July 25, '61.   Died April 8, '64, of wounds recd. [at Raymond, Miss.
Bech, Jno. M., July 25, '61.   Disch'd Sept. 8, '62, of wounds at [Donelson.
Batin, F., July 25, '61.   Mustered out July 30, '64.
Basler, J. G., July, 25, '61.   "   July 20, '64.
Becker, Wm., July 25, '61.   Died at Vicksburg, June 30, '63.
Bruner, John, July 25, '61.   Died May 25, '63, of wounds recd. [at Champion Hills.
Berlin, D. M., July 25, '61.   Mustered out July 1, '65.
Bruner, J. D., July, 25, '61.
Baner, Jacob, July 25, '61.   Mustered out July 30, '64.
Breitsprecker, W., July 25, '61.   "   "
Culligan, John, July 25, '61.   "   "
Cunningham, S. B., July 25, '61.
Campbell, Jno. E., July 25, '61.   "   May 4, '64.
Durant, F., July 25, '61.   Accidently killed May 20, '62.
Dutcher, Chas., July 25, '61.   Discharged Oct. 14, '61.
Dunham, A., July 25, '61.   Killed at Ft. Donelson Feb. 15, '62.
Everman, J. C., July 25, '61.   Mustered out Aug. 6, '64.
Elliot, Jos., July 25, '61.   Died at Cairo, Ill., (no date.)

Name, and date of Rank.	Remarks.
Flora, Jasper, July 25, '61.	Discharged July 25, '62, by order [of Grant.
Gardenhire, J. M., July 25, '61.	Discharged May 2, '62, by order of [Grant.
Gemer, A., July 25, '61.	Died Aug. 14, '61.
Genert, August, July 25, '61.	
Geswinder, N., July 25, '61.	Mustered out Mar. 21, '66.
Gardenhire, Geo., July 25, '61.	Killed at Donelson Feb. 15, '62.
Humphrey, J. A., July 25, '61.	
Jameson, Joshua, July 25, '61.	Absent at mustering out.
Johnson, Moses, July 25, '61.	Discharged Oct. 14, '61.
Krebs, Chris., July 25, '61.	Disch'd July 24, '62, of wounds at [Donelson and Shiloh.
Keller, Jacob, July 25, '61.	Killed at Donelson Feb. 15, '62.
Kelly, John, July, 25, '61.	Murdered at Norfolk, Mo., Sept. [17, '61.
Lynch, Jas., July 25, '61.	Mustered out July 30, '64.
Leeper, Wm., July 25, '61.	Transferred to N. C. S. as Mus.
Miller, F. C., July 25, '61.	Killed at Donelson, Feb. 15, '62.
Miller, H. A., July 25, '61.	Promoted captain July 14, '64.
Manchon, H., July 25, '61.	Discharged July 10, '63; disabled.
O'Brien, Peter, July 25, '61.	
O'Neil, John, July 25, '61.	Discharged July 25, '64: tm. expd.
Priest, John W., July 25, '61.	Killed at Donelson Feb. 15, '62.
Peters, Geo., July 25, '61.	Mustered out May 4, '64.
Robinett, John, July 25, '61.	" "
Rouse, Geo. W., July 25, '61.	
Rust, M. N., July 25, '61.	Transferred to 12th Ill. infantry.
Switzer, John M., July 25, '61.	Promoted sergt.
Staines, Dutton, July 25, '61.	Promoted corpl.; disch'd Sept. 24, ['62.
Steward, E. O., July 25, '61.	Discharged Oct. 14, '61.
Seiter, John C. July 25, '61.	Mustered out May 4, '66.
Tansey, V. G., July 25, '61.	Discharged Oct. 14, '61.
Wardner, H., July 25, '61.	Transferred to Inv. Corps Sept. 15, ['62.
Warren, J. July 25, '61.	Discharged Nov. 8, '63, of wounds [at Vicksburg.

HISTORY OF MACON COUNTY. 79

Name, and date of Rank.	Remarks.
Wills, Andrew, July 25, '61.	Died Feb. 17, '62, of wounds at [Donelson.

RECRUITS, DRAFTS AND SUBSTITUTES.

Anthons, Josephus, Apr. 5, '64.	Prom. corp.; mustered out May 4, ['66.
Andrish, Antoine, Aug. 17, '61.	Killed at Shiloh April 6, '62.
Beecher, Peter, Aug. 17, '61.	Disch'd Sept. 9, '62, of wounds at [Shiloh.
Brown, Henry, Aug. 29, '61.	Disch'd Sept. 5, '62, of wounds at [Shiloh.
Dunham, Dayton, Aug. 16, '61.	Wounded at Donelson; discharged [April 11, '62.
Dunz, John, Aug. 29, '61.	Mustered out May 4, '65.
Frank, Peter, Sept. 7, '61.	
Fluke, August, Aug. 29, '62.	Discharged Oct. 11, '63.
Grosh, Jacob, Aug. 17, '61.	Mustered out Aug. 5, '64.
Gross, Jacob, Aug. 22, '61.	
Gunter, Hugo, Nov. 27, '61.	Mustered out March 2, '66.
Grob, Jno. J., Jan 5, '64.	" May 4, '66.
Hatchly, Isaac, Nov. 26, '61.	Disch'd May 1, '62. of wounds at [Shiloh.
Hawley, Jno. D., Sept. 19, '61.	
Jones, R. F.	Mustered out May 14, '66.
Kepler, M., Sept. 7, '61.	Disch'd Dec. 15, '62, of wounds at [Shiloh.
Lehman, Jacob, Aug. 8, '61.	Disharged Aug. 7, '64.
Langheld, August, Aug. 5, '61.	Disch'd Aug. 8, '63, of wounds at [Raymond, Miss.
Lynn, Robt., Aug. 29, '61.	Died Oct. 31, '61.
Lankerman, Jacob, Jan. 1, '62.	Mustered out May 4, '66.
Mossman, Wm., Dec. 18, '63.	" "
Magae, Jno. S., April 28, '64.	" "
Mathys, Jno., April 16, '64.	" "
McGorry, Thos., Dec. 1, '61.	Promoted 1st lieut.
O'Connol, J. H., Aug. 13, '61.	
Preston, Thos., Aug. 23, '61.	Disch'd Oct. 15, '63, of wounds at [Vicksburg.

Name, and date of Rank. *Remarks.*

Pfeifer, Frank, April 15, '64. Mustered out July 1, '65.
Reister, Leonard, Sept. 2, '61.
Walker, Michael, Aug. 13, '61. Mustered out May 4, '66.
Webber, Chas., Sept. 28, '61. Killed at Charleston, Mo., Oct. 16, ['61.
Zimm, Jno., April 28, '64. Mustered out May 4, '66.

TWENTY-FIRST ILLINOIS INFANTRY.

The Twenty-first Illinois Regiment Infantry was mustered into the service in the latter part of June, 1861, under command of U. S. Grant. Went to Ironton, Mo. Engaged in battle at Perryville and Chaplin Hill. In a skirmish at Knob Gap. Engaged in battle near Murfreesboro, Tenn.; lost many men in this engagement. Was with Gen. Rosecrans' army, from Murfreesboro to Chattanooga. Engaged in a severe skirmish at Liberty Gap, June 25, 1863. In the battle of Chicamauga, Sept. 19-20, 1863.

After this battle, regiment remained at Bridgeport, Ala., three months.

Mustered out Dec. 16, 1865, at San Antonio, Texas. Arrived at Camp Butler Jan. 18, 1866, for final pay and discharge.

ROSTER TWENTY-FIRST INFANTRY—CO. "A."

Name, and date of Rank. *Remarks.*

COLONELS.

U. S. Grant, June 16, '61. Promoted Brig. Gen. Aug. 5, '61; [Maj. Gen. Feb. 16, '62.
J. W. Alexander, Aug. 23, '61. Killed in battle Sept. 20, '63.
Jas. E. Calloway, May 11, '65. Mustered out Dec. 16, '65.
Wm. H. Jamison, July 13, '65. " "

LIEUTENANT COLONELS.

Geo. W. Peck, Sept 2, '61. Dischd, ill health, Sept. 19, '62.
W. E. McMaken, Sept. 19, '62. Term expired Nov. 16, '64.

MAJOR.

Jno. L. Wilson, June 2, '65. Mustered out Dec. 16, '65.

HISTORY OF MACON COUNTY.

Name, and date of Rank.   *Remarks.*

ADJUTANTS.

Chas. B. Steele, Sept. 6, '61.   Resigned July 20, '64.
J. R. Duncan, July 20, '64.   Prom. capt. company " A;" mustered out Dec. 16, '65.
Jno. A. Pierce, Aug. 21, '65. Mustered out Dec. 16, '65.

QUARTERMASTERS.

Jno. E. Jones, May 15, '61.   Mustered out Aug. 18, '64.
Simeon Paddleford, Aug. 18, '64.   "   Dec. 16, '65.

SURGEONS.

Eden M. Seeley, Aug. 21, '62. Res. May 21, '64.
Jas. J. Reat, May 21, '64.   Mustered out Dec. 16, '65.

CHAPLAIN.

E. D. Wilkins, Oct. 12, '61.   Res. July 9, '64.

CAPTAINS.

S. S. Goode, May 7, '61.   State service, ten regt. bill.
Geo. S. Dunning, May 17, '61. Res. Oct. 24, '62.
Geo. F. Eaton, Oct. 24, '62.   Mustered out July 5, '64.

FIRST LIEUTENANTS.

E. D. Coxe, Oct. 24, '62.   Mustered out July 5, '64.
B. F. Osborne, July 5, '64.   Dismissed July 3, '65.
J. R. Sheperd, Aug. 21, '65.   Mustered out Dec. 16, '65.

SECOND LIEUTENANTS.

J. L. Bowman, May 7, '61.   Res. April 14, '62.
Jos. C. Alvord, Oct. 24, '62. Killed in battle Dec. 31. '62.
Theo. Gross, June 1, '63.   Res. May 12, '65.
Alvin Colmus, Dec. 16, '65.   Mustered out Dec. 16, '65.

FIRST SERGEANT.

Edward D. Coxe, June 15, '61. Promoted 2d lieutenant.

SECOND SERGEANT.

Charles Disbrow, June, 15, '61. Discharged Aug. 10, '62, disability.

Name, and date of Rank.   *Remarks.*

CORPORALS.

Elijah Smith, June 15, '61.	Killed at Stone river Dec. 30, '62.
Wm. R. Wheeler, June 15, '61.	Discharged Sept. 1, '63.
Ben. F. Osborne, June 15, '61.	Re-enlisted as vet.; promoted 1st lieut.
Joseph Wagoner, June 15, '61.	Discharged April 23, '63.
G. W. Stephens, June 15, '61.	Re-enlisted as vet.; mustered out Dec. 16, '65.

MUSICIAN.

J. D. L. Meeks, June 15, '61.   Mustered out July 5, 64.

WAGONER.

Jno. Hanks, June 15, '61.   Mustered out July 5, '64.

PRIVATES.

Joseph Barber, June 23, '61.	Re-enlisted as vet.; mustered out Dec. 16, '65.
Jas. T. Baker, June 15, '61.	Discharged Oct. 16, '62.
Hugh Bacon, June 15, '61.	Killed at Stone river Dec. 31, '62.
Philip Bloss, June 15, '61.	Died at Andersonville prison June 15, '64.
Jacob Conouff, June 15, '61.	Killed at Stone river Dec. 30, '62.
Wm. H. Clipson, June 15, '61.	Re-enlisted as vet.; mustered out July 13, '65. Prisoner of war.
Jas. Clark, June 21, '61.	Re-enlisted as vet·; transferred to eng. corps Aug. 2, '64.
Henry Cruise, July 21, '61.	
David Crawford, June 26, '61.	Re-enlisted as vet.; mustered out July 13, '65. Prisoner of war.
Frank Ernst, June 15, '61.	Dischd Aug. 10, '62; disability.
F. H. Fammer, June 15, '61.	
H. F. Fletcher, June 15, '61.	Mustered out July 5, '64.
Daniel Foley, June 15, '61.	Killed at Chickamauga Sept. 10, '63.
Joseph E. Hobson, June 15, '61.	Mustered out July 5, '64.
Jasper H. Hixson, June 15, '61.	Disch'd March 11, '64; disability.
Wm. H. Higgins, June 24, '61.	Killed at Stone river Dec. 30, '62.
Orlando Hogan, June 24, '61.	Mustered out July 5, '64.

Name, and date of Rank.	Remarks.
Wm. Johnson, June 25, '61.	Discharged Oct. 1, '61.
Thos. E. Jefferson, June 25, '61.	Mustered out July 5, '64.
Jas. R. Kennedy, June 25, '61.	Disch'd Sept. 29, '62, wounds.
Jno. B. Lembeck, June 25, '61.	Transferred to inv. corps March 23, '64.
Jno. Leigh, June 24, '61.	Mustered out July 5, '64.
Wm. McPherson, June 15, '61.	
H. B. F. Martin, June 15, '61.	Re-enlisted as vet.; died Oct. 30, '64.
Jno. McAvoy, June 15, '61.	Re-enlisted as vet.; mustered out July 13, '65. Prisoner of war.
L. D. Morgan, June 23, '61.	Mustered out July 5, '64.
Abe. McKitrick, June 23, '61.	Disch'd April 30, '62; disability.
Wm. McGrath, June 15, '61.	Discharged Oct. 7, '61.
C. M. Pope, June 15, '61.	Mustered out July 5, '64.
Wm. H. Ross, June 25, '61.	" "
C. Rosenberger, June 15, '61.	" " as corp.
Daniel Shutter, June 23, '61.	
Peter Shelt, June 15, '61.	Re-enlisted as vet.; mustered out Dec, 16, '65.
Geo. S. Stuart, Juue 15, '61.	Died at Annapolis, Md., Nov., '64.
Henry C. Stuart, June 15, '61.	Re-enlisted as vet.; mustered out Dec. 16, '65.
Edward Stockton, June 15, '61.	
Jos. Sheperd, June 15, '61.	
John Smith, June 15, '61.	Mustered out July 5, '64.
John Street, June 15, '61.	Re-enlisted as vet.; mustered out Dec. 16, '65, as corporal.
Patrick Shannon, June 15, '61.	Discharged to re-enlist in 15th U. S. Inf., Dec. 24, '62.
Jas. Shepherd, June 22, '61.	Re-enlisted as vet.; prom. 1st lieut.
Wm. H. Stewart, June 23, '61.	Mustered out Dec. 16, '65.
Martin Tibbett, June 15, '61.	Mustered out July 5, '64.
John Thute, June 24, '61.	Re-enlisted as vet.; mustered out Dec. 16, '65.
Jno. L. Whitton, June 15, '61.	Disch'd Aug. 18, '63—disability.
Benj. F. Witts, June 22, '61.	Died Jan. 7, '63—wounds.

Name, and date of Rank.	Remarks.
Wm. H. Witts, June 24, '61.	Mustered out July 5, '64.
Rodolph Zorger, June 22, '61.	Died Jan. 22, '63, of wounds.

RECRUITS.

John Cram, Oct. 12, '61.	Died Nov. 10, '62.
John Eckart, Jan. 22, '62.	Mustered out Jan. 28, '65.
Martin Fitzpatrick, Oct. 12, '61.	" " Feb. 12, '65.
Taylor Florey, Oct. 12, '61.	" " April 27, '65.
Albert Fowkes, Oct. 12, '61.	
Silas W. West, Aug. 13, '61.	Discharged Feb. 1, '62—disability.

COMPANY "K."

CAPTAINS.

A. M. Pattison, May 16, '61.	Resigned Nov. 21, '62.
John L. Wilson, Nov. 21, '62.	Promoted Major.
Sydney B. Wade, July 18, '65.	Mustered out Dec. 16, '65.

SECOND LIEUTENANT.

John F. Weitzel, Jan. 31, '63. Killed at Chickamauga, Sep.19,'63.

PRIVATES.

Pat. S. Curtis, June 14, '61.
John F. Weitzel, June 25, '61. Promoted sergeant and 2d lieut.

UNASSIGNED RECRUITS.

John Barrett, Dec. 19, '63.

THIRTY-FIFTH ILLINOIS INFANTRY.

The Thirty-fifth Illinois Infantry was organized in Decatur, on the third day of July, 1861. On the twenty-third it was accepted by the Secretary of War, as Col. G. A. Smith's Independent Regiment of Illinois Volunteers. Left Decatur August 4th; arrived at Jefferson Barracks, Mo., the 5th; thence to the Marine Hospital, St. Louis; moved to Jefferson City, Mo.; next to Otterville; marched to Sedalia and joined Gen. Siegel's advance on Springfield, arriving there the 26th; moved from Springfield to Rolla; returned to Springfield the 13th of February, 1862. In an engagement at Pea Ridge, Col. G. A. Smith was severely wounded. The principal places of action were at Rocky-faced Ridge, Resaca, Dallas, Mud Creek, Kenesaw, Perryville, Stone River and Chickamauga. Mustered out at Springfield, Ill., on the 27th day of September, 1864.

ROSTER THIRTY-FIFTH REGIMENT INFANTRY.

Name, and date of Rank.   *Remarks.*

COLONELS.

G. A. Smith, July 2, '61.   Prom. Brig.-Gen. Sept. 19, '62; discharged Sept. 22, '63.
W. P. Chandler, Sept. 22, '63.   Term expired Sept. 27, '64; was Lieutenant Colonel.

MAJOR.

John McIlwain, July 3, '61.   Killed at Kenesaw Mountain, June 22, '64.

ADJUTANTS.

W. J. Usrey, Sept. 1, '61.   Resigned April 15, '62.
Uriah Fox, April 15, '62.   Resigned Nov. 17, '63.
Samuel W. Bird, Nov. 17, '63.   Term expired Sept. 27, '64.

QUARTERMASTER.

John G. Miles, July 3, '61.   Term expired Sept. 27, '64.

SURGEONS.

W. J. Chenoweth, Sep. 25, '61.   Resigned Dec. 14, '62.
S. B. Hawley, Dec. 9, '62.   Term expired Sept. 27, '64.

FIRST ASSISTANT SURGEON.

D. C. Titball, Sept. 25, '61.   Term expired Sept. 27, '64.

SECOND ASSISTANT SURGEON.

Jonathan D. Wylie, Dec. 8, '62.   Term expired Sept. 27, '64.

CHAPLAINS.

P. D. Hammond, July 3, '61.   Resigned May 12, '62.

Name, and date of Rank.	Remarks.
R. E. Harris, May 12, '62.	Left at Florence, Ala., Aug. 18, '62; not heard from.

NON-COMMISSIONED STAFF.

SERGEANT MAJOR.

Geo. B. Peake, July 3, '61.	Prom. 2d lieut. Co. A, and capt'n.

HOSPITAL STEWARD.

Jos. T. DeWatney, July 3, '61.	Reduced, and returned to Co. A.

PRINCIPAL MUSICIANS.

Newlin B. Davis, July 3, '61.	
Archibald Monroe, July 3, '61.	Promoted to principal musician.

SECOND CLASS MUSICIAN.

Joseph Ricketts, July 3, '61.

COMPANY "A."

CAPTAINS.

B. M. Tables, July 3, '61.	Resigned Dec. 20, '61.
Pierre W. Thomas, Dec. 25,'61.	Resigned Jan. 31, '64.
Geo. B. Peake, July 3, '61.	Term expired Sept. 27, '64.

FIRST LIEUTENANTS.

George F. Deitz, Dec. 25, '61.	Died July 8, '63.
John W. Peen, Jan. 31, '64.	Term expired Sept. 27, '64.

SECOND LIEUTENANT.

Jas. Shoaff, July 3, '61.	Resigned Feb. 3, '62.

PRIVATES.

Augusta Glatz, July 3, '61.	Discharged Aug. 9, '62—wounds.
Conover Hatfield, July 3, '61.	Disch'd Dec. 12, '61—disability.
Wm. C. Stewart, July 3, '61.	Disch'd June 15, '62—disability.
Andrew Stewart, July 3, '61.	
Joseph McMullen, July 3, '61.	
John D. McFadden, July 3, '61.	
John Hager, July 3, '61.	
Curtis Austin, July 3, '61.	Transferred to 59th reg't.
Frank Rea, July 3, '61.	

Name, and date of Rank. *Remarks.*

COMPANY "F."

N. L. F. Monroe, July 3, '61.   Disch'd March 24, '63—disability.

FORTY-FIRST ILLINOIS INFANTRY.

The Forty-first Infantry Illinois Volunteers was organized at Decatur, Illinois, in the month of August, 1861, by Col. Isaac C. Pugh. Moved to St. Louis August 7; 29th moved to Bird's Point, Mo., and assigned to the command of General Prentiss; September 8th moved to Paducah, Ky., and assigned to General B. F. Smith's command; February 5th, '62, moved to Fort Henry; 11th marched to Fort Donelson, and was engaged, 13th, 14th and 15th in the siege, under Colonel McArthur; March 10 moved for Pittsburg Landing, arriving the 14th; engaged in the battle of Shiloh, April 6th and 7th, 1862; engaged in the siege at Corinth; marched to Memphis, arriving July 11, and remained until Sept. 6; moved for Bolivar; moved from Bolivar to LaGrange, Nov. 3; Arrived at Memphis, Tenn., March 10, 1863; sent to Hernando, Miss.; in an engagement at Coldwater; returned to Memphis; moved to Vicksburg May 12th, etc.; was at last consolidated with the Fifty-third regiment.

ROSTER FORTY-FIRST REGIMENT INFANTRY.

Name, and date of Rank. *Remarks.*

COLONEL.

Isaac C. Pugh, July 27, '61.   Mustered out Aug. 20, '64.

LIEUTENANT COLONELS.

Ansel Tupper, July 27, '61.   Killed at Pittsburg Landing April 6, '62.
Jno. Warner, April 8, '62.   Discharged Nov. 26, '62.
Jno. H. Nale.   Mustered out Aug. 2, '64.

Name, and date of Rank.   *Remarks.*

MAJORS.

F. M. Long.   Killed in action July 12, '63.
R. H. McFadden.   Transferred to field staff as consolidated.

ADJUUTANTS.

B. G. Pugh, Dec. 12, '61. Res. March 17, '62.
Wm. C. Gillespie.   Mustered out Aug. 20, '64.

QUARTERMASTERS.

H. C. Bradsby, July 27, '61. Res. June 9, '62.
I. R. Pugh, Sept. 30, '62.   Res. Aug. 1, '63.
John Boughman.   Mustered out Aug. 20, '64.

SURGEONS.

Wm. M. Gray.   Mustered out March 29, '62.
Chas. Carle.   "   Aug. 20, '64.

FIRST ASSISTANT SURGEON.

Geo. W. Short, July 27, '61.   Resigned.
O. M. Warmoth, April 12, '62. Transferred to field and staff as consolidated.

SECOND ASSISTANT SURGEON.

Jno. W. Coleman, Sept. 30, '62. Term expired '66.

COMPANY "A."

CAPTAINS.

Jno. H. Nale, July 27, '61.   Promoted.
M. F. Kanan, April 8, '62.   Transferred to Co. A as consolidated.

FIRST LIEUTENANTS.

Geo. R. Steele, April 8, '62. Res. Aug. 3, '63.
Rolando Bell, April 8, '62.   Prom. from 2d lieut.; must'd out Aug. 20, '64.

Name, and date of Rank.   *Remarks.*

NON-COMMISSIONED STAFF.

SERGEANT MAJOR.

Bartley G. Pugh, Aug. 5, '61.   Promoted adjutant.

QUARTERMASTER SERGEANT.

Alonzo Burgess, Aug. 5, '61.   Mustered out Aug. 20, '64.

HOSPITAL STEWARD.

Jas. W. Routh, Aug. 5, '61.   Mustered out Aug. 20, '64.

PRINCIPAL MUSICIAN.

Alex. Allsbury, Aug. 5, '61.   Reduced to ranks Sept. 1, '62.

FIRST SERGEANT.

Lewis B. Morton, Aug. 5, '61.   Died at Paducah, Ky., Sep. 19,'61.

SERGEANTS.

Roland Bell, Aug. 5, '61.   Promoted 2d lieut.
Bryant Kelsey, Aug. 5,'61.   Died June 20, '63; wounds.
W. E. Winholtz. Aug. 5, '61.   Mustered out Aug. 20, '64, as 1st sergt.; wounds.
David S. Morse, Aug. 5, '61.   Died at Moscow, Tenn., Jan. 23, '63.

CORPORALS.

Wm. H. Hecocks, Aug. 5, '61.   Sergt., killed at Jackson, Miss., July 12, '63.
Moses A. Stare, Aug. 5, '61.
Henry C. Payne, Aug. 5, '61.   Mustered out Aug. 20, '64.
H. M. Streever, Aug. 5, '61.   "   "   as sergt.
Jno. W. Sheperd, Aug. 5, '61.   Discharged Nov. 10, '62; wounds.
Fred. O. Spooner, Aug. 5, '61.   Killed at Shiloh, April 6, '62.
Horace W. Clark, Aug. 5, '61.

PRIVATES.

Anderson, Jas. W., Aug. 5, '61.   Mustered out Aug. 20, '64.
Asher, Robert, Aug. 5, '61.   "   "
Albert, John, Aug. 5, '61.   "   "
Bryant, James, Aug. 5, '61.   "   "

—12

Name, and date of Rank.	Remarks.
Boring, John, Aug. 5, '61.	Mustered out Aug. 20, '64.
Beamer, Marion, Aug. 5, '61.	" "
Betzer, Geo. W., Aug. 5, '61.	Discharged Sept. 28, '62; wounds.
Bell, Albert, Aug. 5, '61.	Mustered out Aug. 20, '64.
Bridleman, Sam., Aug. 5, '61.	" "
Bear, Sam. W., Aug. 5, '61.	Disch'd Oct. 18, '62; disability.
Brancet, Marion, Aug. 5, '61.	Mustered out Aug. 20, '64.
Buck, Latham, Aug. 5, '61.	Re-enlisted as vet.; transferred to Co. A, vet. bat.
Cole, Aaron, Aug. 5, '61.	Re-enlisted as vet.; wounded.
Chambers, Henry, Aug. 5, '61.	Disch'd June 10, '62; disability.
Collady, Hen. S., Aug. 5, '61.	Discharged for disability.
Crandall, Chris., Aug. 5, '61.	Mustered out Aug. 20, '64.
Clark, Henry G., Aug. 5, '61.	Died Nov., '61.
Culver, L, L., Aug. 5, '61.	Mustered out Aug. 20, '64.
Cox, Jas. S., Aug. 5, '61.	Killed at Shiloh April 6, '62.
Drennen, J. B., Aug. 5, '61.	Killed at Donelson Feb. 15, '62.
Dubois, M. C., Aug. 5, '61.	Died at home Sept. 23, '63; w'nds.
Delany, Elijah, Aug. 5, '61.	Mustered out Aug. 20, '64.
Davis, Geo. W., Aug. 5, '61.	" "
Davis, John M., Aug. 5, '61.	Disch'd Nov. 24, '61; disability.
Edmundson, J. W., Aug. 5, '61.	Mustered out Aug. 20, '64.
Ebord, Adam, Aug. 5, '61.	" " w'nded.
Fuller, Henry, Aug. 5, '61.	
Fike, John, Aug. 5, '61.	Mustered out Aug. 20, '64.
Fennor, Elijah B., Aug. 5, '61.	" "
Forin, John L., Aug. 5, '61.	" "
Greene, Enoch D., Aug. 5, '61.	" "
Giblin, Michael, Aug. 5, '61.	Supposed died at Decatur, Ill.
Glassie, R. W., Aug. 5, '61.	Mustered out Aug. 20, '64.
Guthbred, Richd., Aug. 5, '61.	" "
Greene, Wm. H., Aug. 5. '61.	" " as corp.
Hays, John, Aug. 5, '61.	Discharged Aug. 6, '61, by writ of habeas corpus.
Hull, John R., Aug. 5, '61.	Discharged April 8, '63, as corp.; disability.
Hull, James E., Aug. 5, '61.	Died in hands of enemy; w'nded.
Harter, Thos. J., Aug. 5, '61.	Disch'd Dec. 5, '62; wounds.

HISTORY OF MACON COUNTY. 91

Name, and date of Rank.	*Remarks.*
Huston, Walt. B., Aug, 5, '61.	Mustered out Aug. 20, '64.
Huston, Norv., Aug. 5, '61.	Killed at Shiloh April 6, '62.
Hackney, Thos., Aug. 5, '61.	Disch'd Sept. 19, '62; wounds.
Jordan, I. N., Aug. 5. '61.	Wounded at Shiloh; killed at Vicksburg June 7, '63.
Jennison, Geo., Aug. 5, '61.	Captured, paroled.
Kelse, Oscar A., Aug. 5, '61.	W'nded at Donelson; disch'd Oct. 23, '63, as corp., and prom.
Kile, Isaac W., Aug. 5, '61.	Mustered out Aug. 20, '64, as corp.
Kummisson, J.W. Aug. 5, '61.	" "
Longabaugh, R., Aug. 5, '61.	Trans. to inv. corps Sept. 15, '63.
Longabaugh, C., Aug. 5, '61.	Re-enlisted as vet.; transferred to Co. A, vet. bat.
Morlan, Wm. M., Aug. 5, '61.	Disch'd Nov. 7, '62; wounds.
Manderville, Geo., Aug. 5, '61.	Mustered out Aug. 20, '64.
Moore, Jas. W., Aug. 5, '61.	Died at Paducah, Ky., Feb. 7, '62.
McDonald, Hugh, Aug. 5, '61.	
Monohon, J. M., Aug. 5, '61.	Died at Paducah, Ky., Dec. 28, '61.
Parr, Wm., Aug. 5, '61.	Must'd out Aug. 20, '64 (vet. bat.)
Ray, Jos., Aug. 5, '61.	Wounded at Shiloh; re-enlisted as vet.; transferred to Co. A.
Smick, Aaron, Aug. 5, '61.	M. O. Aug. 20, '64, as sergeant; wounded.
Sides, Jas. M., Aug. 5, '61.	Mustered out Aug. 20, '64.
Stookey, H. L., Aug. 5, '61.	Discharged Aug. 2, '64; wounds.
Stookey, Wm. H., Aug. 5, '61.	Died at Alexandria, La., Ap.17,'64.
Strope, Thos. B., Aug. 5, '61.	Disch'd April 27, '62; disability.
Smith, Wm. W., Aug. 5, '61.	Discharged Sept. 19, '62; wounds.
Sweet, Michael, Aug. 5, '61.	
Senseman, Daniel, Aug. 5, '61.	Discharged Sept. 20, '63, as corp.; wounds.
Smith, Wm. H., Aug. 5, '61.	Serg't; died April 16,'62; wounds.
Short, William T., Aug. 5, '61.	Disch'd Feb. 27, '63; disability.
Spainhower, D., Aug. 5, '61.	Disch'd Sept. 18, '62; disability.
Stewart, Jas. H., Aug. 5, '61.	M. O. Aug. 20, '64; wounded.
Troxell, Jas. B., Aug. 5, '61.	" " " "
Todd, Geo. E., Aug. 5, '61.	Disch'd April 7, '62; disability.
Tuttle, George, Aug. 5, '61.	Killed at Shiloh, April 6, '62.

Name, and date of Rank.	Remarks.
Thompson, G. W., Aug. 5, '61.	Disch'd Nov. 17, '62; disability.
Timmons, S. H., Aug. 5, '61.	Mustered out Aug. 20, '64.
Timmons, M. F., Aug. 5, '61.	Died at Natchez Oct. 20, '63, of wounds.
Tansy, Alex. W., Aug. 5, '61.	Disch'd Nov. 25, '62; disability.
Vaughan, Wm. D., Aug. 5, '61.	Disch'd Aug. 4, '62; disability.
Westcott, W. H., Aug. 5 '61.	Mustered out Aug. 20, '64.
White, John R., Aug. 5, '61.	Re-enlisted as vet.; transferred to Co. A., Vet. Bat.
Williams, Andrew, Aug. 5, '61.	Transferred to invalid corps, Sept. 15, '63.
Williams, John E., Aug. 5, '61.	Died at Jackson, Tenn.
Wilson, Hiram R., Aug. 5, '61.	Disch'd Aug. 2, '62; wounds.
Ward, John J., Aug. 5, '61.	Mustered out Aug. 20, '64.
Whitesell, Wm. H., Aug. 5, '61.	" " "

RECRUITS.

Crain, Jas. H.	Died at home, Oct. 27, '63.
Hull, Joel.	Mustered out Aug. 20, '64.
McDonald, Samuel A.	Deserted.
Robey, Kilburn H.	Disch'd Nov. 24, '61; disability.
Schroll, George B.	Disch'd Sept. 18, '62; wounds.
Wheeler, William.	Mustered out May 3, '66, to date Aug. 25, '62.

COMPANY " B."

CAPTAINS.

A. B. Lee, July 27, '61.	Resigned Aug. 11, '63.
John H. Davis, Aug. 15, '63.	Term expired Aug. 20, '64; was 1st lieutenant.

FIRST LIEUTENANT.

Wm. H. Palmer, Aug. 15, '63.	Transferred to Co. B, as consolidated; was 2d lieutenant.

SECOND LIEUTENANT.

Jackson A. Alelick, July 27, '61. Died at Mound City, Mar. 1, '62.

HISTORY OF MACON COUNTY.

Name, and date of Rank.	Remarks.

PRIVATE.

Good, John C., Jan. 3, '64.   Transferred to Co. B, Vet. Bat.; transferred to Co. G, 53d.

COMPANY "E."

CAPTAIN.

Jno. L. Armstrong, July 27, '61.   Died Dec. 11, '61.
W. S. Oglesby, Dec. 12, '61.   Killed in action, April 6, '62; was 1st lieutenant.
Oscar Short, Sept. 1, '62.   Term expired Aug. 20, '64.

FIRST LIEUTENANTS.

Robert Warnick, Dec. 12, '61.   Dismissed as 2d lieut.
Jas. A. Wilson, April 18, '62.   Term expired Aug. 20, '64.

SECOND LIEUTENANTS.

Jas. M. Taylor, Dec. 12, '61.   Resigned April 26, '62.
S. R. Appleton, Sept. 30, '62.   Resigned Nov. 18, '62.
Jos. Catherwood, Nov. 18, '62.   Term expired Aug. 20, '64.

SERGEANT.

Pasley, Buckner H., Aug. 5, '61.   Mustered out Aug. 20, '64.
Wilson, Jas. A., Aug. 5, '61.   Promoted 1st lieutenant.
Yick, Joseph, Aug. 5, '61.   Died April 8, '62; wounds.

CORPORALS.

Rose, Albert D., Aug. 5, '61.   Disch'd Sept. 6, '62; disability.
Bennett, Jno. H., Aug. 5, '61.   Disch'd April 18, '62; disability.
Strait, Oscar, Aug. 5, '61.   Promoted sergeant, then captain.
Stevens, Henry, Aug. 5, '61.   M. O. Aug. 20, '64, as private.
Graham, Harrison, Aug. 5, '61.   Drowned near Decatur, June 19, '62.

Stevens, Jas. M., Aug. 5, '61.   Mustered out Aug. 20, '64.
Burke, Jas. W., Aug. 5, '61.   Discharged Oct. 9, '62.
Graham, Jacob, Aug. 5, '61.   Killed at Shiloh, April 6, '62.

PRIVATES.

Armstrong, T. J., Aug. 5, '61.   Mustered out Aug. 20, '64.
Austin, Edmiston, Aug. 5, '61.   "   "

94 HISTORY OF MACON COUNTY.

Name, and date of Rank.	Remarks.
Botts, Wm. D., Aug. 5, '61.	Disch'd Sept. 19, '62; disability.
Berry, Jesse R., Aug. 5, '61.	Died Nov. 11, '63; wounds.
Barrell, John P., Aug. 5, '61.	Disch'd Mar. 2, '63; disability.
Bennett, Wm., Aug. 5, '61.	Mustered out Aug. 20, '64.
Blair, Wm., Aug. 5, '61.	Re-enlisted as vet.; transferred to Co. A, Vet. Bat.
Beshle, John, Aug. 5, '61.	Died Aug. 6, '62; wounds.
Berry, Benjamin, Aug. 5, '61.	Serg't; died at Keokuk, July 1,'62.
Brookshire, J. P., Aug. 5, '61.	Disch'd April 10, '63; disability.
Barker, C. S., Aug. 5, '61.	
Bentley, Charles, Aug. 5, '61.	Re-enlisted as vet.; transferred to Co. A, Vet. Bat.
Brewington, H. I., Aug. 5, '61.	Re enlisted as vet.; transferred to Co. A.
Clark, Benjamin, Aug. 5, '61.	In marine service; said to have been discharged.
Clark, Martin, Aug. 5, '61.	Mustered out Aug. 20, '64.
Crouch, Alex., Aug. 5, '61.	Re-enlisted as vet.; transferred to Co. A, Vet. Bat.
Carmean, Pearson, Aug. 5, '61.	Disch'd Dec. 7, '61; disability.
Davis, David M., Aug. 5, '61.	Killed at Shiloh, April 2, '62.
Douglas, Edward, Aug. 5, '61.	Re-enlisted as veteran.
Dillon, Job A., Aug. 5, '61.	Mustered out Aug. 20, '64.
Evans, Robert, Aug. 5, '61.	Disch'd June 19, '63; disability.
Graham, Wm. J., Aug. 5, '61.	Prisoner of war; mustered out of regiment.
Griffee, Levi, Aug. 5, '61.	Disch'd Jan. 8, '62; disability.
Gull, John Z., Aug. 5, '61.	Died at Albany, Ind., June 9, '62.
Hemstead, Henry, Aug. 5, '61.	
Herring, Thomas, Aug. 5, '61.	Serg't; died July 18, '62; wounds.
Jostis, Henry, Aug. 5, '61.	Mustered out Aug. 20, '64.
Jostis, William, Aug. 5, '61.	" "
Jones, David, Aug. 5, '61.	Disch'd June 17, '62; disability.
Kirbaugh, Wm., Aug. 5, '61.	Re-enlisted as veteran.
Langdon, S., Aug. 5, '61.	Died at Paducah, Ky., Dec. 2, '61.
Long, Jas. W., Aug. 5, '61.	Died July 21, '63; wounds.
Little, James W., Aug. 5, '61.	Mustered out Aug. 20, '64.
Lutrelle, John, Aug. 5, '61.	Died at Columbus, Ky., Dec. 4, '62.

Name, and date of Rank.	Remarks.
McQuality, Jas. Aug. 5, '61.	Disch'd Nov. 25, '62; disability.
Malon, Perry, Aug. 5, '61.	
Nicholson, J. N., Aug. 5, '61.	Mustered out Aug. 20. '64.
Odor, Henry C., Aug. 5, '61.	Missing since Feb. 10, '62; supposed dead.
Ordleb, Lewis, Aug. 5, '61.	
Peck, Geo. A., Aug. 5, '61.	Sergeant; died at Mound City, March 8, '62.
Pasley, Jos. A., Aug. 5, '61.	Mustered out Aug 20, '64.
Pasley, M. L., Aug. 5, '61.	Died at Paducah, Ky., Dec. 4, '61.
Pope, John, Aug, 5, '61.	Trans. to inv. corps Dec. 1, '63.
Read, John, Aug. 5, '61.	Killed at Ft. Donelson.
Ralls, Geo. W., Aug. 5, '61.	Mustered out Aug. 20, '64.
Rose, Wm. C., Aug. 5, '61.	Died April 13, '62; wounds.
Scott, John, Aug. 5, '61.	Mustered out in the field.
Shortel, John, Aug. 5, '61.	
Stephens, Jos. F., Aug. 5, '61.	Disch'd Dec. 20, '61; disability.
Stith, Geo. W., Aug. 5, '61.	Killed at Shiloh April 6, '62.
Sinnard, Ben. P., Aug. 5, '61.	Disch'd Feb. 14, '63; disability.
Smith, Simon D., Aug. 5, '61.	Disch'd Sept. 1, '62, as corp.; disability.
Ulmer, Chas., Aug. 5, '61.	Mustered out Aug. 20, '64.
Ward, John, Aug. 5, '61.	" " as sergeant; wounded.

RECRUITS.

Allsbury, Alex.	Re-enlisted at vet.
Green, Aaron.	Mustered out Aug. 20, '64, as 1st sergt.
Murray, Patrick.	Transferred to Co. A. vet. bat.
Nevins, Chas.	Re-enlisted as vet.
Perdue, James T., Dec. 22, '63.	
Stevens, F. M.	Mustered out Aug. 20, '64.
Stevens John D.	" "
Smith, Joseph.	Died at Memphis, Tenn., April 3, '63.
Walker, Joseph L., Jan. 5, '64.	Trans. to Co. A, vet. bat.
Wheeler, And. M.	Mustered out May 29, '65.

HISTORY OF MACON COUNTY.

Name, and date of Rank.   *Remarks.*

COMPANY "F."

CAPTAINS.

David P. Brown, July 27, '61.   Res. March 28, '62.
J. C. Lewis, March 28, '62.   Resigned Oct. 16, '62; was 1st lieut. and 2d lieut.
Jesse F. Harrold, Oct. 16, '62. Term expired Aug. 20, '64; was 1st lieut.

FIRST LIEUTENANTS.

H. C. McCook, July 27, '61.   Promoted chaplain.
Henry Bevis, Oct. 1, '61.   Res. Feb. 10, '62.
Wm. H. Taylor, Oct. 16, '62.   Term expired Aug. 20, '64; was 2d lieutenant.

SECOND LIEUTENANT.

Ed. C. Sackett, Oct. 16, '62.   Term expired Aug. 20, '64.

PRIVATES.

Rogers, Henry, Aug. 7, '61.   Re-enlisted as vet.
Petrey, Solomon.   Mustered out Aug. 20, '64.
Rouse, Levi.   Disch'd May 5, '62; disability.

COMPANY "G."

CAPTAINS.

Francis M. Long, July 27, '61. Prom. major.
Daniel H. Hall, Sept. 1. '62.   Prom. by President May 26, '64; was 1st lieut.
T. J. Anderson, May 27, '64.   Term expired Aug. 20, '64; was 1st lieut. and 2d lieut.

FIRST LIEUTENANTS.

John B. Butler, Sept. 1, '62.   Res. June 18, '63; was 2d lieut.
Chas G. Young, May 27, '64.   Term expired Aug. 20, '64.

SECOND LIEUTENANT.

John C. Cox, July 27, '61.   Died April 9, '62; wounds rec'd at Pittsburg Landing.

Name, and date of Rank.   *Remarks.*

PRIVATES.

Reddy, Wm. H., July 26, '61.   Killed at Shiloh April 6, '62.
Ready, John W.   Disch'd Sept. 18, '62; disability.

COMPANY "H."

CAPTAINS.

H. Blackstone, July 27, '61.   Res. Jan. 14, '62.
John H. Huffner, Jan. 28, '62. Killed in battle April 6, '62; was 1st lieut.
Luther H. Wilber, April 7, '62. Died April 28, '62; was 1st lieut.
Wm. F. Turney, April 29, '62. Term expired Aug. 20, '64; was 2d lieut.

FIRST LIEUTENANTS.

James S. Steen, July 27, '61. Res. Dec. 21, '61.
D. M. Turney, April 29, '62.   Term expired Aug. 20, '64.

SECOND LIEUTENANTS.

H. H. Hardy, Dec. 25, '61.   Res. May 21, '62.
Chris. Corneley, May 22, '62. Killed in action July 12, '63.

PRIVATES

Pugh, Isaac R.   Prom. regimental quartermaster.

COMPANY "I."

CAPTAINS.

Ben. B. Bacon, July 27, '61.   Res. Mar. 4, '62.
F. M. Green, Mar 5, '62.   Term expired Aug. 20, '64; was 2d lieutenant.

FIRST LIEUTENANTS.

B. R. Parrish, July 27, '61.   Res. Sept. 28, '62.
Leander Green, Nov. 5, '62.   Term expired Aug. 20, '64; was 2d lieut.

SECOND LIEUTENANT.

P. J. Frederick, Sept. 28, '62. Term expired Aug. 20, '64.

Name, and date of Rank.   Remarks.

PRIVATES.

Carmon, Jno. P., Aug. 5, '61.   Promoted commissary sergt.
Gross, Sam'l E., Aug. 5, '61.   Discharged Aug. 16, '61.
Jacobs, Geo., Aug. 5, '61.   Mustered out Aug. 20, '64.
Wells, Elijah, Aug. 5, '61.   "   "
White, Henry, Aug. 5, '61.   Died accidental w'nds Sept. 13, '62.
Wellhouse, Peter, Aug. 5, '61. Mustered out Aug. 20, '64.

VETERANS.

Conrad, Edward, Jan. 21, '64.   Transferred to Co. A, vet. bat.
Frazee, Ben. F., Dec. 18, '63. Transferred to vet. bat.
Jones, James, Jan. 5, '64.   "   "
Snyder, Henry, Dec. 18, '63.   "   "
Smith, Wm. H., Dec. 18, '63.   "   "
Woodward, Sam., Feb. 10, '64.   "   "
Davidson, Jo., April 5, '64.
Gaines, Maxwell, Oct. 31, '63.
Stingley, Daniel, Jan. 15, '64.

SIXTY-THIRD INFANTRY.

The Sixty-third Infantry, Illinois Volunteers, was organized at Camp Dubois, Anna, Illinois, in the month of December, 1861, by Colonel Francis Moro, and mustered into United States service April 10, 1862. Ordered to Cairo April 27; to Henderson, Ky., July 12; returned to Cairo 22d. August 4th moved to Jackson, Tenn., and assigned to Fourth Brigade, Seventh Division, Seventeenth Army Corps, Col. John D. Stephenson, Seventh Missouri Infantry, commanding brigade, Brig.-Gen. John A. Logan commanding division. November 10 moved to LaGrange; 28th moved against Pemberton, and returned to LaGrange January 16, 1863. May 10th, 1863, ordered to Vicksburg, Miss.; on picket duty at Young's Point till May 21st; June 7th assigned to Mower's Brigade, and moved to Millikin's Bend. In an engagement at Richmond, La.; returned to Young's Point, thence to Vicksburg; July 5th, 1863, moved to Helena, Ark; 28th moved to Memphis;

moved towards Chattanooga; November 16th arrived at Bridgeport, Ala.; arrived at Chattanooga November 20th; engaged in battle at Mission Ridge, 23d and 24th of November, 1863; arrived at Huntsville Dec. 26th, and went into winter quarters. Ordered to Illinois on veteran furlough, April 3, and returned to Huntsville, May 21st, 1864. June 22d moved to Kingston; command ordered to join Gen. Sherman; December 10th, 1864, arrived at Savannah, and moved to Miller's Station, on the Gulf Railroad; started on a trip through the Carolinas; returned to Savannah. Participated in the battle of Bentonville, N. C., March 21st, and entered Goldsboro March 24, 1865; moved to Raleigh; moved from Raleigh April 29th, and arrived at Richmond May 10; went to Alexandria; participated in the grand review at Washington, May 24; moved to Parkersburg, on the Ohio river, thence to Louisville, Ky. July 13, 1865, mustered out of United States service, and left for Camp Butler, Illinois, arriving there July 16th, after having traveled 6,453 miles.

ROSTER SIXTY-THIRD INFANTRY.

Name, and date of Rank.   *Remarks.*

COLONELS.

Francis Moro, Dec. 1, '61.   Resigned Sept. 29, '62.
Jos. B. McCown, Sept. 29, '62.   M. O. April 9, '65; was Lt.-Col.
James Isaminger, July 12, '65.   M. O. July 12, '65; was Lt.-Col

LIEUTENANT COLONEL.

Henry Glaze, Sept. 24, '62.   Res. June 30, '63; was Major.

MAJORS.

Joseph K. Lemen, Sept. 29, '62. Mustered out April 9, '65,
J. R. Stanford, June 4, '65.   "   July 13, '65.

ADJUTANTS.

C. S. Chambers, April 10, '62.   Resigned Dec. 16, '62.
W. P. Richardson, Dec. 16, '62. Mustered out April 9, '65.
Theodore Elfes, June 6, '65.   "   July 13, '65.

Name, and date of Rank. *Remarks.*

QUARTERMASTERS.

John M. Maris, Feb. 28, '62. Mustered out April 9, '65.
Benj. Robertson, June 6, '65.   " July 13, '65.

SURGEONS.

Wm. M. Gray, May 26, '62. Resigned Sept. 12, '62.
J. W. McKinney, Sept. 15, '62. Mustered out April 9, '65.
Alex. A. Lodge, June 6, '65. M. O. July 13, '65; was 1st asst. surgeon and 2d.

FIRST ASSISTANT SURGEON.

Lyman Hall, April 10, '62. Resigned Dec. 31, '62.

CHAPLAINS.

Stephen Blair, April 10, '62. Died.
John Glaze, Feb. 2, '63. Commission canceled.
George Compton, May 22, '63. Mustered out July 13, '65.

COMPANY "H."

CAPTAINS.

S. G. Parker, April 10, '62. Discharged July 14, '63.
John M. Davis, July 14, '63. Discharged April 30, '64; was 1st lieutenant.
Geo. W. Baxter, July 12, '65. M. O. July 12, 65; was 1st lieut.

FIRST LIEUTENANTS.

Wilson F. Cox, July 14, '63. M. O. May 24, '65; was 2d lieut.
A. J. Bixler, July 12, '65. M. O. July 13, '65.

SECOND LIEUTENANTS.

James Houselman, April 10, '62. Discharged Dec. 2, '62.
Thos. Abernethy, July 12, '65. Mustered out July 13, '65.

FIRST SERGEANT.

Snides, Daniel D., Dec. 16, '61.

SERGEANTS.

Cox, Wilson T., Dec. 16, '61. Promoted 2d lieut.
Baxter, Geo. W., Dec. 16, '61. Re-enlisted as veteran.

HISTORY OF MACON COUNTY. 101

Name, and date of Rank. *Remarks.*

Freeman, R., Dec. 16, '61. Re-enlisted as veteran.
Mettlin, Jas. C., Dec. 16, '61. " "

CORPORALS.

McQuay, Jos., Dec. 16, '61.
Peterson, J. M. B., Dec. 16,'61. Died at Jackson, Tenn., Sept. 15, '62.
Dawson, D. L., Dec. 16, '61. Re-enlisted as veteran.
Kohr, Samuel W., Dec. 16, '61. " "
Robinson, David, Dec. 16, '61. Died, Jackson, Tenn., Sept. 14,'62.
Lawrence, Y. P., Dec. 16, '61. Mustered out April 9, '65.
Hill, Joel, Dec. 16, '61.
Holmes, W. H., Dec. 16, '61. Disch'd Nov. 14, '62; disability.

WAGONER.

Rowe, Absalom, Dec. 16, '61. Disch'd Nov. 14, '62; disability.

PRIVATES.

Ayers, Dan. C., Dec. 16, '61. Re-enlisted as vet.; mustered out July 13, '65.
Armstrong, S. A., Dec. 16, '61. Died at Cairo, May 12, '62.
Abbott, Josiah, Dec. 16, '61.
Abernethy, Thos., Dec. 16, '61. Re-enlisted as vet.; mustered out July 13, '65, as serg't.
Asbury, Levi, Dec. 16, '61. Re-enlisted as veteran.
Barnes, Wm. H., Dec. 16, '61. " "
Brockway, A., Dec. 16, '61.
Brockway, D. L., Dec. 16, '61. Disch'd Nov. 14, '62; disability.
Bixler, A. J., Dec. 16, '61. Re-enlisted as vet.; mustered out July 13, '65, as 1st serg't.
Bruce, Franklin, Dec. 16, '61. Mustered out May 31, '65.
Brower, Godfrey, Dec. 16, '61.
Bozarth, Jno. S., Dec. 16, '61. Re-enlisted as vet; mustered out July 13, '65.
Burch, George, Dec. 16, '61. Re-enlisted as vet.; mustered out July 13, '65.
Barnhart, Jacob, Dec. 16, '61. Died at Anna, Ill., April 27, '62.
Baily, Samuel, Dec. 16, '61. Discharged June 28, '64.
Crawford, Eli, Dec. 16, '61.

Name, and date of Rank.	Remarks.
Crawford, Wm., Dec. 16, '61.	Re-enlisted as vet.; mustered out July 15, '65.
Crawford, S., Dec. 16, '61.	Disch'd Nov. 14, '62; disability.
Culver, S. M., Dec. 16, '61.	Mustered out April 9, '65.
Campbell, S. D., Dec. 16, '61.	Died at Nashville, Tenn., Jan. 3, '64.
Cadwallader, A., Dec. 16, '61.	Re-enlisted as vet.; mustered out July 13, '65.
Church, George, Dec. 16, '61.	
Cline, Simon, Dec. 16, '61.	Disch'd Nov. 14, '62; disability.
Crigler, Wm. H., Dec. 16, '61.	
Doolen, J. L., Dec. 16, '61.	
Day, Richard, Dec. 16, '61.	Mustered out April 9, '65.
Earles, Joshua, Dec. 16, '61.	Disch'd Sept. 9, '62; disability.
Earls, Booker, Dec. 16, '61.	Re-enlisted as veteran.
Ebbert, John J., Dec. 16, '61.	
Ford, Wm. C., Dec. 16, '61.	Re-enlisted as veteran.
Flaherty, Jno., Dec. 16, '61.	
Harrigan, Jno., Dec. 16, '61.	Re-enlisted as vet.; mustered out July 12, '65.
Holly, Michael, Dec. 16, '61.	
Harman, Jesse, Dec. 16, '61.	Re-enlisted as vet.
Hogan, John, Dec. 16, '61.	Re-enlisted as vet.; mustered out July 15, '65.
Jones, James H., Dec. 16, '61.	
Lynch, Myter, Dec. 16, '61.	Mustered out April 9, '65.
Lacost, John, Dec. 16, '61.	Retained to make good the time lost.
Lord, Andrew, Dec. 16, '61.	Mustered out April 29, '65.
Meddleton, B., Dec. 16, '61.	
McWilliams, H., Dec. 16, '61.	
Moore John, Dec. 16, '61.	
Morgan, Samuel, Dec. 16, '61.	
Newton, Wm., Dec. 16, '61.	Mustered out April 11, '65.
Platt, Phinneas, Dec. 16, '61.	
Querry, Wm., Dec. 16, '61.	Re-enlisted as vet.; mustered out July 15, '65.
Roberts, Jos., Dec. 16, '61.	

Name, and date of Rank.	*Remarks.*
Sheets, Joseph, Dec. 16, '61.	
Sheets, Isaiah, Dec, 16, '61.	
Smith, James, Dec. 16, '61.	
Smith, George, Dec. 16, '61.	Died at Mound City May 20, '62.
Sparling, And., Dec. 16, '61.	
Sparling, Isaac, Dec. 16, '61.	Re-enlisted as vet.; mustered out July 13, '65.
Suck, Jacob, Dec. 16, '61.	Re-enlisted as vet.
Sullivan, Orren S. Dec. 16, '61.	" " mustered out July 13, '65.
Umbert, Chas. F., Dec. 16, '61.	Re-enlisted as vet.
Wimmer, B., Dec. 16, '61.	Mustered out April 9, '65.
Wilson, W. A., Dec. 16, '61.	Disch'd July 19, '62; disability.
Wilson, John B., Dec. 16, '61.	Mustered out April 9, '65.
Wright Harrison, Dec. 16, '61.	Re-enlisted as vet.; mustered out July 13, '65.
Watkins, Joel, Dec. 16, '61.	
Waller, Eli, Dec. 16, '61.	
Weiver, Isaac, Dec. 16, '61.	Re-enlisted as vet.
Waggoner, Thos., Dec. 16, '61.	
Waggoner, R., Dec. 16, '61.	
Young, George, Dec. 16, '61.	Discharged July 23, '62.
Young, Jas. B., Dec. 16, '61.	Re-enlisted as vet.

RECRUITS.

Abbott, Isaiah, Dec. 16, '61.	Mustered out July 13, '65.
Beach, Harmon, Feb. 27, '64.	" "
Davis, Allen, Feb. 27, '64.	" "

ONE HUNDRED AND FIFTEENTH REGIMENT ILLINOIS INFANTRY.

This regiment left Camp Butler the 4th of Oct., 1862; reported to Gen. Wright, at Cincinnati, the 6th, and crossed over into Kentucky and reported to Brig. Gen. A. J. Smith, and was assigned to Second Brigade Second Division, Army of Kentucky. Passed to

Richmond, Kentucky, and remained there about two months. About the 21st of December, went to Danville, Ky.; from Danville to Louisville, thence to Nashville, Tenn., and went into camp. From Nashville to Franklin, and went into camp. In March, '63, under Baird and Atkins, they assisted in driving VanDorn across the Duck river, and then returned to camp and remained until June 1st, 1863. Went to Triune, Tenn., and June 24, with the Army of the Cumberland, drove Gen. Bragg across the Tennessee. Went into camp at Tullahoma, but soon marched towards Chattanooga, with a forced march across the Cumberland mountains to Rossville, Ga. On the 19th and 20th of September, engaged the enemy on the field of Chickamauga. In this engagement, lost five men from Macon county. After the engagement marched against Dalton, Ga.; returned to camp near Cleveland, Tenn.; remained there until the 3d day of May, then joined Sherman's Army on the Atlantic campaign. This regiment led the charge at Tunnel Hill, Ga., and engaged in battle at Resaca, Ga., on the 15th and 16th of May, 1864. This regiment took an active part in the engagements of November and December, 1864, which resulted in the destruction of Bragg's old veteran army, known as the Army of the Tennessee, under Gen. Hood. The Brigade to which the 115th Illinois was attached for nearly two years was known as the "Iron Brigade."

On the 23d of December, 1864, while pursuing Hood in his retreat from Nashville, Col. J. H. Moore of the 115th Illinois took command of this Brigade, of which the 115th was a part. This position he kept until the regiment was mustered out of service at the close of the war. The regiment went to Huntsville, Ala., and went into camp the 5th of Jan., 1865. On the 14th of March went into East Tennessee, then to Nashville, where it remained until it was mustered out of service at the close of the war, June 11, 1865. Arrived at Camp Butler, Ill., June 16; received pay, and discharged, June 23.

ROSTER ONE HUNDRED AND FIFTEENTH REGIMENT INFANTRY.

Name, and date of Rank.   *Remarks.*

COLONEL.

Jesse H. Moore, Sept. 13, '62.   Promoted Brevet Brig.-Gen., May 15, '65.

LIEUTENANT COLONELS.

Wm. Kinman, Sept. 13, '62.   Killed in battle, Sept. 20, '63.
Geo. A. Poteet, Sept. 20, '63.   Must'd out June 11, '65; was Maj.

MAJOR.

Jno. W. Lapham, Sept. 20, '63.   Mustered out June, 11, '65; was Capt. Co. A.

ADJUUTANTS.

John H. Woods, Sept. 13, '62.   Resigned April 10, '63.
A. Litsinberger, April 10, '63.   Resigned Oct. 26, '63.
W. W. Peddecord, Oct. 26, '63.   Mustered out June 11, '65.

QUARTERMASTERS.

B. F. Farly, Sept. 13, '62.   Resigned April 1, '63.
Chas. W. Jerome, April 1, '63.   Mustered out June 11, '65.

SURGEONS.

Enoch W. Moore, Oct. 4, '62.   Resigned April 17, '63.
Chas. W. Higgins, June 8, '63.   Declined commission.
Garner H. Bane, June 17, '63.   Mustered out June 11, '65.

FIRST ASSISTANT SURGEONS.

N. G. Blalock, Sept. 13, '62.   Resigned July 27, '63.
Clark E. Loomis, Aug. 17, '64.   Mustered out June 11, '65.

SECOND ASSISTANT SURGEON.

James A. Jones, Oct. 3, '62.   Murdered by guerrillas, Tunnel Hill, Ga., July 11, '64.

CHAPLAINS.

Arthur Bradshaw, Sept. 23, '62. Resigned Dec. 30, '62.

Name, and date of Rank.	Remarks.
Richard Holding, Jan. 1, '63.	Declined commission.
Wm. S. Crissey, July 20, '63.	Mustered out June 11, '65.

COMPANY "A."

CAPTAIN.

Jesse Hannon, Sept. 20, '63.	Mustered out June 11, '65; was 1st lieut. and 2d lieut.

FIRST LIEUTENANTS.

A. C. Bankson, Sept. 13, '62.	Resigned Dec. 30, '62.
Jos. B. Gore, Sept. 20, '63.	Mustered out June 11, '63; was 2d lieut.

PRIVATE.

Wm. Reese, Aug. 11, '62.	Died at Nashville, Tenn., Oct. 12, '63; wounds.

COMPANY "E."

CAPTAINS.

John M. Lane, Sept, 13, '62.	Resigned May 11, '63.
Jas. A. Whitaker, May 11, '63.	Mustered out June 11, '65; was 1st lieut.

FIRST LIEUTENANTS.

David S. Moffitt, Sept. 13, '62.	Resigned Mar. 25, '63.
Jesse F. Hedges, May 11, '63.	Mustered out June 11, '65; was 2d lieut.

SECOND LIEUTENANTS.

Adam C. Allison, Sept. 13, '62.	Resigned Feb. 28, '63.
I. H. C. Royse, May 11, '63.	Mustered out June 11, '65.

PRIVATES.

Abrams, F. M., Aug. 3, '62.	Mustered out June 11, '65.
Armstrong, J. A., Aug. 13, '62.	" "
Armstrong, M. S., Aug. 13, '62.	Died at Nashville, Tenn., Sept. 3, '63.
Ashmead, M. J., Aug. 13, '62.	Killed at Chickamauga, Sept. 20, '63.

HISTORY OF MACON COUNTY. 107

Name, and date of Rank.	Remarks.
Amsler, John, Aug. 22, '62.	Disch'd June 20, '63; disability.
Biddle, Alex. W., Aug. 22, '62.	Trans. to V. R. C., April 30, '64.
Breeden, Jno. M., Aug. 22, '62.	Discharged Jan. 5, '63; disability.
Breeden, C. M., Aug. 22, '62.	Mustered out June 11, '65, as corp.
Barnes, John A., Aug. 22, '62.	" " "
Bivens, Robert, Aug. 22, '62.	Disch'd Mar. 23, '65; wounds.
Clements, D. T., Aug. 22, '62.	Missing in action, Sept. 20, '63.
Clements, M. H., Aug. 22, '62.	Disch'd Dec. 14, '62; disability.
Clements, Philip, Aug. 22, '62.	Must'd out June 11, '65, as corp.
Cummings, Jno., Aug. 22, '62.	Absent, sick, at muster out of reg.
Cummings, J. H., Aug. 22, '62.	Mustered out June 11, '65.
Crocks, G. W., Aug. 15, '62.	Died in Christian county, Ill., Nov. 6, '62.
Crafton, John, Aug. 22, '62.	Died at Nashville, Tenn., March 4, '63.
Clements, E. T., Aug. 13, '62.	Must'd out June 11, '65, as sergt.
Douglas, A. C., Aug. 13, '62.	Promoted hospital steward.
Darmer, Jno. O., Aug. 15, '62.	Disch'd May 15, '65; wounds.
Darmer, Wm. C., Aug. 15, '62.	Mustered out July 1, '65; was prisoner,
DeAtley, A. H., Aug. 13, '62.	Died at Nashville, Tenn., March 3, '63.
Gay, David H., Aug. 13, '62.	Disch'd April 3, '63; disability.
Hight, James L., Aug. 13, '62.	Corporal; transferred to V. R. C. April 30, '64.
Hedges, Jesse T., Aug. 13, '62.	1st sergt; promoted 2d lieut.
Johnson, Jos., Aug. 11, '62.	Corporal; killed at Chickamauga, Sept. 20, '63.
Jacobs, Jas. C., Aug. 22, '62.	Mustered out June 11, '65.
Markwell, W. A., Aug. 22, '62.	Mustered out June 11, '62.
Myers, Jno. W., Aug. 15, '62.	" "
Martin, Jas. M., Aug. 13, '62.	" " as sergt.
Pope, Zachariah, Aug. 13, '62.	Died at Lexington Ky., Nov. 10, '62.
Pope, James M., Aug. 13, '62.	Died at Danville, Ky., Dec. 31, '62.
Quick, Sam. W., Aug. 13, '62.	Mustered out June 11, '65.
Roberson, Jer., Aug. 13, '62.	Transferred to eng. corps Aug. 11, '64.

Name, and date of Rank.   *Remarks.*

Rose, John V., Aug, 13, '62.   Died at Resaca, Ga., May 26, '64.
Ruby, Henry J., Aug. 13, '62.   Killed at Chickamauga Sept. 20, '63.
Ruby, Jas. A., Aug. 13, '62.   Mustered out June 11, '65.
Rugh, Samuel, Aug. 13, '62.   " "
Wood, Newell, Aug. 13, '62.   " "
Whitaker, J. A., Aug. 15, '62.   Promoted 1st lieut.
White, Levi, Aug. 13, '62.   Disch'd Aug. 6, '63; disability.
Waterman, G. A., Aug. 13, '62.

RECRUITS.

Deatley, Jos. A., Jan. 22, '63.   Transferred to Co. A, 21 Ill. Inf.
Elder, Wm. F., Jan. 28, '63.   Disch'd Jan. 2, '65; wounds.
Hugle, John.   Died at Nashville, Tenn., Sept. 14, '63.

COMPANY "F."

CAPTAINS.

F. L. Hays, Sept 13, '62.   Prom. by President to major and payment, April 6, '64.
Chas. Griffith, April 7, '64.   Mustered out June 11, '64.

FIRST LIEUTENANTS.

Jas. Smith, Sept. 13, '62.   Res. Feb. 6, '63.
Mat. Freeman, Feb. 6, '63.   Died March 30, '63; was 1st lieut.
Wm. F. Slocum, Mar. 30, '63.   Res. Nov. 28, '63; was 1st lieut.
Jacob Porter, Nov. 28, '63.   Killed May 15, '64.
Gordon W. Mills, May 15, '64.   Resigned Feb. 14, '64.
C. C. McComas, March 13, '65.   Mustered out June 11, '65.

SECOND LIEUTENANT.

David Reed, March 30, '63.   Died Sept. 27, '63; wounds.

PRIVATES.

Carter, Jas. F., Aug. 7, '62.   Mustered out July 12, '65.
Lutrell, Alex., Aug. 12, '62.   Killed at Chickamauga Sept. 20, '63.

HISTORY OF MACON COUNTY.

Name, and date of Rank.	Remarks.
Goodman, Chas., Aug. 16, '62.	Mustered out June 11, '65,
Moore, Edward, Aug. 18, '62.	Disch'd Aug. 6, '63; disability.
Sanderson, J. D., Aug. 21, '62.	Mustered out June 11, '65.
Cline, Andy, Aug. 6, '62.	Disch'd May 30, '63; disability.
Chew, Wm. L., Aug. 13, '62.	Disch'd April 1, '63; disability.
Freeland, G. C., Aug. 12, '62.	Mustered out June 11; '65, as corp.
Garver, Abe. M., Aug. 14, '62.	" "
Imboden, C. M., Aug. 6, '62.	Disch'd Feb. 29, '64; wounds.
Kramer, Elias, Aug. 6, '62.	Disch'd Oct. 4, '62; disability.
Kepler, Andrew, Aug. 11, '62.	Mustered out June 11, '65.
Kaufman, I. S., Aug. 12, '62.	" " as sergt.
Kaufman, M. S., Aug. 11, '62.	" " as corp.
Kolp, Wm. H., Aug. 9, '62.	Prom. principal musician.
Lutrell, The., Aug. 6, '62.	Disch'd Dec. 16, '63; disability.
Moore Albert T., Aug. 6, '62.	Mustered out June 11, '65; sergt.
Meridith, Jas. W., Aug. 7, '62.	" "
Oglesby, C. E., Sept, 11, '62.	" "
Priest, John, Sept. 6, '62.	" "
Pierce, Wm. W., Aug. 11, '62.	" "
Roe, Geo. L., Aug. 11, '62.	Died at Franklin, Tenn, Apr. 6,'63.
Ross, Jos., Aug. 15, '62.	Disch'd April 14, '63; disability.
Roberts, Richard, Aug. 9, '62.	Disch'd Jan. 22, '63; disability.
Shively, Alf., Aug. 11, '62.	Sergt.; killed at Chickamauga Sept. 20, '63.
Shull, Richard, Aug. 11, '62.	Mustered out June 11, '65.

COMPANY "H."

CAPTAINS.

Henry Pratt, Sept. 13, '62.	Res. April 16, '63.
J. O. Reardon, April 24, '63.	Mustered out June 11, '65; was 1st lieut. and 2d lieut.

FIRST LIEUTENANTS.

Silas Parker, Sept. 13, '62.	Res. Nov. 12, '63.
Jos. J. Slaughter, April 24, '63.	Mustered out June 11, '65.

SECOND LIEUTENANT.

S. R. Hatfield, March 12, '63.	Mustered out June 11, '65.

Name, and date of Rank.   *Remarks.*

PRIVATES.

Boze, Alvis H., Aug. 15, '62.   Discharged March 31, '63.
Plitsenberger, A., July 6, '62.   Promoted com. sergt.
Peddecord, W.W. Aug. 5, '62.   Promoted sergt. major.
Quinlan, John, Aug. 7, '62.   Discharged March 20, '63.
Weatherford, W., Aug. 13, '62.   Mustered out June 11, '65.

COMPANY "K."

CAPTAINS.

Jas. Steele, Sept. 13, '62.   Dismissed March 3, '63.
Alanson Pierce, March 3, '63.   Resigned Sept. 24, '64.
Philip Riley, Sept. 24, '64.   Mustered out June 11, '65; was 1st lieut. and 2d lieut.

FIRST LIEUTENANTS.

Sylvester Baily, Sept. 13, '62.   Resigned Dec. 28, '63.
Sam. Alexander, Sept. 24, '64.   Mustered out June 11, '64.

PRIVATE.

Throckmorton, J. W.

ONE HUNDRED AND SIXTEENTH ILLINOIS INFANTRY.

The One Hundred and Sixteenth Regiment Illinois Volunteers was made up almost entirely from Macon county. The campanies began to go into camp in the fair ground, near Decatur, about the 15th August, 1862. They were sworn into the United States service on the 6th day of September, but ranks not being full, were only mustered as a battalion. On the 31st were mustered as a regiment. Left Decatur November 8th, arriving at Cairo on the 9th; left on the same evening for Memphis, where it remained until the 26th, during which time the Fifteenth Army Corps was organized under the command of Gen. W. T. Sherman, and was assigned to the First Brigade, Second Division. The commander of this division was Maj.-Gen. Morgan L. Smith, and the brigade commander, Gen. Giles A. Smith. From Memphis marched to Tallahatchie, which was reached December 13th. On the 20th started down the Mississippi; entered the mouth of the Yazoo the 26th, and landed about fifteen miles above the mouth of that river. On the next day the battle of Chickasaw began, and continued until the 30th. This was the first engagement of the regiment. About the 1st of January, 1863, passed down the Yazoo, and sailed up the Mississippi and Arkansas rivers to Arkansas Post, where was fought the second battle in which this regiment was engaged, January 10 and 11. On the 22d landed at Young's Point, La., opposite Vicksburg. During the winter made attempts to get around Vicksburg by canals, etc. In the spring crossed the river near Port Gibson, and were under fire at Black River and Champion Hills, and were engaged in the bloody charges upon the works in the rear of Vicksburg, May 18 and 22, and were present at the surrender of that place, July 4th. The next morning started in search of Gen. Johnston, who was stationed beyond Black river; followed him until he took refuge in Jackson, Miss. By several engagements, drove him beyond the Pearl river. Went into camp near Black river, July 25th; the camp was called Camp Sherman. Here the regiment remained until about the first of October, then removed to Vicksburg, then sailed to Memphis, and then went to Corinth, and then marched for Chattanooga, which was reached November 21st. On the night of the 23d the 116th, in company with the 6th Missouri, embarked in pontoon boats, floated down the Tennessee and landed at the mouth of the Chickamauga, within less than one mile of the enemy's entrenchments on Missionary Ridge, and held the position until the balance of the corps was brought over, and captured all of Bragg's pickets. Then marched to the foot of the ridge on the evening of the 24th; engaged in a skirmish in which Gen. Giles A. Smith was wounded, the command of the brigade devolving on Col. Tupper. On the 25th were present at the storming of Missionary Ridge. After this victory this regiment was marched to the relief of Knoxville, and was constantly on the move until the 9th of January, 1864; then went into winter quarters at Larkensville, Ala.; remained in quarters until May 16, and was engaged in the charge and capture of Resaca; was at the battles of Dallas, May 25 to 28, and Big Shanty; next at Kenesaw Mountain, on 27th of June; thence crossed the Chattahoochie and fought the battle of Stone Mountain, and drove the enemy to the immediate vicinity of Atlanta, where the battle of June 22d was fought, recapturing the works after the enemy had taken them from us.

On the 28th fought the battle of Ezra Chapel, in which the enemy was badly beaten and driven back; moved up and formed lines within 800 yards of enemy, August 3d, at Atlanta, and engaged in the siege of that place, fighting the battle of Jonesboro, the 14th, which was virtually an end of the siege. After the battle of Jonesboro, went into camp at Atlanta; remained there until orders were given to break camp and begin " Sherman's March to the Sea," with occasional skirmishes on the march, until the vicinity of Savannah was reached; then participated in the capture of Fort McAllister, on December 13. Then the regiment marched to Savannah, and entered that city December 21, and went into camp. Then took shipping and went to Beaufort, S. C., and marched thence to Pocatalago, and fought a battle there, and had general skirmishing until the city of Columbia was reached; went into camp after the burning of that city; moved thence to Bentonville, N. C., and had a severe battle; went into camp; moved thence to Raleigh, which surrendered without opposition; thence ordered to Washington, and went into camp and remained until ordered home to be mustered out of service, which was done June 7, 1865.

For some unaccountable reason, no mention is made of the noble record of this regiment in the Adjutant General's Reports. A similar omission is made in the Patriotism of Illinois. The brief history of the regiment above given, the author has prepared partly from the recollection of Capt. William Grason, and partly from memoranda furnished by Chaplain N. M. Baker, and Surgeon Ira N. Barnes. The citizens of Macon county have erected to the memory of the brave Col. Tupper, in Greenwood Cemetery, a monument, as a recognition of his services; and the long list of killed and wounded in battle, given below, will forever speak, louder than words, of the splendid record of the 116th.

REGIMENTAL ROSTER.

Name, and date of Rank. *Remarks.*

COLONELS.

N. W. Tupper, Sept. 30, '62. Died at Decatur, Mar. 10, '64.
John E. Maddux, June 7, '65. Mustered out June 7, '65; was Lieutenant Colonel.

LIEUTENANT COLONELS.

J. P. Boyd, Sept. 6, '62. Resigned Jan. 28, '64.
Anderson Froman, Jan. 28, '64. Died June 16, '64; was Major.
John A. Windsor, May 15, '65. Must'd out June 7, '65; was Maj.

MAJORS.

Austin McCleery, Jan. 28, '64. Resigned Sept. 26, '64.
Nich. Geshwind, June 7, '65. Mustered out June 7, '65, as Capt. Company F.

ADJUTANTS.

Chas. H. Fuller, Sept. 30, '62. Resigned June 27, '63.
Wm. E. Crissey, June 27, '63. Discharged Jan. 30, '65.
Myron Holcomb, Jan. 30, '65. Mustered out June 7, '65.

QUARTERMASTERS.

Lyman King, Sept. 3, '62. Resigned Mar. 2, '63.
Chas. F. Emery, Mar. 2, '62. Prom. by President, Jan. 9, '64.
John H. Porter, Jan. 9, '64. Mustered out June 7, '65.

SURGEON.

Ira N. Barnes, Mar. 26, '63. Mustered out June 7, '65.

FIRST ASSISTANT SURGEON.

J. A. Heckleman, Sept. 17, '62. Mustered out June 7, '65.

SECOND ASSISTANT SURGEON.

J. A. W. Hostetler, Oct. 1, '62. Mustered out June 7, '65.

CHAPLAINS.

N. M. Baker, Sept. 30, '62. Mustered out June 7, '65.

Name, and date of Rank. *Remarks.*

NON-COMMISSIONED STAFF.

Crocker, R. C., Aug. 7, '62.	Sergt. major; trans. to Co. D.
Holcomb, Myron.	Promoted adjutant.
Ward, Thos. J., Aug. 9, '62.	Mustered out June 7, '65; was prisoner.
Porter, John J.	Promoted reg. quartermaster.
Hopkins, Allen F., Aug. 9, '62.	Quartermaster sergt; mustered out June 7, '65; was quar. sergt.
Crissey, Wm. E., Aug. 9, '62.	Com. sergt.; promoted adjutant: was com. sergt.
Jennings, I. D., Aug. 7, '62.	Com. sergt.; mustered out June 7, '65.
Lukens, Edward, Aug. 13, '62.	Hospital steward; mustered out June 7, '65.
Barret, Martin L., Aug. 14, '62.	Principal musician; mustered out June 7, '65.
Henneby, Francis, Aug. 7, '62.	Mustered out June 7, '65; principal musician.

COMPANY "A."

CAPTAINS.

W. F. Brown, Sept. 6, '62.	Resigned April 20, '63.
Guston F. Hardy, April 20, '63.	Died June 12, '63; was 2d lieut.
Wm. Grasson, June 12, '63.	Mustered out June 7, '65; was 1st lieut.

FIRST LIEUTENANTS.

John B. Perdew, Sept. 6, '62.	Died March 27, '63.
J. L. Shellabarger, June 12, '63.	Mustered out June 12, '65; was 2d lieut.

SECOND LIEUTENANT.

Jas. Boswell, June 7, '65.	Mustered out June 7, '65.

SERGEANTS.

Boswell, Jas. H., July 26, '62.	Sergt.; mustered out June 7, '65.
Stephens, A. C., Aug. 4, '62.	Mustered out June 7, '65.
Farrow, Geo. L., Aug. 4, '62.	

HISTORY OF MACON COUNTY.   115

Name, and date of Rank.   *Remarks.*

CORPORALS.

Harrington, R. H., Aug. 9, '62.   Disch'd Feb. 2, '63; disability.
Cox, Jerome A., Aug. 8, '62.   Mustered out May 20, '65.
Stine, Jas., Aug. 6, '62.   Discharged Feb. 2, '65, as sergnt.;
Eads, James, Aug. 6, '62.   Mustered out June 7, '65.
Baty, Samuel, Aug. 6, '62.   Killed at Vicksburg May 19, '63.
Purdeu, Wm. M., Aug. 4, '62.   Mustered out June 7, '65.

MUSICIANS.

Widick, Jas. H., Aug. 6, '62.   Must'd out June 7, '65, as private.
Lyons, Geo. W., Aug. 7, '62.   "   "   "

WAGONER.

Steel, Wm. M., Aug. 4, '62.   Disch'd March 4, '63; disability.

PRIVATES.

Agen, Monathan, Aug. 8, '62.   Mustered out June 7, '65.
Allen, Elisha, Aug. 2, '62.   Died of wounds received Arkansas Post, Jan. 11, '63.
Balch, Alex. H., July 26, '62.   Died at Van Buren, Ark., June 1, '63.
Bear, Wm., Aug. 6, '62.   Died at Young's Point, March 5, '63.
Bear, Henry C., Aug 9, '62.   Absent, wounded at mustering out of regiment.
Beamer, Jacob E., Aug. 21, '62.   Died at Memphis Sept. 23, '63.
Bilby, Geo., Aug. 14, '62.   Mustered out June 7, '65.
Bowen, Daniel, Aug. 9, '62.   "   "
Bowdle, Wm. H., Aug. 6, '62.   Discharged Dec. 21, '64; wounds.
Bowman, Sol. S., Aug. 6, '62.   Transferred to V. R. C., Jan. 10, '65.
Brackney, Eli, Aug. 4, '62.
Brown, Wes. M., Aug. 6, '62.   Mustered out June 7, '65.
Brown, Thos. W., Aug. 13, '62.   Trans to inv. corps, Aug. 1, '63.
Bundy, Hardin, Aug. 9, '62.   Died at Benton Barracks July 17, '63.
Burke, Thos. F., Aug. 6. '62.   Mustered out June 7, '65, as sergt.

Name, and date of Rank.	*Remarks.*
Caulk, Albert, Aug. 9, '62.	Andersonville prison record says died.
Cheek, Alonzo, Aug. 26, '62.	Died at Young's Point, La.
Davis, Geo. W., Aug. 2, '62.	Sergt; killed at Atlanta, Ga., July 22, '64.
Green, Michael, Aug. 6, '62.	Mustered out June 7, '65.
Glaze, Wm., July 26, '62.	Absent, sick, at mustering out.
Guffy, Nathaniel, Aug. 6, '62.	" " "
Guffy, Jacob, Aug. 14, '62.	Transferred to inv. corps August 1, '63.
Hickman, Wm., Aug. 6, '62.	Mustered out June 7, '65, as corp.
Hollandsworth, W. Aug. 6, '62.	Died at Young's Point April 19, '63.
Houseman, John, Aug. 6, '62.	Mustered out June 7, '65.
Houseman, N., Aug. 21, '62.	Absent, sick, at mustering out of regiment.
Houseman, W., Aug. 6, '62.	Transferred to V. R. C., Aug. 10, '64.
Jabine, Jas. T., Aug. 12, '62.	Mustered out June 7, '65, as corp.
Littleton, T. M., Aug. 28, '62.	" "
Long, Jas., Aug. 6, '62.	" "
Long, Thos., M.	Transferred to inv. corps, Sept. 1, '63.
McKee, And., Aug. 7, '62.	Mustered out June 7, '65.
Makey, Horace D., Aug. 8, '62.	" " 26, '65.
Marsh, Samuel D., Aug. 22, '62.	Died at St. Louis April 29, '63.
Michener, J. A., Aug. 6, '62.	Died at Camp Butler, Ill., Jan. 4, '64.
Miller, Daniel, Aug. 24, '62.	Died at Young's Point March 4, '63.
Morris, Lewis, Aug. 5, '62.	Sergt.; wounded; transferred to inv. corps Feb. 15, '64.
Morris, Wm. T., Aug. 8, '62.	Died at Marietta, Ga., Aug. 3, '64; wounds.
McCurdy, Chas., Aug. 7, '62.	Died at Memphis June 28, '63.
Nelson, Samuel, July 30, '62.	Disch'd March 16, '63; disability.
Neyhard, John J., Aug. 6, '62.	Mustered out June 7, 65.
Nichols, John W., Aug. 6, '62.	Disch'd Feb. 6, '64; wounds.

Name, and date of Rank.	Remarks.
Perdew, Joel F., Aug. 9, '62.	Absent, sick, at mustering out of regiment.
Page, Moses B., Aug. 21, '62.	Mustered out June 7, '65.
Peck, John, July 21, '62.	Sergt.; died at home Sept. 28, '63.
Peck, Jacob, July 24, '62.	Mustered out June 7, '65.
Pasley, Arthur, Aug. 6, '62.	Transferred to inv. corps, Dec. 1, '63.
Palmer, Jos. V., Aug. 8, '62.	Died June 4, '63; wounds.
Porter, Jno. H., Aug. 20, '62.	Promoted quartermaster sergt.
Reason, Wm. J., Aug. 6, '62.	Mustered out June 7, '65.
Rimmell, H. M., Aug. 9, '62.	Died at Memphis, Tenn., Jan. 21, '63.
Ritter, Jno. M., Aug. 11, '62.	Mustered out June 7, '65, as sergt.
Rose, Elijah T., Aug. 7, '62.	Died May 22, '63, wounds at siege of Vicksburg.
Rundle, Chas. W., Aug. 6, '62.	Mustered out June 7, '65.
Rogers, Jno. W., Aug. 6, '62.	Killed near Kingston, N. C., Mar. 8, '65.
Scheer, F. W., Aug. 23, '62.	Mustered out June 7, '65.
Skinner, John R., Aug. 6, '62.	Disch'd Sept. 16, '63; of wounds.
Stafford, Nelson, Aug. 6, '62.	Mustered out June 7, '65.
Stapp, David, Aug. 6, '62.	Died at Lawson hospital May 5, '63.
Stewart, Thos. C., Aug. 6, '62.	Mustered out June 7, '65; was prisoner.
Walker, Henry, Aug. 11, '62.	Died at Memphis Tenn., April 3, '64.
Walker, Peter, Aug. 9, '62.	Mustered out June 7, '65; w'nded.
Wear, Jonathan, Aug. 6, '62.	" " as corp.
Wilson, George, Aug. 6, '62.	Absent, sick, at mustering out of regiment.
Wright, C. F., Aug. 6, '62.	Died at Jefferson barracks July 2, '63.

RECRUITS.

Moffet, Jos. E., Feb. 1, '64.	Trans. to Co. H, 55th Ill. Inf.
Walters, Wm. J., Feb. 1, '64.	Died at Kennesaw Mountain June 27, '64; wounds.

Name, and date of Rank.   *Remarks.*

John Leslie.	Died of w'nds rec'd at Kennesaw June 27, '64.
Joseph Blythe.	Wounded at Kennesaw June 27.
W. H. Clay.	" Ft. McAllister.
John W. Steward.	Died in hospital.
Josiah D. Steward.	Killed at Jonesboro Aug. 13.
M. M. Betzer.	Transferred to 55th Ill.
James Peck.	" "
John McKee.	" "
James McKee.	" "

COMPANY "B."

CAPTAINS.

Austin McClurg, Sept. 6, '62.	Promoted Major.
C. Reibsame, Jan. 28, '64.	Mustered out June 7, '65; was 1st Lieutenant.

FIRST LIEUTENANTS.

John S. Taylor, Sept. 6, '62.	Killed Jan. 8, '63.
Chas. E. Bolles, Jan. 28, '64.	Commission canceled; was 2d lieut.
John H. Miller, Jan. 28, '64.	Mustered out June 7, '65; was 2d lieut.

SECOND LIEUTENANT.

A. J. Williams, Sept. 6, '62.	Resigned Mar. 17, '63.

FIRST SERGEANT.

Isaac D. Jennings, Aug. 7, '62.	Promoted com. sergeant.

SERGEANTS.

Miller, John H., Aug. 7, '62.	Promoted 2d lieut.
Menaugh, W. T., Aug. 7, '62.	Absent, sick, at muster out of regt.
Songer, John A., Aug. 9, '62.	Mustered out July 10, '65, as priv.
Songer, Adiniron, Aug. 9, '62.	

CORPORALS.

Brown, K. A., Aug. 7, '62.	Mustered out June 7, '65.
Funk, William, Aug. 8, '62.	" "
Rogers, Reuben, Aug. 9, '62.	" " as priv.

Name, and date of Rank.	Remarks.
Shirley, Geo. W., Aug. 9, '62.	Absent, sick, at muster out of reg.
Troutman, J. W., Aug. 9, '62.	Mustered out June 7, '65.
Troutman, Sam., Aug. 9, '62.	" "

MUSICIANS.

Carter, H. W., Aug. 8, '62.	Discharged Jan. 28, '63.
Goodman, J. E., Aug. 11, '62.	Discharged Sept. 20, '63.

WAGONER.

Welty, Geo. H., Aug. 12, '62.	Mustered out June 7, '65.

PRIVATES.

Adams, James, Aug. 5, '62.	Mustered out June 7, '65.
Andrews, J. B., Aug. 9, '62.	Absent, sick, at muster out of reg.
Boles, Chas. E., Aug. 13, '62.	Mustered out June 7, '65, as sergt; com'd lieut.
Billings, Milton, Aug. 8, '62.	Mustered out June 7, '65.
Bear, John M., Aug. 6, '62.	Sergeant; absent, sick, at muster out of regiment.
Bradon, John E., Aug. 11, '62.	Mustered out June 7, '65.
Burgess, T. J., Aug. 5, '62.	
Baily, John W., Aug. 15, '62.	Mustered out July 1, '65, as corp.; wounded.
Beck, William, Aug. 15, '62.	Absent, sick, at muster out of reg.
Bills, R., Jr., Aug. 14, '62.	Killed at Arkansas Post, January 11, '63.
Braden, S. R., Aug. 12, '62.	Absent, wounded, at muster out of regiment.
Bradshaw, S. C., Aug. 9, '62.	Died at Young's Point, La., April 3, '63.
Burke, Patrick, Aug. 7, '62.	Died at Young's Point, La., April 8, '63.
Burke, William, Aug. 7, '62.	Mustered out June 7, '65.
Bell, Charles V., Aug. 15, '62.	Died in Mississippi, Mar. 23, '63.
Dilliner, James, Aug. 7, '62.	Absent, sick, at muster out of reg.
Daily, Austin, Aug. 19, '62.	Mustered out June 7, '65.
Disbrow, Lewis, Aug. 14, '62.	Sergeant; died at Young's Point, April 15, '63.

Name, and date of Rank.	Remarks.
Dugan, Michael, Aug. 14, '62.	Mustered out July 2, '65.
Earls, Stephen, July 19, '62.	Absent, sick, at muster out of reg.
Enterline, E., Aug. 19, '62.	Discharged March 14, '63.
Enos, Thomas, Aug. 9, '62.	Died at Young's Point, Feb. 11,'63.
Enterline, Conrad, Aug. 9, '62.	Discharged March 20, '64.
Ellis, David A., Aug. 14, '62.	Trans. to V. R. C., Sept. 1, '63.
Frank, S. G., Aug. 6, '62.	Died at St. Louis, April 11, '63.
Foster, John W., Aug. 20, '62.	Mustered out June 7, '65.
Fry, Amos, July 19, '62.	Mustered out July 19, '65; w'nded.
Fuller, Fred., Aug. 7, '62.	Mustered out June 7, '65.
Gill, John, Aug. 9, '62.	" "
Garver, F. M., Aug. 9, '62.	" " as corp.
Garver, C., Aug. 14, '62.	Died at St. Louis, May 17, '63.
Houck, Lewis, Aug. 9, '62.	Mustered out June 7, '65.
Huggins, J. H., Aug. 14, '62.	" " was pris'r.
Henson, R. S., Aug. 9, '62.	" "
Houck, Geo. L., Aug. 9, '62.	" "
Hays, Thompson, Aug. 7, '62.	" "
Henley, or Heneby, F. Aug. 7,'62.	Promoted principal musician.
Hays, John G., Aug. 7, '62.	Discharged Aug. 7, '63.
Hough, John S., Aug. 9, '62.	Absent, sick, at muster out of reg.
Jordan, John W., Aug. 8, '62.	Died at Young's Point, La., Feb. 8, '63.
Jordan, Wm. H., Aug. 8, '62.	Mustered out June 7, '65.
Jordan, Jeremiah, Aug. 9, '62.	Died at Young's Point, February 11, '63.
Kelley, Michael, Aug. 15, '62.	Mustered out June 7, '65.
Larken, T. H., Aug. 7, '62.	" "
Maher, Edward, Aug. 15, '62.	" "
McWhinney, Jno., July 30, '62.	" " as corp.
Myer, William, Aug. 2, '62.	Deserted Nov. 13, '62.
McDonald, R., July 17, '62.	Died at Memphis, Oct. 4, '63.
Nolan, Patrick, Aug. 21, '62.	Mustered out June 7, '65.
Nix, Wm. H., Aug. 7, '62.	Absent, sick, at muster out of reg.
Nesbitt, H. W., Aug. 11, '62.	Died at Keokuk, Ia., Jan. 27, '63.
Olney, Geo. W., Aug. 11, '62	Died at Memphis, Mar. 17, '63.
Pricer, Aaron, Aug. 9, '62.	Mustered out June 7, '65.
Peaker, John W., Aug. 8, '62.	Absent, wounded, at M. O. of reg.

Name, and date of Rank.   *Remarks.*

Patterson, A., Aug. 9, '62.   Mustered out June 7, '65.
Patterson, G. W., Aug. 20, '62.   Killed at Kenesaw Mountain, June 27, '64.
Quackenbush, S., July 30, '62.   Mustered out July 10, '65.
Rogers, R. A., Aug. 9, '62.   Absent, sick, at muster out of reg.
Reibsame, C., Aug. 11, '62.   Promoted sergt., then 1st lieut.
Rutherford, G. W., Aug. 8,'62.   Mustered out June 7, '65.
Smoot, Ben. F., Aug. 9, '62.   Died at Young's Point, February 15, '63.
Sherman, Jas. D., Aug. 20, '62.   Died on steamer City of Memphis, May 25, '63.
Street, Wesley, Aug. 15, '62.   Mustered out June 7, '65.
Stains, John A., Aug. 8, '62.   Died at Young's Point, June 4,'63.
Shelton, Martin, Aug. 11, '62.   Mustered out June 7, '65.
Shepherd, J. H., Aug. 9, '62.   "   "
Sickafonse, J. W., Aug. 15, '62.   "   "
Shepherd, A., Aug. 8, '62.   Killed at Arkansas Post, January 11, '63.
Shutter, Daniel, Aug. 9, '62.   Mustered out June 7, '65.
Tolles, Cyrus N., Aug. 8, '62.
Wall, Richard, Aug. 14, '62.   "   "
Wydick, John, Aug. 9,'62.   "   "
Weikel, Samuel, Aug. 15, '62.   Absent, sick, at muster out of reg·
Westfall, J. W., July 30, '62.   Mustered out June 7, '65, as sergt.
Wheeler, Amos, Aug. 11, '62.   Sick at muster out of regiment.
Warnick, W. C., Aug. 15, '62.   Sick at muster out of regiment.
Wheeler, A. J., Aug. 12, '62.   Mustered out June 7, '65.

RECRUITS.

Sites, Henry, Feb. 25, '64.   Trans. to Co. F, 55th Ill. Inf.
Shutter, Felix, Feb. 24, '64.   "   "   "
Westfall, Jas. K., April 13, '64.   "   "   "

COMPANY "C."

CAPTAINS.

Thos. White, Sept. 6, '62.   Killed in battle May 26, '64.

Name, and date of Rank.	Remarks.
R. M. Foster, June 7, '64.	Mustered out June 7, '65; was 1st lieut. and 2d lieut.

FIRST LIEUTENANTS.

Jas. M. Wallace, Sept. 6, '62.	Resigned March 2, '63.
Z. R. Prather, April 20, '65.	Mustered out June 7, '65; was 2d lieut.

SECOND LIEUTENANT.

Jacob B. Schroll, June 7, '65.	Mustered out June 7, '65.

FIRST SERGEANT.

Ellis, John W., Aug. 9, '62.	Died at Young's Point Feb. 23, '63.

SERGEANT.

Metzler, Abe., Aug. 13, '62.	Wounded at muster out of regt.
Camp, W. P., Aug. 9, '62.	Died at Milliken's Bend June 23, '63.
Montgomery, T., Aug. 9, '62.	Trans. to V. R. C., Feb. 1, '64.
Davidson, John B., Aug. 9, '62.	Died at Young's Point Feb. 8, '63.

CORPORALS.

Dunbar, Elias L., Aug, 9, '62.	Mustered out June 7, '65.
Edwards, J. W., Aug. 9, '62.	Disch'd April 13, '63; disability.
Fenton, Philo S, Aug. 9, '62.	Absent, wounded, at muster out of regiment.
Maeyers, Sam. T., Aug. 9, '62.	Mustered out June 7, '65.
Jones, Jas. H., Aug. 13, '62.	Disch'd Feb., '63; wounds.
Markel, Israel W., Aug. 9, '62.	Died at Memphis Feb. 30, '63.
Prather, Z. R., Aug. 9, '62.	Promoted 2d lieut.
Warnick, R. G., Aug. 9, '62.	Died at Memphis, May 22, '63.

MUSICIANS.

Helpman, D. C., Aug. 9, '62.	Mustered out July 22, '65; was prisoner.
Wallace, W. R., Aug. 6, '62.	Died on steamer D. A. January, March 7, '63.

HISTORY OF MACON COUNTY. 123

Name, and date of Rank.	Remarks.
WAGONER.	
Niles, Erastus, Aug. 9, '62.	Mustered out June 7, '65.
PRIVATES.	
Aaron, James L., Aug. 9, '62.	Mustered out June 7, '65.
Altum, Jas. W., Aug. 13, '62.	Died at Young's Point May 12, '63.
Akers, Wm. A., Aug. 18, '62.	Died at Young's Point Feb. 10, '63.
Black, Robert M., Aug. 9, '62.	Disch'd June 3, '63; disability.
Beedles, Jas. P., Aug. 9, '62.	Died on City of Memphis, March 16, '63.
Bohrer, John W., Aug. 9, '62.	Mustered out June 7, '65.
Bohrer, Geo. W., Aug. 9, '62.	Disch'd Jan. 9, '63; disability.
Champion, A. B., Aug. 9, '62.	Mustered out June 7, '65, as sergt.
Cochran, Jas. A., Aug. 9, '62.	" July, '65, as corporal, prisoner of war.
Coomb, Elijah, Aug. 9, '62.	Mustered out June 7, '65.
Devore, Jos., Aug. 9, '62.	Discharged April 25, '64.
Dickey, Jno. B., Aug. 9, '62.	Trans. to signal corps June 7, '64.
Davidson, Jas. B., Aug. 9, '62.	Disch'd Feb. 5, '63; disability.
Davidson, D. L., Aug. 13, '62.	Mustered out July 11, '65; prisoner of war.
Davis, Wm., Aug. 9, '62.	Mustered out June 7, '65.
Davidson, R. L., Aug. 9, '62.	Died at home Dec. 5, '63.
Dividson, Alex., Aug. 13, '62.	Mustered out June 7, '65.
Davidson, D. P., Aug. 13, '62.	" "
Davidson, T. K., Aug. 15, '62.	Killed near Jonesboro, Ga., Aug. 31, '65.
Ellis, Jas. A., Aug. 9, '62.	Mustered out June 7, '65.
Gregory, David, Aug. 9, '62.	Died at Louisiana April 16, '63.
Grennel, Chas., Aug. 9, '62.	Died at Mound City Dec. 15, '63.
Goff, Edward L., Aug. 9, '62.	Died at Mound City Nov. 2, '63.
Goff, Leonard J., Aug. 9, '62.	Mustered out June 7, '65, as wagoner.
Gault, John M., Aug. 9, '62.	Absent, wounded, at muster out of regt.

124   HISTORY OF MACON COUNTY.

Name, and date of Rank.	Remarks.
Hopkins, A. F., Aug. 9, '62.	Prom. sergt., then quartermaster sergt.
Hill, Joshua F., Aug. 9, '62.	Prisoner of war; died July 23, '63; wounds.
Herrington, D. J., Aug. 11, '62.	Mustered out June 7, '65, as musician.
Howell, E. J., Aug. 11, '62.	Died at Richmond, Va., Feb. 15, '65. Prisoner of war.
Jones, Hugh, Aug. 13, '62.	Died at Memphis, Tenn., Dec. 24, '62.
Krone, Jacob, Sept. 15, '62.	Died at Paducah, Ky., Feb. 20, '64.
McIlheran, John, Aug. 9, '62.	Absent, wounded, at muster out of regt.; prisoner of war.
Maeyers, John, Aug. 9,'62.	Died at Andersonville prison, June 17, '64.
Montgomery, Eli, Aug. 9, '62.	Died at Mound City Dec. 7, '64.
McConnaughty, S. B. "	Died at Walnut Hills, Miss., May 19, '63; wounds.
Myers, Wm. J., Aug. 9, '62.	Disch'd Jan. 24, '63; disability.
May, Henry F., Aug. 13, '62.	Disch'd March 20, '63; disability.
McMurty, J. L., Aug. 13, '62.	Must'd out July 1, '65; was pris.
Pound, D. K., Aug. 13, '62.	" June 7, '65; was pris.
Riber, E., Aug. 13, '62.	" " was prom. sergt.
Stoner, John H., Aug. 9, '62.	Mustered out May 27, '65.
Smith, John R., Aug. 9, '62.	Disch'd Feb. 6, '64; disability.
Smith, Jos. P., Aug. 9, '62.	Disch'd Aug. 4, '63; disability.
Snyder, Sam. W., Aug. 9, '62.	Mustered out June 7, '65.
Stine, Hiram S., Aug. 9, '62.	Disch'd July 7, '63; disability.
Scott, James, T., Aug. 9, '62.	Disch'd Jan., '63; disability.
Scott, Henry C., Aug. 9, '62.	Died at Memphis July 8, '63; wounds.
Schroll, Jacob B., Aug. 9, '62.	Mustered out June 7, '65, as sergt. Com. 2d lieut.; was prisoner.
Spaulding, J. A., Aug. 9, '62.	Died at Camp Sherman, Miss., Aug. 6, '63.
Turpin, Beechem, Aug. 9, '62.	Mustered out June 7, '65.

HISTORY OF MACON COUNTY. 125

Name, and date of Rank.	Remarks.
Thomas, Wm., Aug. 9, '62.	Died at Richmond, Va., Feb. 10, '64; prisoner of war.
Traughber, R. S., Aug. 9, '62.	Died on Stmr. City of Memphis Feb. 8, '63.
Travis, J. D. C., Aug. 13, '62.	Disch'd Feb. 16, '63; disability.
Travis, Isaac W., Aug. 13, '62.	Died at St. Louis Sept. 2, '63.
Travis, Sam. H., Aug. 13, '62.	Died on Stmr. Planet Jan. 5, '63.
Travis, U. D., Aug. 13, '62.	Died in La., April 27, '63.
Timmons, Eph., Aug. 12, '62.	Disch'd Feb. 25, '63; disability.
Timmons, Lam., Aug. 13, '62.	Died at Memphis March 16, '63.
Traughber, H. C., Aug. 18, '62.	Mustered out June 7, '65.
Urbain, John, Aug. 9, '62.	Disch'd Sept. 5, '63; disability.
Vliet, Amos W., Aug. 9, '62.	Mustered out June 7, '65.
Wallace, Wm., Aug. 9, '62.	Disch'd April, '63; disability.
Ward, Thos. J., Aug. 9, '62.	Sergt.; prom. sergt. major; was prisoner of war.
Wilson, Robt. D., Aug. 9, '62.	Mustered out June 7, '65.
Webber, Lewis, Aug. 18, '62.	Died at Richmond, Va., March 16, '64.

RECRUITS.

Aaron, John C., Feb. 11, '64.	Trans. to Co. F, 55th Ill. Inf.
Baker, N. M.	
Devore, Benjamin F.	Trans. to Co. K, before muster in.
Dulaney, John, March 29, '64.	Trans. to Co. F, 55th Ill. Inf.
Johnson, W. H., Feb. 27, '64.	" " "
Kimberlin, John A.	Trans. to Co. K, before muster in.
Kitt, Samuel.	

COMPANY "D."

CAPTAINS.

Joseph Lingle, Sept. 6, '62.	Resigned Feb. 29, '64.
Geo. A. Milmine, Feb. 29, '64.	Discharged Jan. 30, '65; was 1st lieut. and 2d lieut.

FIRST LIEUTENANTS.

Jas. R. Briggs, Sept. 6, '62.	Resigned April 6, '63.

Name, and date of Rank.	Remarks.
Thad. Collins, Feb. 29, '64.	Mustered out June 7, '65; was 2d lieut.

SECOND LIEUTENANT.

Hugh A. Lyons, June 7, '65.	Mustered out June 7, '65.

FIRST SERGEANT.

George, J. W., Aug. 15, '62.	Discharged Aug. 3, '63.

SERGEANTS.

Hoagland, J. E., Aug. 7, '62.	Disch'd June 7, '63; disability.
Williams, G. W., Aug. 7, '62.	Died on steamer City of Memphis Feb. 18, '63.
Collins, Thad., Aug. 7, '62.	Promoted 2d lieut.
Lyons, Hugh A., Aug. 13, '62.	Mustered out June 7, '65, as 1st sergt.; com'd 2d lieut.

CORPORALS.

Armstrong, D. T., Aug. 13, '62.	Sergeant; died at St. Louis April 7, '63.
Bowser, John F., Aug. 9, '62.	Died at Chattanooga May 21, '64; wounds.
Gill, David, Aug. 9, '62.	Died at Chickasaw Bayou Dec. 31, '62.
Watson, A. J., Aug. 9, '62.	Mustered out June 7, '65.
Streever, J. B., Aug. 9, '62.	Died at Annapolis, Md., November 1, '63.
Spore, Seth F., Aug. 9, '62.	Trans. to Co. F, 55th Ill. Inf.
Slifer, N. W., Aug. 9, '62.	Mustered out June 7, '65, as sergt.
Long, J. G., Aug. 9, '62.	Died at Richmond, Va., Feb. 20, '64; prisoner of war.

MUSICIANS.

Barger, Elias, Aug. 9, '62.	Mustered out June 7, '65.
Robertson, Amos, Aug. 13, '62.	Mustered out June 7, '65, as corp.

WAGONER.

Emery, C. F., Aug. 8, '62.	Discharged March 2, '63.

HISTORY OF MACON COUNTY. 127

Name, and date of Rank.   *Remarks.*

PRIVATES.

Armstrong, John, Aug. 15, '62.
Adams, Andrew, Aug. 11, '62.   Corporal; died at Richmond, Va., Jan. 27, '64; prisoner of war.
Antrim, B. F., Aug. 7, '62.   Mustered out June 7, '65, as sergt.
Allen, J. L., Aug. 9, '62.   Mustered out June 7, '65.
Amber, Wm., Aug. 9, '62.   Died at Young's Point January 20, '63.
Amber, H., Aug. 9, '62.   Died at Vicksburg, July 25, '63.
Adams, Joel B., Aug. 9, '62.   Mustered out June 8, '65.
Arbuckle, J. I., Aug. 9, '62. Mustered out June 7, '65, as corp.
Alexander, Sam., Aug. 9, '62.
Briggs, Wm., Aug. 9, '62.   Died at home Dec. 21, '63.
Belford, R. A., Aug. 12, '62. Discharged Feb. 1, '63.
Chism, John A., Aug. 8, '62.   Mustered out June 7, '65.
Chapman, L. N., Aug. 9, '62.   Mustered out June 7, '65, as corp.
Cory, Arthur O., Aug. 9, '62. Mustered out June 7, '65, as prisoner of war.
Cooper, N., Aug. 13, '62.   Died at Memphis, Tenn., March 6, '63.
Craft, John, Aug. 15, '62.   Died at St. Louis April 5, '64.
Corn, A. F., Aug. 9, '62.   Died on steamer City of Memphis Feb. 18, '63.
Crocker, R. C., Aug. 7, '62.   Promoted sergeant major.
Davidson, E. H., Aug. 9, '62. Absent, sick, at muster out of reg.
Daves, Wm., Aug. 9, '62.   Mustered out June 7, '65, as sergt.
Evans, Andrew, Aug. 13, '62.
Emerick, Geo., Aug. 7, '62.   Corporal; died at Annapolis, Md., Aug. 25, '63.
Elliott, J. W., Aug. 15, '62.
Fesler, Isaac, Aug. 9, '62.   Discharged April 3, '63.
Fenner, John W., Aug. 9, '62. Killed at Walnut Hills, Miss., May 19, '63.
Fesler, Larkin, Aug. 15, '62. Mustered out June 7, '65.
Gash, H. B., Aug. 9, '62.   "   "
Huckaboy, Jas., Aug. 7, '62.   Mustered out June 7, '65, as corp.
Kline, John, Aug. 15, '62.   Discharged Jan. 19, '63.

128   HISTORY OF MACON COUNTY.

Name, and date of Rank.   *Remarks.*

Kennedy, John, Aug. 13, '62.
Lukens, Edwards, Aug. 13, '62.   Promoted hospital steward.
Lukens, Wm. F., Aug. 13, '62.   Died in Mississippi June 22, '63.
Liston, J. E., Aug. 13, '62.   Killed at Atlanta, Ga., July 22,'64.
Locke, Philip, Aug. 27, '62.   Mustered out Juue 7, '65.
McKeever, H. D., Aug. 13, '62.   "   "
Miller, John, Aug. 13, '62.   "   "   as pris.
Miller, Clarke, Aug. 7, '62.   "   "
Millmine, E. K., Aug. 9, '62.   "   "
Martin, Robert, Aug. 13, '62.   "   "
O'Neal, Barnett, Aug. 13, '62.   Discharged Sept. 2, '63.
Pope, Richard, Aug. 23, '62.   Discharged Sept. 23, '63.
Payne, Sanford, Aug. 13, '62.   Discharged March 12, '63.
Plater, J. Y., Aug. 7, '62.   Sergeant; died at Memphis April 4, '63.

Querry, James, Aug. 13, '62.   Mustered out June 7,'65; prisoner.
Querry, Eri, Aug. 18, '62.   Mustered out June 7, '65.
Ray, Alonzo, Aug. 8, '62.   Discharged Jan. 19, '63.
Rinehart, Wm., Aug. 15, '62.   Died at Camp Butler, Ill., March 19, '64.

Reed, Squire, Aug. 7, '62.   Mustered out June 7, '65.
Ryan, Joseph, Aug. 7, '62.   "   "
Shannon, W. G., Aug. 22, '62.   "   "
Schenck, B. W., Aug. 7, '62.   "   "   as corp.
Schenck, Wm., Aug. 7, '62.   "   "   "
Sperling, Jacob, Aug. 9, '62.   "   "   as sergt.
Smith, Fred., Aug. 9, '62.   Sergeant; died at Cleveland, Tenn., Jan. 28, '65.

Scott, David, Aug. 7, '62.   Mustered out June 7, '65; was pris.
Sellers, Peter, Aug. 18, '62.   Discharged Aug. 12, '63.
Salters, J. W., Aug. 9, '62.   Mustered out June 7, '65.
Shannon, John, Aug. 9, '62.   "   "
Sandy, Edward, Aug. 9, '62.   Discharged Feb. 6, '64.
Thornburg, Thos., Aug. 7, '62.   Mustered out June 7, '65.
Towers, Wm., Aug. 9, '62.   "   "
Tooly, Charles, Aug. 9, '62.   "   "   as corp.
Vanler, Wm. A., Aug. 5, '62.   Discharged Jan. 16, '63.
VanVoorhees, S. N., Aug. 9,'62. Discharged January, '63.

Name, and date of Rank.	Remarks.
Williams, A. G., Aug. 11, '62.	Died at Richmond, Va., March 5, '64; prisoner of war.
Williams, M. J., Aug. 11, '62.	Died at St. Louis March 26, '63.
Withers, Alex., Aug. 9, '62.	Died at Young's Point March 23, '63.
Withers, Ira, Aug. 9, '62.	Died at Milliken's Bend April 27, '63.
Wright, A. J., Aug. 12, '63.	Died at Young's Point Feb. 17, '63.
Zinn, Jacob, Aug. 15, '62.	Mustered out June 7, '65.

RECRUITS.

Briggs, Alex.	Died on Stmr. Planet Jan. 20, '63.
Gill, Wm. H. H.	
Harris, E.	

COMPANY "E."

CAPTAINS.

Lewis J. Eyman, Sept. 6, '62.	Killed Jan. 11, '63.
J. S. Windsor, Jan. 31, '63.	Promoted major.
R. M. Hamilton, Sept. 26, '64.	Mustered out June 7, '65; was 1st lieut.

FIRST LIEUTENANTS.

S. H. Varney, Sept. 6, '62.	Resigned March 5, '63.
Jos. D. Noon, March 5, '63.	Died June 18, '63.
Wm. N. Streeter, June 3, '63.	Resigned May 27, '64.
Sam. J. Varney, Sept. 26, '64.	Died small pox Feb. 13, '65.
W. H. Dickerson, Apr. 20, '65.	Mustered out June 7, '65.

SECOND LIEUTENANTS.

W. L. Harris, Sept. 6, '62.	Resigned June 28, '63.
Amsi H. Baker, June 7, '65.	Mustered out June 7, '65.

SERGEANTS.

Mackey, L. J., Aug. 15, '62.	Absent, sick, at muster out of regt.
Hamilton, R. M., Aug. 15, '62.	Promoted 1st lieut.

Name, and date of Rank.	Remarks.
Noon, Jos. D., Aug. 6, '62.	Died at Memphis, June 18, '63.
Baker, Amsi H., Aug. 6, '62.	Mustered out June 7, '65; com'd 2d lieut.

CORPORALS.

Eyman, Ed. C., Aug. 6, '62.	Died at Milliken's Bend April 26, '63.
Boyd, E. H., Aug. 2, '62.	Died at Young's Point Feb. 23, '63.
Gepford, Jer., Aug. 2, '62.	Mustered out June 2, '65.
Rinehart, Joel, Aug. 2, '62.	" June 7, '65.
Eyman, John, Aug. 6, '62.	Trans. to V. R. C., Jan. 15, '64.
Danley, John, Aug. 6, '62.	Mustered out June 7, '65.
Parr, Andrew, Aug. 7, '62.	" "
Goodner, Geo., Aug. 7, '62.	" "

MUSICIANS.

Kitch, Robert G., Aug. 6, '62.	Mustered out June 7, '65.
Gepford, Silas, Aug. 10, '62.	

WAGONER.

Nicholson, H. B., Aug. 6, '62.	Mustered out June 7, '65.

PRIVATES.

Allen, Wm. G., Aug. 8, '62.	Mustered out June 7, '65.
Boyd, James H., Aug. 2, '62.	Absent, sick, at muster out of regt.
Benton, Chas. F., Aug. 6, '62.	" " "
Brewer, Geo. W., Aug. 6, '62.	Mustered out June 7, '65.
Bullard, Chas. S., Aug. 6, '62.	Absent, sick, at muster out of regt.
Bruce, Joel, Aug. 8, '62.	Died at Young's Point Feb. 9, '63.
Bruce, Geo. W., Aug. 6, '62.	Died at Decatur Aug. 31, '63.
Benton, E. L., Aug. 8, '62.	Died on hospital boat Mar. 18, '63.
Barnhart, J., Aug. 10, '62.	Mustered out June 7, '65; prisoner of war.
Burt, Silas, Aug. 2, '62.	Mustered out June 7, '65.
Clark, Ira E., Aug. 6, '62.	Died at Decatur, Ill., Nov. 6, '62.
Corn, John W., Aug. 6, '62.	Mustered out June 7, '65.
Cross, Jacob, Aug. 6, '62.	" "
Clark, Chas. H., Aug. 6, '62.	" "
Carver, M., Aug. 7, '62.	Died at Young's Point Feb. 11, '63.

HISTORY OF MACON COUNTY. 131

Name, and date of Rank.	Remarks.
Cox, John H., Aug. 7, '62.	Discharged at St. Louis.
Cross, Israel M., Aug. 9, '62.	Died at Young's Point March 26, '63.
Dickerson, W. H., Aug. 2, '62.	Promoted corporal, sergeant and 1st lieut.
Downey, John, Aug. 6, '62.	Mustered out June 7, '65.
Danley, F. M., Aug. 6, '62.	Died at Young's Point March 5, '63.
Douglas, S. A., Aug. 6, '62.	Mustered out June 7, '65.
Dunham, L. H., Aug. 13, '62.	Trans. to V. R. C. May 1, '64.
Eaton, Michael, Aug. 8, '62.	Discharged Nov. 25, '63.
French, H. W., Aug. 2, '62.	Trans. to inv. corps, Sept 30, '63.
Farnam, M. A., Aug. 2, '62.	Mustered out June 7, '65.
Farnam, Stephen, Aug. 2, '62.	" " as sergt.
Farnam, Chester, Aug. 6, '62.	Corporal; killed at Resaca, Ga., May 14, '64.
Farnam, David, Aug. 6, '62.	Mustered out June 7, '65.
Farnam, Lindsay, Aug. 6, '62.	Absent, sick. at muster out of reg.
Free, James, Aug. 6, '62.	Mustered out June 7, '65.
Fowler, J. W., Aug. 6, '62.	Killed at Walnut Hills, Miss., May 19, '63.
Gooden, Jos., Aug. 6, '62.	Mustered out June 7, '65.
Greeley, M., Aug. 6, '62.	" " as corp.
Graham, Thos., Aug. 7, '62.	" "
Gass, E. M., Sept. 29, '62.	Died at Memphis Oct. 31, '63.
Gepford, W. H., Sept. 16, '62.	Mustered out June 7, '65, as corp.
Hornbeck, S. C., Sept. 18, '62.	" "
Houser, Geo. W., Sept. 18, '62.	" " as corp.
Houston, Wm., Aug. 2, '62.	Killed near Atlanta, Ga., July 22, '64.
Hunt, Wm., Aug. 2, '62.	Mustered out June 7, '65.
Holcomb, Byron, Aug. 2, '62.	Promoted sergt. major.
Hawk, James M., Aug. 6, '62.	Mustered out June 7, '65, as corp.
Hobbs, Jacob J., Aug. 6, '62.	Sergt.; died July 30, '64; wounds.
Havener, Jos., Aug. 6, '62.	Mustered out June 7, '65.
Harrison, Ben., Aug. 6, '62.	Died at Camp Butler Feb. 24, '64.
Hatchett, Jno. H., Aug. 6, '62.	Mustered out June 7, '65; sergt.
Jones, Young P., Aug. 7, '62.	

HISTORY OF MACON COUNTY.

Name, and date of Rank.	Remarks.
Johnson, F. M., Aug. 6, '62.	
Jones, Wm. G., Aug. 7, '62.	Absent, sick, at muster out of reg.
Johnson, E. M., Aug. 7, '62.	Died at Decatur, Ill., Oct. 16, '63.
James, J. L., Aug. 8, '62.	Discharged June 14, '63.
Kitch, Solomon, Aug. 6, '62.	Mustered out June 7, '65, as corp.
Kile, Edward M., Aug. 6, '62.	" "
Kelsey, Harper, Aug. 13, '62.	Died at Memphis Aug. 5, '63.
Kile, John W., Aug. 6, '62.	Mustered out June 7, '65.
Land, Moses, Aug. 6, '62.	Died at Cherry Grove, Ill., Nov. 25, '63.
Nelson, Eli, Aug. 7, '62.	Disch'd Feb. 18, '65; disability.
Pettit, Geo., Aug. 6, '62.	Died near Dallas, Ga., May 31, '64.
Parr, James H., Aug. 6, '62.	Died at Young's Point March 2, '63.
Rittenhouse, I. W., Aug. 6, '62.	Corp.; died at Decatur, Ill., Sept. 29, '64; wounds.
Rager, Wm. H., Aug. 2, '62.	Mustered out June 7, '65.
Shartzer, A., Aug. 2, '62.	" "
Sprague, Jas. H., Aug. 2, '62.	" "
Stocton, R. M., Aug. 6, '62.	" " as sergt.
Sollars, R. G., Aug. 6, '62.	Discharged Sept. 16, '64.
Stout, Leonard, Aug. 6, '62.	Discharged March 28, '64.
Sprague, Nat., Aug. 5, '62.	Mustered out June 7, '65, as corp.
Smalley, Allen, Aug. 6, '62.	Died at Camp Sherman, Miss., Aug. 31, '63.
Snyder, Thos. A., Aug. 18, '62.	Died at St. Louis July 3, '63.
VanGundy, Geo., Aug. 6, '62.	Died at Young's Point Mar. 16, '63.
Varney, Sam. J., Aug. 14, '62.	Sergt; com'd 1st lieut.; not must'd; died at Annapolis Feb. 3, '65.
Wheeler, Larkin, Aug. 2, '62.	
White, Lewis E., Aug. 2, '62.	Discharged Aug. 14, '63.
Wood, Basil, Aug. 6, '62.	Mustered out June 7, '65.
Young, Jos. H., Aug. 6, '62.	Died at Memphis April 13, '63.

RECRUITS.

Benton, William P.	Died at Memphis, January, '63.

Name, and date of Rank.　　　　　*Remarks.*

COMPANY "F."

CAPTAINS.

Sam'l N. Bishop, Sept. 6, '62.　Resigned April 12, '63.
N. Geschwind, April 12, '63.　Promoted Major.
Wm. P. Goodner, June 7, '65.　Mustered out June 7, '65.

FIRST LIEUTENANTS.

John B. Tutt, Sept. 6, '62.　Died Jan. 26, '63.
S. R. Riggs, April 12, '63.　Resigned Dec 11, '64.
John A. Cochran, June 7, '65.　Mustered out June 7, '65.

SECOND LIEUTENANTS.

E. R. Pratt, Sept. 30, '62.　Died March 30, '63.
J. C. Stansbury, April 28, '63.　Died April 19, '63.
John P. Lewis, June 7, '65.　Mustered out June 7, '65.

PRIVATES.

Lourish, Benj., Sept. 5, '62.　Died at Young's Point February 15, '63.
Lourish, David, Aug. 11, '62.　Discharged March 20, '63.
Young, Geo. E., Sept. 14, '62.　Absent, sick, at muster out of reg.

COMPANY "G."

CAPTAINS.

Alonzo B. Davis, Sept. 30, '62.　Died Dec. 22, '63.
Harvey Mahannah, Dec. 22, '63.　Mustered out June 7, '65; was 1st lieut.

FIRST LIEUTENANT.

Jas. P. Barnett, Dec. 22, '63.　Mustered out June 7, '65.

SECOND LIEUTENANTS.

Lafayette Helm, Sept. 30, '62.　Died Feb. 16, '63.
Byron Barrett, Mar. 15, '63.　Mustered out June 7, '65.

Name, and date of Rank. *Remarks.*

FIRST SERGEANT.

Barnett, Jas. P., Aug. 11, '62.　Prom. 1st lieut.

SERGEANTS.

Landis, D. B., Aug. 18, '62.　Wounded; transferred to V. R. C. Sept. 15, '63.
Davis, Wm. B., Aug. 12, '62.
Doyle, Michael, Aug. 9, '62.　Mustered out June 7, '65.
Burdick, Z. C., Aug. 12, '62.　　"　　　　　"

CORPORALS.

Smith, Wm., Aug. 11, '62.　Mustered out June 7, '65, as sergt.
Rouse, Oren S., Aug. 12, '62.　　"　　　　　"　　　　"
Kitrick, Abe., Aug. 14, '62.　Mustered out June 7, '65.
Bragg, John E., Aug. 12, '62.　　"　　　　　"

MUSICIAN.

Rea, David, Aug, 12, '62.　Mustered out June 7, '65.

WAGONER.

Horton, Wm. H., Aug. 12, '62.

PRIVATES.

Andrews, Elijah, Sept. 28, '62.
Andrews, Elias, Sept. 28, '62.
Barret, M. L., Aug. 14, '62.　Promoted principal musician.
Barrett, Chas., Sept. 14, '62.　Died at Young's Point February 22, '63.
Brooks, Wm., Aug. 12, '62.
Baird, Joseph C., Aug. 12, '62.　Discharged March 31, '63.
Cotterell, Thos., Aug. 12, '62.　Mustered out June 7, '65.
Crissey, Wm. E., Aug. 12, '62.　Promoted com. sergeant.
Dickey, Wm. W., Aug. 15, '62.　Killed at Atlanta, Ga., July 22,'64.
Dickey, D. A., Sept. 9, '62.　Corporal; killed at Atlanta, Ga., July 22, '64.

HISTORY OF MACON COUNTY.   135

Name, and date of Rank.   *Remarks.*

Fry, Wm., Sept. 9, '62.
Fuller, Lafayette, Sept. 29, '62.   Absent, sick, at muster out of reg.
Gant, Jackson, Sept. 11, '62.   Died at Memphis, Tenn., October 10, '63.
Higgins, Jno. T., Aug. 14, '62.   Detached at muster out of reg.
Howell, Brice, Aug. 12, '62.
Howell, Lewis, Aug. 15, '62.
Hoots, Alex., Aug. 12, '62.   Mustered out June 7, '65, as corp.
Helm, John S., Aug. 18, '62.   "   "
Harper, C. R., Aug. 11, '62.   Died Jan. 12, '65; wounds.
Hooker, Wm. C., Aug. 15, '62.   Died at Memphis March 30, '63.
Huston, Servantus, Aug. 13, '62.   Mustered out June 7, '65.
Huusley, C. E., Aug. 14, '62.   "   "
Henson, J., Aug. 20, '62.   "   "
Hanks, Dunham, Aug. 12, '62.
Kemp, Isaac, Aug. 12, '62.
Kemp, Philip, Aug. 15, '62.   Mustered out June 7, '65, as sergt.
Lyons, Wm., Aug. 12, '62.   Absent, sick, at muster out of reg.
Lickliter, G. W., Sept. 29, '62.   Died at Memphis May 1, '63.
Lukens, John, Aug. 14, '62.   Mustered out June 7, '65; woun'd.
Latham, Henry, Aug. 2, '62.   "   "
Moore, David, Aug. 20, '62.   "   "
Moore, Wm., Aug. 15, '62.
Mahannah, H., Aug. 11, '62.   Mustered out June 7, '65.
Mott, Geo. W., Sept. 11, '62.   Discharged Feb. 18, '65, as sergt.; wounds.

Rosa, S. W., Aug. 12, '62.
Rhodes, Wm. H., Sept. 18, '62.   Discharged March 11, '63.
Smith, A. L., Aug. 12, '62.   Discharged Dec. 18, '62.
Smith, Wm. C., Aug. 21, '62.   Died at Young's Point January 27, '63.
Shupp, Samuel, Aug. 26, '62.   1st sergt.; absent, sick, at muster out of regiment.
Shasted, Wm. E., Aug. 14, '62.   Died at Young's Point February 20, '63.
Smith, T. W., Aug. 11, '62.   Mustered out June 7, '65.
Startsman, L., Aug. 18, '62.   "   "

Name, and date of Rank.   *Remarks.*

Secrist, Wm., Aug. 12,'62.   Died at Mound City, Ill., August 1, '63.
Smith, Jno. W., Sept. 18, '62.   Discharged Sept. 12, '63.
Schmitz, M., Sept. 13, '62.   Mustered out June 7, '65.
Spear, Wm., Aug. 14, '62.   Discharged March 3, '65.
Troxell, John A., Aug. 14, '62.   Transferred to V. R. C. June 15, '63.
Willett, Jas. L., Aug. 12, '62.   Mustered out June 7, '65, as corp.
Williams, L. A., Aug. 17, '62.   Transferred to V. R. C. December 15, '63.
Wheeler, Wesley, Aug. 12, '62.   Discharged June 6, '63.

Company "H."

CAPTAINS.

J. L. Dobson, Sept. 30, '62.   Resigned June 13, '63.
John P. Lamb, June 13, '63.   Resigned Dec. 22, '64.
Chas. P. Essick, April 20, '65.   Mustered out June 7, '65.

FIRST LIEUTENANTS.

Isom Simmons, April 28, '63.   Killed Dec. 22, '64.
Jas. Goodwin, April 20, '65.   Mustered out June 7, '65.

SECOND LIEUTENANTS.

The. Short, Sept. 20, '62.   Died Feb. 6, '63.
Wm. W. Winn, June 7, '65.   Mustered out June 7, '65.

MUSICIAN.

Robinson, Jos. Sept. 18, '62.   Trans. to Inv. Corps Dec. 17, '63.

PRIVATE.

Sollars, Chas., Sept. 10, '62.

RECRUIT.

Bacon, Geo. W., Feb. 28, '64.   Trans. to Co. F, 55th Ill. Inf.

Name, and date of Rank.   *Remarks.*

COMPANY "I."

CAPTAINS.

Uriah P. Forbes, Sept. 30, '62. Resigned April 25, '63.
John F. Bishop, April 25, '63. Resigned March 30, '64, was 1st lieut.
Isaac N. Martin, Mar. 13, '64. Mustered out June 7, '65; was 1st lieut.

FIRST LIEUTENANT.

Fred. Schwab, March 13, '64. Mustered out June 7, '65.

SECOND LIEUTENANTS.

Irwin Miller, Sept. 30, '62. Dismissed Jan. 19, '65.
Joshua K. Carr, June 7, '65. Mustered out June 7, '65.

SERGEANTS.

Sheppard, F. M., Aug. 13, '62. Mustered out June 7, '65, as priv.
Carr, Joshua K., Aug. 6, '62. " " as 1st sergt.; com. 2d lieut.
Workheiser, E., Aug. 14, '62. Mustered out June 7, '65, as priv.
Phillips, W. H., Aug. 22, '62. Priv.; detached at muster out of regiment.

CORPORALS.

Vermillion, M., Aug. 14, '62. Priv.; died Larkinsville, Ala., Feb. 4, '64.
Carter, J. E., Aug. 8, '62. Mustered out June 7, '65, as priv.
Martin, Geo., Aug. 12, '62. " " as sergt.
Hammond, J. H., Aug. 14, '62. " " as priv.
Schuh, Peter, Aug. 13, '62. " "
Kingsberry, Asa, Aug. 8, '62. Absent, sick, at muster out of reg.
Scott, John, Aug. 14, '62. Mustered out June 7, '65, as priv.
Mendenhall, G. W., Aug. 8, '62. " " was pris.

MUSICIAN.

Whelan, Henry, Aug. 22, '62. Mustered out June 7, '65.

Name, and date of Rank.   *Remarks.*

PRIVATES.

Art, Joseph, Aug. 12, '62.	Died on hospital boat March 15, '63.
Barth, Jacob, Aug. 22, '62.	Died on hospital boat March 15, '63.
Bratz, Jacob, Aug. 14, '62.	Died at Young's Point, La., Feb. 22, '63.
Bailey, G. C., Aug. 18, '62.	Mustered out June 7, '65.
Barnett, Samuel, Sept. 27, '62.	" "
Conaly, M. C., Aug. 13, '62.	" "
Collins, E. R., Aug. 8, '62.	" " as corp.
Cline, Henry, Aug. 15, '62.	" " as sergt.
Cothen, Cors, Aug. 14, '62.	" "
Church, Geo. W., Aug. 11, '62.	Transferred to Co. A, 55th Ill. Inf.
Drain, Joseph, Aug. 22, '62.	Disch'd May 5, '65; disability.
Enkie, Jno. Q., Aug. 14, '62.	Disch'd April 8, '63; disability.
Ebert, Henry, Aug. 14, '62.	Sergt.; absent, sick, at muster out of regiment.
Fry, Michael, Aug. 8, '62.	Mustered out June 7, '65, as corp.
Flaherty, J. J., Aug. 13, '62.	" "
Fulk, Henry, Aug. 16, '62.	Absent, sick, at muster out of reg.
Flaherty, M., Aug. 27, '62.	Must'd out June 7, '65; was pris.
Fulk, John W., Aug. 22, '62.	Died at Young's Point, La., Jan. 29, '63.
Fry, John, Aug. 22, '62.	Trans. to Co. A, 55th Ill. Inf.
Guthrie, David, Aug. 14, '62.	Mustered out June 7, '65.
Guthrie, Wm. S., Aug. 14, '62.	Died at Young's Point Feb. 9, '63.
Gehrt, Ferd., Aug. 21, '62.	Absent, sick, at muster out of reg.
Garver, Dan. H., Sept. 19, '62.	
Gloden, Michael, Aug. 14, '62.	Mustered out June 7, '65, as corp.
Goodpasture, J., Aug. 9, '62.	Discharged Oct. 9, '62; writ habeas corpus.
Hammond, T. R., Aug. 9, '62.	Mustered out June 7, '65, as sergt.
Hoff, Michael, Aug. 9, '62.	" " as corp.
Harris, Henry, Aug. 22, '62.	" "
Heinold, And., Aug. 12, '62.	Died at Quincy, Ill., Mar. 25, '65.
Herrindeen, O., Sept. 27, '62.	Died on hospital boat March 13, '63.

Name, and date of Rank.	Remarks.
Jenkins, S. T., Sept. 10, '62.	Disch'd Jan. 24, '63; disability.
Keller, Mathias, Aug. 9, '62.	Died at Quincy, Ill., Oct. 25, '63.
Kitchen, J. B., Aug. 12, '62.	Disch'd March 27, '63; disability.
Koehler, Ernest, Aug. 12, '62.	Died at Chattanooga, Tenn., Feb. 19, '64.
Latch, J., jr., Aug. 8, '62.	
Latch, Geo. B., Aug. 8, '62.	
Latch, Theo. R., Aug. 8, '62.	
Morganthall, J., Aug. 8, '62.	Absent, sick, at muster out of reg.
Martin, John, Aug. 14, '62.	
Miller, Alex., Aug. 9, '62.	Killed at Resaca, Ga., May 14, '64.
Miles, Samuel, Aug. 13, '62.	Mustered out June 7, '65.
Mang, John, Sept. 26, '62.	Disch'd Sept. 2, '63; disability.
Miller, Henry S., Aug. 9, '62.	Mustered out June 7, '65.
Morrel, Andrew, Aug. 14, '62.	Killed at Arkansas Post Jan. 11, '63.
Mendenha, H., Aug. 20, '62.	Disch'd March 6, '63; disability.
Nier, Fred., Aug. 12, '62.	Mustered out June 7, 65.
Odle, Wm., Aug. 12, '62.	Disch'd March 11, '63; disability.
Reynolds, S. V., Aug. 13, '62.	Died at Decatur Oct. 8, '62.
Smith, Val., Aug. 14, '62.	Mustered out June 7, '65.
Smoot, M. A., Aug. 14, '62.	Died on str. Planet Feb. 18, '63.
Strickland, Jos., Aug. 15, '62.	Died at Evansville Jan. 10, '65.
Shinnaman, H., Aug. 19, '62.	Died at St. Louis March 4, '63.
Stumpff, John, Aug. 19, '62.	Mustered out June 7, '65.
Smith, Fred., Aug. 22, '62.	
Smith, E., Sept. 13, '62.	Mustered out June 7, '65, as corp.
Tool, Geo., Aug. 22, '62.	
Vogle, Philip A., Aug. 14, '62.	Trans to V. R. C. May 1, '64.
Veail, David, Aug. 13, '62.	Disch'd May 22, '63; disability.
Witt, Michael, Aug. 29, '62.	Mustered out June 7, '65.
Westerhaver, H., Aug. 8, '62.	Wagoner; absent, sick at muster out of regiment.
Younger, Josiah, Aug. 12, '62.	Corp.; killed at Vicksburg July 2, '63.
Younger, J. Q., Aug. 14, '62.	Disch'd Mar. 28, '63; disability.

140   HISTORY OF MACON COUNTY.

Name, and date of Rank.   *Remarks.*

Young, Wm., Aug. 12, '62.   Corp.; absent, wounded, at muster out of regiment.

RECRUIT.

Miller, Wm. H., Aug. 12, '62.   Trans. to Co. A, 55th Ill. Inf.

COMPANY "K."

CAPTAINS.

John E. Maddox, Sept. 30, '62.   Promoted Lieut. Col.
Jas. H. Glore, June 15, '64.   Mustered out June 7, '65; was 1st lieut. and 2d lieut.

FIRST LIEUTENANTS.

John S. Windsor, Sept. 30, '62.   Promoted captain Co. E.
Jos. D. Mackey, June 15, '64.   Mustered out June 7, '65.

SECOND LIEUTENANTS.

N. W. Wheeler, Sept. 30, '62.   Killed March 19, '63; siege of Vicksburg.
H. G. Eppler, June 7, '65.   Mustered out June 7, '65.

SERGEANTS.

Green, G. W., July 17, '62.   Absent, sick, at muster out of reg.
McCann, Thos.   Died at Milliken's Bend, La., May 8, '63.
Dermot, Jas., July 9, '62.   Disch'd March 20, '64, as priv.

CORPORALS.

Tedroe, Wm. L., July 26, '62.   Mustered out June 7, '65; was pris.
Stackhouse, John, Aug. 6, '62.   "   "
Purtroff, John, July 29, '62.   Died at Mound City Sept. 7, '63.
Young, J. J. H., July 14, '62.   Discharged April 11, '63.
Harbour, M. V., Aug. 14, '62.   Sergt.; absent, wounded, at muster out of regiment.
Thompson, Wm., Aug. 14, '62.   Absent, sick, at muster out of reg.
Herrin, John, Aug. 14, '62.   Died at Young's Point May 24, '63.
Griffin, Wm. T., Aug. 6, '62.

Name, and date of Rank.   *Remarks.*

MUSICIANS.

McIntyre, Dan., Aug. 15, '62.   Discharged July 3, '64.
Berickman, B. C., Aug. 19, '62.

WAGONER.

Young, Wm., Aug. 6, '62.   Absent, sick, at muster out of reg.

PRIVATES.

Name	Remarks
Ater, Geo., Aug. 7, '62.	Trans to Inv. Corps Sept. 1, '63.
Ashberry, J. W., Aug. 24, '62.	Corp.; died at Rome, Ga., Sept. 9, '64; wounds.
Brewer, Wm. J., Aug. 14, '62.	Mustered out June 7, '65.
Burt, G. W., Aug. 15, '62.	Transferred to Invalid Corps Jan. 17, '64.
Baird, C. M., July 25, '62.	Died at Young's Point February 23, '63.
Badger, James, July 22, '62.	Absent, sick, at muster out of reg.
Brooks, Jasper, Aug. 24, '62.	Died at Young's Point February 3, '63.
Brooks, R. K., Aug. 24, '62.	Mustered out June 7, '65, as sergt.
Chafin, Amos, Aug. 15, '62.	
Coleman, Adam, Aug. 15, '62.	Died at Memphis March 21, '63.
Clarke, Michael, Aug. 28, '62.	Died at Memphis Jan. 31, '63.
Carr, Clark, Aug. 22, '62.	
Clay, Wm., Aug. 2, '62.	
Collins, Naman, Aug. 8, '62.	Mustered out June 7, '65, as sergt.
Cook, N. T., July 15, '62.	" "
Clark, Hugh, July 22, '62.	" "
Cox, Jerome, Aug. 8, '62.	Discharged July 1, '63.
Chafin, Joseph, Aug. 25, '62.	
Deboy, George, Aug. 13, '62.	Died at Atlanta, Ga., July 25, '64; wounds.
Devore, Benj., Aug. 9, '62.	Died at Decatur Nov. 18, '63.
Eldridge, B., Aug. 19, '62.	Absent, sick, at muster out of reg.
Epler, Hiram.	Mustered out June 7, '65, as sergt.
Follis, Levi, Aug. 11, '62.	Mustered out June 7, '65.
Follis, Alex., Aug. 11, '62.	Died on hospital boat May 23, '63.
Fry, Jesse, Aug. 7, '62.	Discharged January 8, '65.

Name, and date of Rank.	Remarks.
Gingle, Andrew, Aug. 6, '62.	Missing since May 31, '65; supposed insane.
Hunter, J. S., Aug. 15, '62.	Discharged May 6, '65, as corp.
Hix, Richard, Aug. 27, '62.	Died on hospital boat Jan. 31, '63.
Hampshire, Wm., Aug. 22, '62.	Absent, sick, at muster out of reg.
Herrold, J. A., Aug. 22, '62.	Transferred to Invalid Corps Sept. 30, '63.
Hegar, or Haaka, H. Aug. 28, '62.	Died at Big Shanty June 23, '64; wounds.
Heck, John, Aug. 2, '62.	Mustered out June 7, '65.
Holder, Wm., Aug. 1, '62.	Died at Chattanooga June 14, '64.
James, Jacob, Aug. 11, '62.	Killed near Atlanta, Ga., July 22, '64.
James, Daniel, Aug. 11, '62.	Died at St. Louis July 20, '63.
Johnson, J., Aug. 25, '62.	Died at Decatur Nov. 25, '62.
Jones, J., Aug. 2, '62.	Mustered out June 7, '65.
Kimberland, J. A., Aug. 15, '62.	" "
Luster, Wm., Aug. 11, '62.	" "
Leigh, G. W., Aug. 2, '62.	Died at Memphis Nov. 26, '62.
Mattox, Maley, Aug. 14, '62.	Corporal; died at Young's Point Feb. 1, '63.
McGloughlin, M., Aug. 6, '62.	Mustered out June 7, '65.
Murphy, Patrick, Aug. 20, '62.	Discharged Dec. 4, '63.
McCantus, Owen, Aug. 22, '62.	
Maples, Jacob, Aug. 15, '62.	Absent, sick, at muster out of reg.
McCune, Wm., Aug. 22, '62.	" " "
O'Neil, John, Aug. 25, '62.	Discharged Sept. 29, '63.
Poindexter, S. H., Aug. 22, '62.	Absent, sick, at muster out of reg.
Poyner, S., Aug. 16, '62.	Died at Pana, Ill., June 20, '64.
Purkey, David, Aug. 7, '62.	Transferred to Invalid Corps Sept. 1, '63.
Ryan, James, Aug. 15, '62.	Sergeant; died at Big Shanty, Ga., July 17, '64; wounded.
Reed, J. W., Aug. 8, '62.	Died at Keokuk, Iowa, Oct. 5, '63.
Reed, T. J., Aug. 22, '62.	Died at Young's Point February 11, '63.
Staines, Daniel, Aug. 15, '62.	Died at Young's Point February 7, '63.

Name, and date of Rank.	*Remarks.*
Shields, John, Aug. 15, '62.	Mustered out June 7, '65.
Shoemaker, David, Aug. 8, '62.	" "
Shaw, Henry, July 15, '62.	Discharged April 15, '63.
Smith, C. R., July 25, '62.	Mustered out June 7, '65.
See, William, Aug. 27, '62.	Discharged April 10, '63.
Terril, David B., Aug. 9, '62.	Mustered out June 7, '65, as corp.
Vest, Toliver, July 17, '62.	Com. in 2d Miss. Colored Inf.
Wannell, Jas. W., Aug. 9, '62.	Mustered out June 7, '65.
Wallace, David, Aug. 12, '62.	" "
Wood, Jas. W., Aug. 18, '62.	Died at Young's Point January 31, '63.

RECRUITS.

Chappin, E. C., Nov. 3, '62.	Killed at Resaca, Ga., May 14, '64.
Dobson, John.	
Hines, Wm., Feb. 15, '64.	
Richardson, Isaac.	Died at Camp Butler Mar. 26, '64.

CHAPTER V.

"THE DEEP SNOW."

Among the memorable events associated with the early history of the county, is the "deep snow." This is one of the land-marks of the early settler. It is his mile-stone, from which he counts in dating preceding or succeeding events. He reckons the date of his coming, his marriage, and the births of his children, from it. You ask him the age of John, Sarah or Susan, and he seldom fails to fix their births at so many years before or after the deep snow. You may locate a certain event as occurring Anno Domini, so and so, and your ante-deep-snow resident will at once commence counting on his fingers the intervening years between the deep snow and the particular time in question, in order to verify your date. The fact is, that the deep snow was an important and very extraordinary phenomenon. There has been nothing equal to it in this latitude for the last hundred years—if the Indian traditions are correct as to what occurred before the white man's advent. According to their traditions, as related to the first white settlers, a snow fell, from fifty to seventy-five years before the settlement by the white people, which swept away the immense herds of buffalo and elk that then roamed over our vast prairies. This tradition was verified by the vast quantity of buffalo and elk bones remaining in different localities upon our prairies when first visited by white men.

The deep snow under consideration occurred in the winter of 1830-'31.

It commenced snowing early in the fall, and continued, at intervals, throughout the entire winter. The snow falls would be succeeded by heavy sleets, forming crusts of ice between the layers of snow. There were weeks that the sun was not visible, and the cold was so intense that not a particle of snow would melt upon the sides of the houses facing the south. People were for weeks absolutely blockaded or housed up, and remained so until starvation compelled them to go forth in search of food, or to procure corn and to get it ground at the few horse mills then in the country. It may be of interest, in this connection, to relate an incident connected with the early history of the late Abraham Lincoln, who was at that time a resident of Macon county. Late in the winter, Mr. Lincoln and John Hanks, with great difficulty made their way across the Sangamon to a horse mill owned by Robert Smith, five and a half miles southwest of Decatur, for the purpose of getting some corn ground. They found Mr. S. in the field gathering corn. He had succeeded in getting a road opened to the field, and would drive a yoke of oxen, attached to a sled, to the end of the road, lift the sled around, turning the cattle in the direction from which they came, and then, with baskets, gather the corn that was exposed above the snow, and carry it and deposit it in the sled. Mr. S. was engaged at this when Mr. Lincoln made his appearance, requesting his " grist " to be ground. Mr. Lincoln was asked if he had to labor under such difficulties on his side of the river. " Yes," said he, "we have to do worse than that, for we have used up all of our corn, and now have to go to our neighbors for assistance."

It is not known that any one starved or was frozen during this trying ordeal; but suffering, hunger and untold hardships were endured by the people. Game, such as prairie chickens, quails, deer, etc., prior to that time, had been abundant, but for years afterwards was very scarce, having perished in the snow. Deer were often caught and killed without the aid of guns or other fire-arms, being unable to get through the snow or walk on top. Later in winter, when the mass of snow and ice had become compact, fences that were staked and ridered were driven over with heavily loaded vehicles, and, in fact, in places could not be seen. The snow is usually estimated at three feet deep at places where it was not drifted, and of course would have been much deeper than that if it had fallen in a short space of time. In the spring, when this immense amount of snow melted, the river and streams were very

—19

high, and, for this reason, it was almost as difficult to get from a place as it was during the winter.

THE "SUDDEN FREEZE," OR "SUDDEN CHANGE."

In January, 1836, occurred an extraordinary atmospheric phenomenon experienced by the residents of this county, known as the "sudden freeze." It was attended with loss of life to both man and beast, and the most intense suffering from cold. Incidents are related in connection with this "sudden change," that, to the incredulous, seem marvelous and highly colored, and as some have expressed it, "rather fishy." Immediately preceding the storm the ground had been covered with snow, which, from rain falling on the day of the occurrence, had become "slushy." The storm came from the northwest, and the clouds, upon its approach, assumed a very threatening and extraordinary aspect, those above being dark, and those below of a white, frosty appearance. The air seemed to be filled with innumerable particles of frozen mist, and the moment the storm struck the unfortunate person away from shelter, he seemed to be instantaneously transferred from a temperate to a most frigid zone. The father of the writer, as this storm approached, was going on an errand, not over a quarter of a mile distant. As he went, the ground was covered with sleet and water; on his immediate return home, the ice had formed sufficient in thickness that he could walk on top.

"The late Gen. I. C. Pugh left town on horseback in the rain, for his home on the Bloomington road, and when he reached the large pond which formerly lay on the east side of North Water street, the cold was so intense that long needles of ice were shooting over the surface of the pond in every direction, presenting a very singular appearance, and in a few moments it was frozen entirely over. The late Dr. Thomas Read came near freezing to death on the prairie, on his way to Shelbyville, on horseback, at that time, and several persons did lose their lives by being on the prairie and unable to reach a shelter. Cattle that were in the fields were held fast by the "slush" freezing about their feet, and it became necessary to cut away the ice to liberate them. Ducks and geese were imprisoned in the same way. It was scarcely fifteen minutes from the time the cold wave swept over the place, before the water and melting snow were hard enough to bear up a horse."*

Another instance is related of a man who came into his house and remained but a few minutes, when some member of the family came in and remarked that the ice and snow had frozen so hard that it would bear a person up. The man at once flatly contradicted the assertion, and accused the person making it of prevarication, and was only convinced when he had made the experiment himself.

METEOROLOGICAL.

In connection with the above atmospheric phenomena, we would desire to extend our observations, but there have been no records kept in this locality until within the last two years. Meteorology is a science entitled to as much consideration as astronomy or other natural sciences. It owes its origin to the observations and study of meteors and their connection with the planetary system. It has extended its field so as to embrace atmospheric phenomena, and their climatology, as well as the changing influences of nature on land and sea. Records are now being made and tabulated, from which much very valuable information may be derived by the great agricultural west. We have no doubt but a few years more of observation and study of this science, will result in the prediction of all unusual and extraordinary atmospheric phenomena, with almost as much certainty as eclipses, transits, etc., are foretold. We give below tables of observations made at Decatur for the last twenty-one months, which, so far as we know, is the only record kept in the county.

*Historical sketch of Macon County, read at Decatur, July 4, 1876.

SYNOPSIS

Of Meteorological Record for the twenty-one months commencing April 1st, 1875, and ending December 31st, 1876; Decatur, Ill.; latitude, 39 deg. 53 min.; longitude, 88 deg. 50 min.; elevation of barometer above mean sea level, 685.17 feet.

TABLE NO. I.

1875.	BAROMETER.				THERMOMETER.				Monthly mean humidity.	Number of days on which rain fell.	Amount of rain-fall in inches, including melted snow.	Number of days in which snow fell.	Monthly depth of snow-fall, in inches.
	Monthly mean.	Range.		Difference in inches.	Monthly mean.	Range.		Different degrees.					
		Highest.	Lowest.			Maximum observed.	Minimum observed.						
April	29.923	30.252	29.469	.783	52.17	82	20	62		10	1.81	2	.71
May	29.895	30.432	29.261	1.171	62.68	88	30	58	78	14	9.42		
Mean of 2 spring months, 1875	29.909				57.42					24	11.23	2	.71
June	29.927	30.232	29.595	.637	71.40	92	44	48	84	16	6.41		
July	29.868	30.223	29.650	.573	77.03	95	60	35	81.4	18	12.49		
August	29.888	30.239	29.539	.700	71.38	88	50	38	80.12	11	4.77		
Mean of sum'r.	29.894				73.47				81.84	45	23.67		
Sept	30.029	30.276	29.654	.622	64.53	90	33	57	77.13	6	2.23		
October	30.005	30.474	29.390	1.084	52.02	80	27	53	74.38	7	2.82		
November	30.055	30.646	29.619	1.027	39.64	67	13	54	75.07	6	1.25		
Mean of fall	30.029				52.06				75.52	19	6.30		
December	29.945	30.393	29.377	1.016	40.32	74	—4	78	75.74	8	1.37	6	1.8
Mean of 9 m'ths ending Dec. 31,'75	29.948	30.646	29.261	1.385	59.08	95	—4	99	78.23	96	42.57	8	1.79
1876.													
January	30.096	30.638	29.336	1.302	37.12	69	4	65	71.11	10	3.86	2	1.1
February	30.067	30.510	29.428	1.082	36.61	70	—5	75	67.08	6	3.56	5	3.
Mean of winter 1875-'76	30.036				38.01				71.31	24	8.19	13	5.9
March	29.976	30.459	29.113	1.346	37.38	74	10	64	72.16	11	5.84	11	18.8
April	29.952	30.249	29.363	.931	54.06	82	30	52	61.88	11	3.57		
May	29.925	30.299	29.632	.667	66.23	89	36	53	61.49	8	3.13		
Mean of spring.	29.951				52.55				65.17	30	12.54	11	18.8

TABLE NO. 1.—*Continued.*

1876.	BAROMETER. RANGE.				THERMOMETER. RANGE.					Monthly mean humidity.	Number of days in which rain fell.	Amount of rain-fall in inches, including melted snow.	Number of days in which snow fell.	Monthly depth of snow fall, in inches.
	Monthly mean.	Highest.	Lowest.	Difference in inches.	Monthly mean.	Maximum observed.	Minimum observed.	Different degrees.						
June	29.852	30.075	29.469	.606	71.65	89	49	40		73.86	20	9.35	...	....
July	29.942	30.149	29.714	.435	78.	94	56	38		73.	13	3.46	...	....
August	29.976	30.197	29.744	.453	77.26	93	53	40		71.63	12	3.80	...	....
Mean of sum'r.	29.923				75.64	...	...	...		72.83	45	16.61	...	....
September	29.968	30.241	29.657	.584	65.83	85	43	42		74.66	13	7.37	...	....
October	29.958	30.483	29.395	1.085	52.79	80	27	53		64.51	9	4.40	...	....
November	30.011	30.262	29.489	.773	38.98	74	16	58		74.44	6	1.96	6	3.6
Mean of fall	29.979				52.53	...	...	...			28	13.73	...	....
December	30.129	30.536	29.664	.872	19.95	49	−12	61		71.14	0	37	6	3.7
Mean of year	29.988	30.638	29.113	1.525	52.99	94	−12	106		69.74	119	50.07	30	30.2

Compiled by J. STEBBINS KING, M. D.,
Observer Signal Service, U. S. Army.

STATEMENT

Showing how many times wind was observed blowing from the eight cardinal points of the compass, during each month, from April 1, 1875, to Dec. 31, 1876; also, aspect of the sky.

TABLE No. 2.

	April, 1875.	May, 1875.	June, 1875.	July, 1875.	August, 1875.	September, 1875.	October, 1875.	November, 1875.	December, 1875.	January, 1876.	February, 1876.	March, 1876.	April, 1876.	May, 1876.	June, 1876.	July, 1876.	August, 1876.	September, 1876.	October, 1876.	November, 1876.	December, 1876.	Total.	Grand total of observations.
North	2	11	10	5	8	13	9	11	0	4	3	12	5	10	4	4	9	7	6	7	10	150	
Northeast	20	6	15	13	5	6	5	13	2	3	2	8	14	18	8	14	10	16	1	3	8	188	
East	4	7	2	5	7	4	3	7	7	2	3	5	3	5	4	6	15	13	6	3	2	113	
Southeast	5	11	6	10	3	2	5	8	17	6	6	15	8	4	13	14	17	12	12	13	6	193	
South	4	17	22	14	21	21	28	15	17	25	35	14	12	26	24	18	24	13	23	15	12	400	
Southwest	16	18	15	31	17	17	26	9	16	22	3	8	22	15	21	25	10	6	22	10	24	343	
West	12	7	5	5	12	9	19	9	18	17	13	10	14	8	13	4	1	6	12	20	12	226	
Northwest	14	5	7	14	17	16	20	16	14	18	24	19	11	4	8	6	6	16	11	19	19	284	
Calm	13	11	10	10	14	7	4	2	4	1	1	2	2	3	1	1	1	1	0	0	0	91	1988
Clear	32	32	17	19	38	42	36	27	23	37	28	19	26	32	18	29	41	29	44	14	34	617	
Fair	18	24	32	26	27	18	26	15	11	7	26	16	26	31	24	34	28	19	19	14	17	458	
Partly cloudy	14	19	22	17	16	17	25	12	16	17	17	16	23	16	23	16	12	12	13	12	15	350	
Cloudy	26	18	19	31	12	13	23	35	42	31	16	42	15	14	25	14	12	30	17	50	27	512	1937

EXPLANATION OF TABLES, ETC.

Clear indicates no clouds, or not more than one-tenth cloudy.

Fair, two to four tenths, inclusive.

Partly cloudy, five to eight-tenths of clouds.

Cloudy, nine-tenths and upwards.

Regula's observations are taken at 6.48 A. M., 3.48 and 10.13 P. M., each day, Decatur mean time, which corresponds with Washington, D. C., mean time of 7.35 A. M., 4.35 and 11 P. M., that being the hour at which all observations are taken at Regula's Signal Service Stations, corrections being made for local time to correspond therewith.

Other observations of the instruments, direction of the wind, etc., are taken as may be demanded. It will be seen, by Table 2, that 1988 observations of direction of wind were noted, and but 1937 of aspect of the sky ; the difference is caused by observations taken during the approach of storms, when the wind has shifted often, while the aspect of the sky has remained unchanged and not mentioned. In Table 1, in column mean of seasons, nine months and of year, the mean of the barometer, thermometer and hygrometer are given, while in the other footings in said columns the range, difference and sums are given.

The minus mark, thus —, placed before figures pertaining to the thermometer, indicates below zero

SUMMARY OF THE NINE MONTHS ENDING DEC. 31, 1875.

Highest observed thermometer	95, 3.48 P. M., July 16.
Lowest " "	—4, 6.48 A. M., Dec 17
Difference	99 deg.
Highest daily mean thermometer	87.2, July 16.
Lowest " "	3.25, Dec. 17.
Difference	83.95 deg.
Highest monthly mean thermometer	77.63, July.
Lowest " "	39.63, November.
Difference	38.00 deg.
Highest observed barometer	30.646, 10 A. M., Nov. 24.
Lowest " "	29.261, 7.35 A. M. May 1.
Difference	1.385 inches.
Highest daily mean barometer	30.558, November 21.
Lowest " "	29.391, May 7.
Difference	1.167 inches.
Highest monthly mean barometer	30.055, November.
Lowest " "	29.868, July.
Difference	.187 inches.

Last freeze of spring, May 16; ice one-thirty-second of an inch formed. Last white frost, May 17; no ice. First frost and ice in fall, September 21; ice thickness of letter paper. First cold day of fall, freezing during entire 24 hours, November 16. First snow, December 7. River frozen over for first time, December 17th; on 19th ice was four inches thick. All ice and frost had disappeared on the 21st. Latter part of December was warm and pleasant; on the 30th and 31st frogs were heard croaking in numerous ponds near the city; and at adjoining railroad stations, some farmers plowing on the 30th.

Heaviest fall of rain in 24 hours, on May 23d, on which day 4.60 inches fell from 3.24 P. M., to 10.10 P. M., of which 2.08 inches fell in 31 minutes, viz: from 3.24 to 3.55 P. M.

No snow storms during these nine months. Light snows fell on eight days, during the months of April and December; as will be seen by reference to table 1, less than two inches fall.

Summary of the Year 1876.

Highest observed thermometer........	94, 2 P. M., July 19.
Lowest " "	—12, 6.48 A. M., Dec. 9.
Difference	106 deg.
Highest daily mean thermometer	86.25, July 19.
Lowest " "	—2.66, Dec. 9.
Difference	88.91
Highest monthly mean thermometer ..	78 July.
Lowest " " ..	19.9, December.
Difference	58.1 deg.
Highest observed barometer	30.536, Dec. 4th.
Lowest " "	29.113, March 16.
Difference	1.423 inches.
Highest daily mean barometer	30.446, Dec. 3.
Lowest " "	29.378, March 16.
Difference	1.068 inches.
Highest monthly mean barometer	30.129, December.
Lowest " "	29.852, June.
Difference	.277 inches.

Last freeze of spring, May 1; thin ice formed. Last white frost observed in city, May 3d; no ice. May 23d, a light white frost was reported from some low lands in the country.

First white frost in fall, September 27th; no injury done to vegetation. First killing frost, with thin ice, October 7th. First ice of any thickness, October 15; ½ inch thick. First cold day, freezing during same, November 18. First snow, November 14. River frozen over on the 8th of December; from that to 31st ice formed to thickness of 10 inches.

During the winter of 1874–5, ground was frozen to an average depth of 38 inches; winter of 1875–6, 6 inches; and thus far in winter of 1876–7, 12 inches.

HIGH WATER.

It is said said that the greatest rain-fall that has occurred in this country was in the year 1835. There was no record kept of the amount that fell by any of the methods of to-day, and all we have to judge by is the high water in the river and creeks. The Sangamon is said to have been higher than at the breaking up of the deep snow in the spring of 1831, or at any time since. The rains commenced falling in the early spring, and continued throughout the early summer. There have been, perhaps, other seasons just as wet, but the streams were never so high at any other time. There were a great many hard rains, and a storm of rain, thunder and lightning occurred in the early part of July, that, for severity, has scarcely ever been excelled. It extended throughout the west, as far as information extended. Our prairies, then undrained, resembled an immense lake, and fish were abundant in almost every locality, It may not be known to many, but it is a well attested fact, that the large ponds upon our prairies, in early days, contained fish, large enough for domestic purposes, almost every spring, and that, too, when the ponds would annually dry up entirely. How the presence of such fish was to be accounted for surpassed the comprehension of ye old settler, except that they were "rained down when small." During this year but little in the way of crops was attempted to be raised. Hogs were fattened in the fall upon the mast, and those that were not killed for food had to subsist during the winter upon the acorns. With them it was literally "root hog or die." Cattle wintered upon buds, the trees being cut down for that purpose. Eighteen hundred and forty-two and 1858 are also notable as years of great rain-fall. During the early history of the county, when there were no bridges, much difficulty was experienced in getting from place to place in the spring time, on account of the high waters. The people, however, were nearly all expert swimmers, and it was seldom that life was lost from the high water. We are sometimes at a loss to know why ferries were established and licensed on the Sangamon; but it should be remembered the river "was up" a great deal longer in those days, when the land was not improved, and when there were no drains to carry the water off rapidly. The water then had to seek the natural drainage, and its course was retarded by many obstructions. We are disposed to believe that the elements "cut more capers," in the shape of deep snows, sudden changes, severe storms, when this whole western country was a wild waste. They say civilization is a great leveler; and perhaps it has had something to do in toneing down the elements. And we had no signal service bureau then, charged by the government with the duty of looking after those matters. "Old Probabilities" didn't then put out his daily weather bulletin at the corner of the postoffice to warn us of the approaching " cold snap," so that we were then often caught without any oil in our lamps, so to speak.

CHARACTERISTICS OF EARLY SETTLERS.

For true and genuine hospitality, the pioneers of this western country were remarkable. This, no doubt, is attributable, in part, to inherent characteristics of the people, but largely so to the peculiar surroundings and circumstances in which they were placed. The sympathetic emotions of man become more and more obtuse as he is placed in situations of independence. Selfishness is not wholly a characteristic of the individual. Cosmopolitan ideas are assumed as wealth and independence place a person beyond the demands of succor and help from others. The requirements of want and deprivation are calculated to make one feel kind and hospitable to all. Napoleon, as an exile at Helena, was not the austere commander at Austerlitz and Mount Tabor. The haughty child of fortune may, and often does, become, when old age and misfortune have overtaken him or her, the very embodiment of kindness and universal friendship. While the wants and necessities of pioneer life are few and simple, yet their supply is none the less exacting. Hence, we find the pioneers of Macon county, governed by the same law, and manifesting the same spirit of generosity that actuates the human breast, under similar circumstances, everywhere. Chapter after chapter of individual acts of kindness might here be related, of those who took part in the early settlement of this county, if we only had the space to devote. No doubt lessons of profit might be learned therefrom by us, in this golden age of steam, of improvement, and civilization. We sometimes laugh at what we call the simplicity and old-fogy notions of our fathers; but whatever we may say on that point, of their generosity, their devotion to each other, of their friendship, of their kind treatment of strangers, as well as acquaintances and neighbors, the less we say, by way of comparison, the better. To divide they were always willing; and to give all, in cases of extreme sympathy, was not uncommon. To charge a stranger for a night's loding was an act of gross impropriety not to be tolerated.

Twenty miles was a short distance to ride, over the then bad roads, to see a sick neighbor. It was never too cold or wet to lend assistance to the needy. If a neighbor, by sickness or other misfortune, was unable to plant his corn, sow or reap his wheat, they all "turned in" and assisted or did it for him. It was never too far to go to assist a " new comer " to " raise " his house, or help rebuild one destroyed by fire. The tools of one man were almost property in common. The refusal to lend almost any article of personal property, was an act of hostility that the whole neighborhood resented. They did not all drink, but among those who did, a refusal to drink with a friend was the unkindest cut of all; it was an act of social ostracism. Another peculiarity of the early pioneers was the readiness they manifested in resenting real or imaginary wrongs or insults. They are said to have been always ready for a fight. The court dockets show that they were as ready for a legal contest, and the amounts involved seems to have had but little weight in the institution of legal proceedings. It was the wrong they sought to correct, and not the amount involved that determined whether they would resort to litigation or not. Slander suits were quite common. Of the four suits brought at the first term of the Macon county circuit court, two were for slander; and of the six at the next term, four were for the same thing.

From the results arrived at, in the cases mentioned, we presume the suits were not very meritorious; yet it is a well established fact that in those early days the people were very jealous in guarding their reputations and that of their families. Character was not to be assailed without just cause. Aside from the fact that in sparsely settled communities every person knows every other person's business, and is for that reason perhaps more disposed to talk, we do not believe the tongue of slander is more energetic or more disposed to injure, under such surroundings, than in densely populated districts; and probably not so much so. The disposition to resent insult, real or seeming, is, however, more marked. There was another characteristic of the pioneers that it is proper to mention in this connection, and which we still see among the survivors, and that was the implicit confidence reposed in each other in their promises and business relations. It is true their contracts were few and simple, and their business transactions by no means complicated, yet there was usually the most implicit confidence reposed in the honor and integrity of those with whom they dealt. A man's promise upon his honor was sure to be met, no matter what sacrifices were required. His word was as good as his bond, if the last cow or hog had to be given up to make it so. Promissory notes were given sometimes, but the person required to give one thought it was a slight reflection upon his integrity. He looked upon it as a transaction tinged a little bit with suspicion and doubt in the mind of the payee, and he usually managed to "take up" that note as soon as possible. He regarded it as a dangerous instrument, and he breathed freer when he had borrowed the money from a neighbor and got his name torn off the note. Of course, there were exceptions to these characteristics, but the general rule, nevertheless, prevailed. The old credit system, existing in early days in this country, grew out of the confidence reposed in the public by the merchants. The necessities of the times, growing out of the scarcity of money, the lack of markets and the few commodities for sale or exhange, of course, had much to do with making a credit system the only system. The merchants bought on long time and sold on long time, and usually at profits that would justify it.

We should make one remark further in this connection, with reference to the state of society during the early settlement of the county. Notwithstanding on muster-days, holidays and Saturdays, when the people generally came together, there was always more or less quarreling or fighting, yet there was none of the reckless lawlessness we find in some parts of the country. It was seldom the parties resorted to knives or pistols; that was gross cowardice. When two men became enraged, or disputed about anything, there was no resort to the "code of honor," now, happily almost entirely banished from the United States, but it was settled in the fisticuff style, and the fellow that was beaten said so, and they quit, shook hands and were friends again. Those who were privileged, by reason of opportunity, to see the fight, looked on as spectators, anxious to see who was the best man, and exerted themselves, not to part the combatants, but to see that they had a "fair fight." It was a common remark made by the early settlers that such and such a man would rather fight than eat. But, while they were disposed to be "on their muscle," and fighting was quite common among these pioneers, there was seldom anything more serious resulting than a black eye or a swollen nose, or a few bruises that lasted but a few days. The first murder that ever occurred in the county was that of Wesley Bohrer, who was murdered by Samuel Huffman, in 1846, seventeen years after the organization of the county. There was but little of the outlawry and bloodshed that has disgraced other portions of the country in the early days, or later days, for that matter. It is said that but one challenge for a duel was ever given and accepted, and that the result of that was not very sanguinary, more laughable in fact than bloody.

"HARD TRIALS AND TRIBULATIONS."

None but those who have experienced them can duly appreciate the difficulties to be surmounted, the hardships to be met and endured, the deprivations and wants experienced that are incident to pioneer life. We talk of the depressions in trade; we bemoan the scarcity of a circulating medium; we talk of the absolute stagnation of the markets for this produce or that; we become enraged at the excessive charges for freights and transportation; we talk of poverty and starvation staring us in the face; we hear political aspirants proclaiming from the rostrums (the stumps of pioneer life) the absolute necessity of the naked, starving, downtrodden oppressed people arising in their might and throwing off the yoke of oppression, or hurling from power this administration or that, which they insist is dragging the people down to poverty and ruin. There yet live in this county men who not only have seen trade depressed, but absolutely no trade; have seen money so scarce that letters from friends had to remain in the post office for days and weeks for want of money to pay the postage; who have hauled their wheat to Chicago, St. Louis and Springfield, in wagons drawn by oxen, over roads termed highways that did not deserve the name of cartways, and when they reached their destination could get but little more than half enough for a bushel of wheat to buy a yard of calico; who have been compelled to live for weeks upon homney, and if bread at all it was bread made from corn ground in hand mills or pounded up with mortars; whose children have been destitute of shoes during the entire winter; whose families had no clothing except what was carded, spun, wove and made into garments by their own hands; schools, they had none; churches, they had none; afflicted with sickness incident to all new countries, sometimes the whole family at once; luxuries of life, they had none; conveniences of modern life, they had none; the auxilliaries, improvements, inventions and labor-saving machinery of to-day they had none; and what they possessed was obtained by the hardest of labor, and the sweat of individual exertions; yet they bore these things without murmuring, hoping for better times to come, and often too, with but little prospect of realization. These were times that tried mens' souls. We often hear it remarked by these old settlers and pioneers that it will do for the young men to go west to the new countries and help build them up, but for them there is no anxiety to try the vicissitudes incident to the early settlement again. They have been there. To them there is no novelty about the thing enticing enough to induce them to leave a home of comfort.

We hear people talk about the old fogy ideas and fogy ways, and want of energy of the old men who have gone through the experiences of pioneer life. Sometimes, perhaps, such remarks are just, but, considering the experiences, education and whole life of such men, such remarks are just as well unsaid. They have had their trials, misfortunes, hardships and adventures, aud shall we, now as they are passing far down the western declivity of life, and many of them gone, point at them the finger of derision and laugh and sneer at the simplicity of their ways? Let us rather cheer them up, revere and respect them, for beneath those rough exteriors beat hearts as noble as ever throbbed the human breast. Senator Oglesby, in his fourth of July address of 1876, surrounded by the few remaining pioneers, paid them a most glowing tribute of respect. He said that we of this generation could never duly appreciate the great sacrifices of those people. They had toiled on and on through adversity and untold trials, that we their distant and remote successors might enjoy the fruits of their sacrifices. He said it was a serious question of the hour, and one that addressed itself to each of us, whether or not we are not so swallowed up in materialism, so wrapped up in personal gain and the acquisition of filthy lucre, as to lose sight of the sturdy women and men who laid the foundations of the republic and placed in the solid earth the corner stones upon which had been reared the fabrics of our material and political prosperity. He made further prediction, which, he said, had haunted him for years, as he had contemplated the condition and tendencies of our affairs, which was this: that when we as a people in the vain pursuits of life, struggling for wealth, distinction and fame, allowed the love of the past to die out in our hearts, then the republic would have taken its first downward step.

As it is in our political affairs and the enjoyment of our civil and religious liberties, so it is with our material comforts. We are blessed with a rich soil, splendid harvests, medium climate and many other things that make us a contented, prosperous and happy people; but we owe much to those who opened up these avenues that have led to our present condition and happy surroundings. Unremitting toil and labor have driven off the sickly miasmas that brooded over our swampy prairies. Energy and perseverance have peopled every section of our wild lands, and changed them from wastes and deserts to gardens of beauty and profit. Where but a few years ago the howling wolves made the night hideous with their wild shrieks, now is heard only the lowing and bleating of domestic animals. But fifty years ago the wild whoop of the Indian was heard where now is heard the engine and rumbling trains of cars, bearing away to the east and to the old world the products of our labor and soil. Then the savage built his rude hut on the spot where rises the dwellings and school-houses and church spires of civilized life. Transformation indeed! And all done not through the chimerical process of Kubla Kahn, but the incessant toil and aggregated labor of thousands of tired hands and brave hearts, and the impulses of such as make any country great. No, we will not forget what we owe to the pioneers of our country. They had their faults, but who does not? If charity be an attribute of the human heart, let us throw around them that mantle as one by one they depart. Let us drop a sympathetic tear over their last resting places as they are gathered, we hope, to a better land, where the rude blasts of winter do not penetrate their abodes, and where storms and winds and sickness and fatigue are unknown.

What will another half century accomplish? These old men who are yet lingering among us as connecting links of the past with the present, what do they think as with their dim eyes they view the scenes that surround them? They have seen the old and new worlds connected with cords that pulsate with the life of industry and progress. They have seen the oceans bound together with metalic bonds, and the whole country traversed with highways of commerce. They have seen the nation rise in majesty and become an influence felt and respected throughout the world. They have seen the spirit of liberty grow up and assert itself to its present commanding influence. They have seen the initiation of that principal of universal brotherhood which dictates the settlement of international disputes by arbitration, rather than a resort to war. They may yet see the same spirit of equity and fairness assert itself in the adjustment of our own domestic affairs. They may live to see the machinery of government so adjusted as that no jars and thunderings of civil war will be felt and heard upon the result of presidential contests. They have seen the religious intoleration that existed to some extent in the early history of the country almost entirely obliterated, so that all men everywhere worship according to the dictates of their own consience, as it was designed they should. They have seen what we are pleased to term the civilization of the nineteenth century permeating every department of human experience, and asserting its influence in all directions for the general good of mankind. They have seen complete revolutions in almost every branch of industry. They have seen the steamboat and railroad supplant the old-time methods of travel. They have seen the reaper and mower and corn-planter succeed the sickle, scythe and hoe. They have seen their households invaded by Howe and Wheeler & Wilson and Singer, and all that long list of labor and time saving machinery that have driven away the stitch, stitch, stitch, so truthfully portrayed by Hood. They view the surroundings with the same strange, wondering astonishment as did Rip Van Winkle on his return from his long sleep in the mountains. Again we ask, what will the next half century accomplish? With the advantages that surround us, what is expected of us? With the capital we have, what shall be expected as our increase? The late Senator Harris frequently remarked to his students of the grave responsibilities resting upon them with the advantages they posssessed. He said, though then near 70 years of age, he could scarcely realize that he was not a young man, the opportunities the times brought were so enticing, so fraught with interest to every one who sought to lead a life of usefulness.

With tears in his eyes he dismissed his students with the motto for each, that:—

"'Tis infamy to die and not be missed."

None of us can do much of ourselves, but what has been done in the last thirty, forty or fifty years has been by the accumulated labor of all that have come and gone before us. What we accomplish will be in the same way, and with doubts and anxious solicitude we leave it for the future historian to record.

A RETROSPECT.

BY A. J. WALLACE.

Fair Genius of the West, whose magic wand
Spreads fadeless beauty o'er this western land—
Where nature o'er the rude and savage wild
Reigned, ere the city or the farm-house smiled;
Or yet was waked the echoes of the horn,
Or dreams of wealth in these wide wastes were born,
Bid thou the light of recollection flow
Back o'er the scenes of fifty years ago.

The savage, then, with never yielding will
Pursues the frightened deer with sleuth-hound skill
And tireless feet, till, with unerring aim,
The fateful arrow slays the panting game;
Or shadows, with a panther's step, his foe—
The hated pale-face—cause of all his woe;
Turns deaf his ear at each imploring cry,
And shouts with joy to see his victim die;
Then, with the nightfall seeks his dusky mates,
And all his triumphs of the day relates;
Or, urged by soft infatuations pent,
The same which heav'n to all mankind has sent,
He quits the crown, to gentle conquest moves,
And worships at the feet of her he loves.

Hard by the borders of yon sheltering wood
We pass the spot where once a cabin stood;
But see no sign—save that the grain-stalk spears

More rankly o'er the garnered mould of years.
Gone, with the builder gone—and yet how dear
The rough-hewn cottage of the pioneer!
Its doors unshut, and generous all its laws,
Broad as the ingle-place its welcome was.
Warm as the hearthstone, ever cleanly swept,
So warm the heart that with each sufferer wept.
Bright as the flame that up the chimney flew,
So bright the joy that round the fireside grew;
And when the night with silent step advanced
On slumb'rous couch the household sank entranced;
And dreams as blissful filled each sleeper's head
As e're filled prince's in his downy bed.
Rough were the men who ploughed the virgin lea,
Swept by the billows of a grassy sea.
Rewarded was their toil; the golden grain
Waved answering undulations o'er the plain.
Uncouth their manners, cordial as the day,
No unfed beggar toiled his weary way.
The traveler unknown, belated, lost,
E'er found a welcome and a kindly host.

These gallant men with ax and plough and spade,
The deep foundations of the nation laid;
And built so well that ages hence will see
An ever-widening home for all the free.
The patriots ever as the poet's heart
Hoards up the memories as the years depart;
Leaps with the joy and feels the battle thrill
That Putnam felt at glorious Bunker Hill.
The rarest gems in nature's rich array
Are valued ever by the price we pay;
Forgot the cost, and we forget the trace
That lends the magic to the diamond's face;—
So when the nation, all ungrateful grows,
Forgets the past, its struggles, and its woes,
In swift retreat 'twill take, with hurried breath,
Its first step downward to the shores of death.

If evil with unrighteous rule prevails,
'Tis not the heritage the past entails.
The wanton child of Luxury and Lust,
Unknown to shame or virtuous distrust,
Runs riot through the heart's enchanted ground,
And leaps its walled defenses at a bound.
The "fast" young man, less noble than his sire,
A slave to wealth and to untamed desire,
In youth decayed, in trembling age unblessed,
Sinks unregretted to his solemn rest.

See Fashion all-adored, though lovely less
Than maiden nature in her homespun dress.
What is the flame her tinseled robes inspire
To fervid nature's fierce magnetic fire?
See wild Ambition, on his fiery car
(Behind him famine, pestilence and war,)
Lift high the flaming truncheon in his hand,
And to destruction doom a smiling land.
Thus great the evil, not without some good;
Or else the prospect is a blackening flood.

Sure, Science in her study brooding brings
Some compensation on the agile wings
Of Enterprise, that mobile as the wind,
Seeks every good that blesses human kind;
And Art enraptured, beautiful and true,
Whose magic pencil steals the sunset hue,
Whose chisel stroke the heroe's living mold,
Doth fix forever in the marble cold,
Smooths down unpolished nature to the line,
And in designing proves itself divine.

Then, reigned a rude and simple rustic grace,
And, now, Refinement sits with smiling face,
A hundred comforts fill our daily store
To one that blessed the pioneer of yore.
His life is past, his labor all is done,
And we now reap the harvest that he won.

NAVIGATION UNDER DIFFICULTIES.

It may not be known to many of our present residents that the Sangamon has ever been navigated. Such is the fact, however. A small sized steamboat is said to have come up as far as Springfield at one time, but experienced considerable difficulty in turning around, and the captain probably abandoned further efforts in that direction in disgust. The legislature at one time declared the Sangamon navigable, but the law did not make it so in fact and soon became a "dead letter." In 1845 the navigation fever struck this vicinity, and a flat-boat was built and went down the river, commanded by Capt. Wm. Rea. In 1846 five more boats were built destined for New Orleans, and were loaded with hogs and corn. They got as far as Long Point (a short distance south of Niantic) that year, and landed for the winter, awaiting high water in the spring of 1847. That spring three of the boats were fitted up and the loads of the other two transferred to them, and another attempt made to get to their destination, with more success. Two were loaded with hogs and one with corn. At Beardstown, the river becoming deeper and the loads being too light, a large quantity of bran was bought and taken on board, partly, perhaps, as ballast and partly as an article of merchandise. Two of the boats went through to New Orleans, and one stopped at Natchez. The captains of these several vessels were Uncle John Hanks, J. G. Braden and Hosea Armstrong. The latter became tired of seafaring at Beardstown and transferred his command to Moses Spencer. The firm engaged in this laudable enterprise was composed of the following gentlemen: Hosea Armstrong, J. J. Peddecord and Henry Prather. We have tried to ascertain the profits derived from these shipments, but have only been able to ascertain that they were not very large. The losses, however, were not very large, for the prices paid for the corn was not to exceed eight cents per bushel, and the hogs were purchased far about one dollar per head. The people along the river were very much interested in the success of this flat-boat experiment. "Uncle Henry Prather," in the autumns of 1845 and 1846, went along down the river and made speeches, urging the necessity of the people turning out and assisting in removing the obstructions in the river. They did so, many of them working for days in cutting out the logs and drifts that had accumulated so that during the high water of the spring following the obstructions would float out in advance of the arrival of the boats When the boats were passing, crowds of people would be found congregated upon the banks of the river to observe the passing flotilla of commerce, so to speak. the people even followed the boats in some instances for miles, to see that no harm should overtake the infant enterprise, and to assist in getting the boats over the logs and mill-dams that impeded their progress. After this effort, all further attempts at navigating the Sangamon ceased.

DEER HUNTINGS.

It was also customary to have neighborhood huntings, when all the men, young and old, would meet together at some appointed place with their hounds, generally on Saturday afternoon, and engage in hunting. The locality was selected, and the participants placed in their positions, which were called "stands;" then the "driver" with the hounds would go out to "start up" the deer, which, when started, would pass the stands where it was generally shot, for there were but few of the early settlers but were "good shots," and rarely failed to bring down their game. It should be mentioned in this connection that deer have their regular runs or courses they follow, and it was necessary in these hunts to be familiar with them, in order to secure positions or stands the game would pass.

Wolf hunts and fox hunts were also quite common. In the early settlement of the county wolves were very common, especially prairie wolves. They could be heard at night in droves, barking like so many dogs. They were very destructive of sheep, and no farmer ever dared leave his out of the "sheep house" over night, and they were often attacked in day time in close proximity to the dwelling. As a means of exterminating these ravenous creatures, a reward of one dollar was provided for by an act of the legislature in 1837, for each wolf scalp exhibited to the clerk of the county court. The black wolves, which were very large, when hungry, have ben known to attack persons, but they were never plentiful in this county. Wolf "chases" were among the many amusements of the early inhabitants, and were a source of protection as well. Wolves ordinarily run very fast, and their endurance was wonderful, the chase often being given up as fruitless when hounds and horses had been completely exhausted. They, even when taken very young, could not be tamed.

The red fox and gray fox were also to be found in this county, though they were not as plentiful as in other localities. The fox chase, owing to the peculiarities of this animal, was always a source of great amusement, not only here, but in all countries. They were often caught and confined for days, until those who desired to take part were ready for the chase, when the excitement of the chase was next to that of " mustering day."

Shooting matches were also very common to the early settlers, and especially so about the holdays. Almost every man was an expert in the use of " fire-arms," especially the rifle. Pioneer life is productive of good marksmen.

COURT DAYS.

Among the notable days in the early history of the county, was court day. The convening of court was one of the events of the year. On that day nearly everybody went to town. If he happened not to be on one of the juries, or a witness, or a suitor, he felt it to be his duty to "go to court" to see and hear what was going on. It answered the place of the shows and circuses of a later day, and perhaps was as instructive if not as entertaining. When court was over in the evening, the judge, lawyers and eitizens congregated in the bar rooms of the taverns, where stories were told, and the evenings spent in conversation, regarded by the "old inhabitants as very entertaining. No doubt but they were, for Lincoln and Douglas and Baker and McDougal and Stuart and Emerson and Lockwood and Treat and Logan and Davis, and others of world-wide reputation, were there and engaged therein. It is said that the immense fund of anecdotes possessed by the late President Lincoln was largely derived from collections made "while on the circuit."

HOUSE RAISINGS.

In the early settlement of the county, the dwellings were mostly built of logs, and those who built houses of such proportions as not to be called " cabins " were compelled to give what was called a " house raising," to which all the inhabitants far and near were invited to assist. The logs were prepared, sometimes hewed and sometimes not, and brought to the place where the house was to be erected, then when the people had all gathered in, those who were the more dexterous in the use of the axe were selected to "carry up the corners," *i. e.* notching the logs so they would fit the one upon the other, and the others would divide off in pairs of corresponding strength, and would carry the logs and place them in position as the building progressed. At the raising of a barn on the farm of the author's father, and which is now the oldest barn standing in the county (erected in 1829), people came the distance of 20 miles to assist in its "raising." At these gatherings in the early days, it was considered improper, in fact an act highly reprehensible, not to have "liquor," as it was then called, to drink. And it may also be noted that while almost every one drank, yet, it was seldom that intoxication was to be seen. Log-rollings and rail-maulings were also common in those days.

THE MAILS.

For a good many years after the organization of the county the mails were not of great dimensions. The arrival of the mail carrier was not a very important event, excepting for a few weeks after election. The news, which was generally by letter, was not fresh and racy when received, as it is to-day. It was more expensive, however, for the postage on a letter cost 25 cents, and it was not always that the recipient could raise the necessary funds to liquidate the government dues. The law was that the postage might be paid at either end of the route, and upon the anti-biblical doctrine that it is more pleasant to receive than to give, the person receiving the letter as a usual thing was compelled to pay the carriage. Letters were often weeks and even months in arriving at their destination. The "fast mails" of "Old Father Taft," though not yet an assured success are of quite late invention. The mails were carried on horseback, usually in a pair of saddle bags more frequently unlocked than locked. The wolves sometimes chased the mail carrier, who was often but a lad, so that at times the mail arrived "ahead of time," which is about the only instance of attempts at fast mail carrying of early days. Sometimes the mail carrier got the ague enroute, or his horse got sick, or the rain or snow stopped him, and then the mail would be "behind time" for a few hours or a few days perhaps. Then instead of the mails coming once or twice a day and from all directions, they came once a week and from Shelbyville only. That was the point of distribution for us. Afterwards and before the era of railroads, the mails were carried by the stage lines, some of which ran east and west and some north and south. This was an improvement, for the mails were then more frequent. We insert the following notice of arrivals and departures of mails in 1851:

ARRIVALS AND DEPARTURES OF THE MAILS.

Arrives from Springfield, Mondays, Wednesdays and Fridays, at 8 o'clock P. M.

From Covington, Indiana, Wednesdays, Fridays and Sundays, at 1 o'clock P. M.

From Bloomington, Fridays, at 12 o'clock M. Returns same day at 1 o'clock P. M.

From Charleston, Thursday, 12 o'clock M. Returning same day at 1 o'clock P. M.

From Ewington, Saturdays, 6 o'clock P. M. Returns Wendesdays, at 6 o'clock A. M.

From Paris, Thursdays, at 6 o'clock P. M. Returns Fridays, at 6 o'clock A. M.

From Edwardsville, Wednesdays, at 6 o'clock P. M. Returns next day at six o'clock A. M.

DECATUR, July, 1851.

P. BUTLER, *P. M.*

ARRIVAL AND DEPARTURE OF MAILS IN 1876.

Post Office Hours.

Office open at 7 A. M.; closes at 8 P. M.
Sundays from 9 to 10 A. M.
Money Order and Registering office open from 7.30 A. M. to 7 P. M.

Mails Close.

For Terre Haute on Ill. M. R. R.................... 9.40 A. M.
" West and St. Louis, on T., W. and W............10.40 A. M.
" East and Chicago, on T., W. and W.............11.30 A. M.
" East, on Ind., D. and S. R. R...................... 1.00 P. M.
" Peoria, on Ill. M. R. R. .... 1.00 P. M.
" Monticello and Champaign, on I., B. and W...... 1.00 P. M.

From Pekin and Peoria, on T., W. and W. R. R...... 2.30 P. M.
" Chicago and St. Louis........................ 8.00 P. M.
" Lafayette and East............. .... 8.00 P. M.
" North, on Ill. Cent. R. R. .... 8.00 P. M.

Mails Arrive.

From South and St. Louis.......... .. .. 5.45 A. M.
" Lafayette, on T., W. and W.... .... 5.45 A. M.
" Peoria, on I. M. R. R......... .. .. 5.45 A. M.
" Pekin and Peoria, on T., W. and W. and Ill. M.
  R. R., ...,...... 10.30 A. M.
" East.... .... 11.20 A. M.
" Monticello and Champaign, on I., B. and W ....11.20 A. M.
" East, on Ind., D. and S. R. R................. 11.20 A. M.
" West and St. Louis, on T., W. and W. .... 12.20 P. M.
" East, on Ill. Mid. R. R.. .... 1.30 P. M.
North on Illinois Central........................... 5.45 P. M.

R. P. LYTLE, *P. M.*

DECATUR, ILL., *May 1, 1876.*

THE STAGES.

But few now here remember those old fashioned stages we used to have, that ran between Terre Haute and Springfield, Shelbyville and Bloomington. The arrival of the stage with its passengers and mails was a more important event than the arrival of the mail carrier. The stage stand in our villages, which was usually the tavern, was a place of very considerable local interest. The stage driver was usually considered as a little larger man and entitled to a few more privileges than ordinary mortals. Albeit he was a man of functionary privileges, and you were required by law to give the entire road to him as he passed.

The passing of his stage was a matter of as much interest as the passing of a new train of cars. He had a peculiar swing and crack of his whip that the little boys would strive to attain. The stage was a peculiar piece of mechanism that rocked prodigiously, as if to keep the passengers awake. It was never full, for in staging it was a proverbial saying that there was always room for one more. It had a "boot" fastened on behind for the storage of the luggage and mails, that was almost as capacious as the stage itself. These stages are still seen in some of our western states and territories, and as in our pre-railroad times are yet carrying the mails. With us, however, they are of the past—gone west, like Greely's young man, or the star of empire, as it were. But we are not to forget them. They were of use and importance in their day and generation, and they were of dignity as well, for Clay, as Senator, and Jackson, as President, rode to Washington in them. They were not remarkable for ease and comfort and not to be compared to the palace cars of to-day, but were endurable nevertheless, for some of our oldest citizens came to the country in them, making an uninterrupted journey of fourteen days and nights. In this day a trip can be made across the continent and back in the same length of time and with immeasurably less fatigue.

CHAPTER VI.

THE CHURCHES, Etc.

> I say the pulpit (in the sober use
> Of its legitimate peculiar powers)
> Must stand acknowledged while the world shall stand
> The most important and effectual guard,
> Support and ornament of virtue's cause.

It would be idle to speculate as to which of the various denominations has done most in bringing about the present condition of society, so far as morals are concerned. Which they have all accomplished in the aggregate there are no methods of ascertaining. If

> "There's a Divinity that shapes our ends,
> Rough hew them as we will,"

We are disposed to believe that He in his providence has devised the church in all its branches for the accomplishment of certain purposes, and the whys and wherefores are matters of little concern to us. If the theological disquisitions and discussions that have taken place in the last hundred years had been devoted to the eradication of evil rather than heated contests, long drawn out, as to whether this denomination or that one was *the* church specially recognized and sanctioned by holy writ, perhaps equally as much good would have been accomplished. If there shall be a time coming when the lamb and lion shall lie down together and a little child shall lead them, then the asperities engendered by the wordy warfares over the *ipse dixits* of creeds and doctrinal points, whether essentials or non-essentials, will have entirely disappeared. The millennium will in all probability obliterate all the speculations of doctrinaries and consign to oblivion many learned theories of innumerable learned D. D.'s. He that shall stand in the light then shining may, perhaps, look into the past centuries and see the paths of at least twelve tribes all converging towards the promised land. There is no royal highway leading up to the New Jerusalem of which any particular corporation has exclusive privileges and sole control. On the contrary there are many ways. That which, for designation, we call the Methodist way, may be a little rough, and its trains may run, at times, at what may seem a reckless speed; and that other way, which we may call the Presbyterian way, may seem more solid and better ballasted, and its trains may run with a more solemn stillness, as it were; yet they both tend to the same point. The trains on each are through trains. The managers of each may speak in terms of praise of the safety and ease and peace of mind vouchsafed by the respective routes, but the passenger, when through, on either, is tired and glad to escape the incidents of travel. It is not our design, therefore, in the very brief sketches of the various denominations mentioned in this chapter to enter into any analogies of their differences, their accomplishments or special characteristics. We give the dates of their organizations, as near as attainable, present membership, etc. Before that, however, we may be pardoned for mentioning specially the

PIONEER PREACHER.

About as far back as we had settlers we had Baptists, Presbyterians, Methodists, etc. By and by along came the preacher, and he selected out his followers. The sheep, though terribly scattered, heard the voice of the shepherd, and came following. Those early shepherds—those pioneer preachers—deserve a passing notice. Their's was no easy lot. Their lives did not fall in pleasant places. Those who stood upon the outskirts of civilization and proclaimed the Word of God, held no enviable positions. It was no place of ease and comfort. It was like picket duty, and just as necessary.

Those early pioneer preachers were men of endurance, and sometimes their hearers as well. They wore their homespun and preached homespun sermons to homespun hearers, in similar logic, and on similar subjects. They had no fine churches with carpeted floors and cushioned seats, and windows of stained glass, and Gothic roofs, frescoed over with bugled angels. None of this. Their meeting houses were often groves, with grass for carpets, rude logs for seats, and the broad canopy of heaven for a covering. Their position, however, was not unenviable. Their songs mingled with the songs of the birds. Their prayers ascended to heaven on breezes bedewed with the perfumes of millions of wild flowers. Their voices echoed through the forests planted and decorated by the hand of God himself. There were no reverberations from painted and papered walls, borne upon an oxidized atmosphere filled with gases from cracked furnaces, and poisonous from diseased lungs. With pure and gentle breezes playing around him, the preacher preached to reprove, persuade and convince, and not to keep his hearers awake. He kept on preaching, too, after his thirty minutes were out, for his hearers came to stay all day. He finished up his subject to his own satisfaction, at the end of an hour, an hour and a half or two hours. It was not necessary to bring part of it up at the next meeting as unfinished business. That subject, or doctrine, was nailed down and riveted. No, the thirty minute executioner didn't stand over your pioneer preacher ready to lop the sermon in two at the end of secondly. The pioneer preacher was also in the habit of speaking out in meeting. No subject laid upon his mind for weeks and months waiting for a favorable opportunity for expression. He had no wrestling with his conscience about whether he ought or ought not to reprove brother or sister so and so. He spoke as he was moved by the spirit, as it were, unmindful of what brother was hit or missed. He preached what he believed to be true, no matter if it ruffled the belief of half his congregation. He had no knack at tempering the winds to shorn lambs. He was bold and fearless in this respect. He could preach Perseverance of the Saints to a whole conference of Methodists. He could preach Falling from Grace to a synod of Presbyterians. When he saw the enemy attempting a flank movement, he moved on him and attacked him in his most vulnerable point. When the devil showed himself he was sure to be struck then and there. There was no coaxing and diplomacy resorted to to dislodge satan from his stronghold. The pioneer preacher never used tufts of grass. He took a stone in the first instance, and he threw it. A two-edged sword was his constant companion, and he kept it whetted sharp.

And then again your pioneer in the wilderness was a man of no great pretensions. He was what he was, and made no effort at appearing to be anything else. While his calling was high, yet, like his Master, he was found among all classes and conditions of society; among the rich and those that dwelt on fine lands and in pleasant surroundings; among the poor and the wretched, where the wolf was continually at their doors. He was a man of simplicity and plainness. What he was upon one day of the week he was sure to be upon all the others. He had no special Sunday cloak that covered up a multitude of weekly sins. His conduct was as the crow flies, straight on, without shadow of turning. He was always a poor man. Like Goldsmith's parson, his income was exceedingly meagre.

THE CIRCUIT RIDER.

The next who followed in the footsteps of the pioneer preacher, was the regularly appointed circuit rider. As the early schoolmaster was a revolving genius, so was the circuit rider, except that his territory was larger and he revolved on horseback. With a bible, hymn book, horse, bridle and saddle, and a pair of saddle bags that contained a change of raiment, the circuit rider's outfit was complete. He had long rides to make across wide prairies and through dense forests. He faced the cold winds like a hero. He battled with the elements with bravery. The rain was scarcely ever too hard or the snow too deep to stop him. Like the train conductor, he felt bound to meet his connections. He studied and practiced on his sermons and "pitched his tunes" on horseback, as he rode from one appointment to another. The good old mothers often stuffed his pockets with new socks, carded, spun and knit with their own hands. Now and then a new pair of trousers were given him as the result of the "chipping in" of two or more neighbors. They did not always fit exactly, for they were made "by guess," but that was a small circumstance, for the circuit rider was none of your fastidious men. He could not afford it and his calling was an embargo in that direction. The pioneer preacher and the circuit rider are about numbered with the things that were. Meetings are no longer held in the private houses as in very early days; nor in the school houses, as in a later day. The substantial and most expensive church houses that exist in our cities, and the neat and modest ones of the country neighborhoods have supplanted them.

THE METHODIST EPISCOPAL CHURCH.

The Methodist church was established when there were but few inhabitants in the country, and has kept pace with the population, constantly advancing until it has reached its present membership.

The first Methodist preaching done in this county, was in the Steven's settlement; and the first organization was effected there by Rev. W. L. Deneen, which formed part of what was then known as the " Salt Creek Circuit," Peter Cartwright being the presiding elder. This organization was formed in the fall of 1829, and consisted of about twelve members, of which the following are some of the names: Buel Stevens and wife, Luther Stevens and wife, Dorus Stevens, Joseph Stevens, Hollenback, David Owen and wife, and John Frazee. In the following year several additions were made to the society from the families of Jonathan and Isaac Miller, who moved to the county.

The same year Dr. Wm. T. Crissey, Alonzo Lapham and their families moved from Edgar county and settled in Decatur and vicinity, and connected themselves with the church.

The first Methodist camp meeting was held the same year, in the Stevens neighborhood, on the farm of David Owens, on what is now known as the Andrew Williams place. This was reserved for a camp ground several years.

In the fall of 1831 the preaching and society were transferred from that neighborhood to Decatur.

So far as is now known, the first preaching by a Methodist minister in Decatur was in May, 1831, by Rev. W. S. Crissey, who came from Indiana on a visit to his uncle, Dr. W. T. Crissey. In the same year several preaching places were established in Macon county.

The first Methodist church building in the county was erected in 1835, in the town of Decatur. It was a frame building, twenty-five feet by thirty feet, and a very rude, insignificant structure compared with those of 1876. From this beginning as seen from its early history, it has progressed to what is shown by following facts concerning its present standing:

There are now in Macon county seven English and two German stations and circuits, making nine, all of which have regular pastors.

There are thirteen English and two German churches in the county.

The entire membership of the county consists of 2030 members. There are fifteen church buildings and five parsonages.

The above church property is valued at $140,000. There are also of this denomination fifteen Sunday schools with about 2000 scholars, and a requisite number of teachers and libraries.

In addition to the above, there is in the city of Decatur an African M. E. church of forty members, with a church house valued at $1500. There is also a flourishing Sunday school of forty members at the same place.

THE FIRST PRESBYTERIAN CHURCH OF DECATUR.

Was organized in the house of Mr. Samuel Powers, on the 1st day of May, 1852, by the Rev. Robert H. Lilly, who was appointed a committee for that purpose by the Presbytery of Palestine. The members at the organization were, David Hopkins, Catherine, his wife, and Lydia, their daughter, Nancy Eagar, Mrs. Mary Lilly, Miss Agness McCormick, John Nicholson and his wife Julia, and Robert Moffit and his wife Elizabeth. David Hopkins was elected and installed first ruling elder. Rev. Augustus F. Pratt gathered up this little church and preached to them one year. After him the Rev. David Manfort, D. D., then quite an old and feeble man, served the church faithfully till October, 1854. About the middle of the next month the church secured the services of the Rev. Erastus W. Thayer, who preached ably to them till the spring of 1857.

The congregation up to about this time worshiped in the old court house, then in the old academy, and in a new building which was erected on east Main street, on a lot belonging to Dr. Roberts and designed ultimately for a store house. About this time, the congregation, having increased in numbers and pecuniary strength, began to take the first steps towards the erection of a church edifice, which resulted in the brick church on Prairie street.

The next minister was the Rev. P. D. Young, who preached one year, and left, for reasons to the writer unknown. Rev. T. M. Oveatt was invited to the charge of the church in July, 1858, and was, in the following spring, installed as the first regular pastor of this church. He continued in the pastoral relation till Jan. 1863, and was succeeded in the following spring by Rev. D. C. Marquis, who was called from this church to the North Presbyterian Church in Chicago, in January, 1866. The church, during the pastorate of these last two men, had a steady and a much more rapid growth. Mr. Marquis, though a young man, just out of the Theological Seminary at Chicago, had preaching powers of no ordinary character. His sermons were evangelical, clear, and profound, and were delivered with great force and animation. If he has had any equal as a sermonizer among the young men in central Illinois, it was his immediate successor, the Rev. Samuel Conn, now of New Albany, Indiana. Both these gentlemen were early honored with the degree of Doctor Divinitatis; because by native power and hard study they earned the distinction. Mr. Conn's health, which was never firm, suffered under the labor and care of the church, and in September, 1868, he closed his labors here. During the last year of Mr. Conn's pastorate a second church was organized in connection with what was called the New School General Assembly, with forty-two members from the First Church, and seven from other quarters. This branch of the church enjoyed the very acceptable services of the Rev. A. L. Brooks till after the union of the two General Assemblies, when he accepted a call to Danville, Illinois, and the two churches united into one harmonious church. The elders of both churches were elected to constitute the session of the re-united church. After Mr. Conn left the Rev. John Brown, D. D., came over on Saturday and supplied this church during the greater part of the next winter.

In the spring of 1869 Rev. James E. Moffatt, a young man from the Chicago Theological Seminary, was settled as pastor, and remained four years. After him came the Rev. Robert McKenzie, and preached a few months over two years.

In September, 1876, Rev. W. H. Prestly accepted a call to this church, and is now preaching most acceptably to full houses.

The church, which began with ten members and one ruling elder, now has about three hundred members, a full bench of ruling elders, and full boards of deacons and trustees.

A large and successful Sunday School is organized under the auspices of this church.

THE CUMBERLAND PRESBYTERIAN CHURCH.

The first sermon by this denomination ever preached in Macon county, was by Rev. John Berry, and was in an old log school house three and a half miles southwest of Decatur, near the present residence of P. M. Wikoff.

The MT. ZION Cumberland Presbyterian Church was organized on the 24th of April, 1830, at the house of the Rev. David Foster, with the following members: Allen Travis, Peggy Travis, Andrew Wilson, Mary A. Wilson, Alexander M. Wilson, Nancy Wilson, Katharine Wilson, James D. Campbell, Lovina Campbell, Andrew Davidson, Asseneth R. Davidson, Elizabeth Bell, Alexander Bell, Nancy Jane Bell, John Davidson, Rhoda Davidson, Rebecca Travis, David Davis, Polly M. Davis, John Smith, Peggy Smith, Samuel Davidson, Elizabeth Davidson, Nancy Davidson, Eleanor Davidson, William D. Baker, Marilla Baker, Robert Smith, Nancy Smith, Robert Foster, Margaret Foster, David Foster, Anna Foster, Wm. C. Foster, Isabel Foster, and Nancy Allen Foster.

The following are the names of the ministers who have had charge of this congregation: David Foster, by whom the church was organized, Neil Johnson, Daniel Traughber, Samuel Ashton, John D. Cowan, J. T. A. Henderson, John C. Smith, R. T. Marlow, R. T. Lester, R. G. Carden, N. M. Baker, and P. H. Crider, the present pastor.

The church has at present about 175 members, and a Sunday School of about 70 members. The first Sunday School in the county was organized at this place by the Rev. David Foster in 1831. The first superintendent was James Scott, and Andrew Wilson, assistant.

The NORTH FORK C. P. Church was organized in April, 1855, by the Rev. John C. Smith, at the Emerson school house, and consisted of 54 members, all but six of which had previously been members of the Mt. Zion congregation.

Present membership, 52.

Present membership of Sunday school, 66.

The successive pastors have been, Daniel Traughber, John C. Smith, Joseph R. Lawrence, G. W. Kinsolving, W. P. Baker, M. Dillow, W. L. Bankson, and N. M. Baker, the present pastor.

The first Sunday school in this vicinity was organized by Miss Charlotte Emerson, sister of the late Judge Emerson, who acted as superintendent and teacher. This was organized in a small house in her father's yard, in the year 1840.

BETHLEHEM C. P. Church was organized in 1850, by the Rev. John C. Smith. It consisted of 51 members; some of which were from Mt. Zion and Mt. Carmel congregations. At present it has 100 members, and a Sunday school of 60 members.

The successive pastors have been John C. Smith, Abner Lansden, James Pantier, N. M. Baker, W. Pinckney Baker, ——Ryan, Thomas Montgomery, J. T. A. Henderson, Robert G. Carden, J. R. Lowrance, T. G. Stansberry, and the present pastor, W. L. Bankson.

The MADISON C. P. Church was organized by the Rev. John C. Smith, from members formerly belonging to the Bethlehem and Mt. Carmel congregations, and has a flourishing membership and Sunday school. The present pastor is Rev. Jesse Beals.

There are also organized churches of this denomination near Argenta, in Friend's Creek township; at Prairie Hall, in Mt. Zion township, and at Shady Grove, in Wheatland township.

THE CHRISTIAN CHURCH.

This chuch was organized in the year 1830, by Elder Joseph Hostetler, of whom a biographical sketch may be found in another part of this book. The place of organization was in the old log court house, which then stood on the west side of the old square, but has since been moved east of Decatur.

The charter members of the organization were, Thomas Cowan and wife, Warner G. Strickland and wife, Elizabeth Cantrall, Stephen Shepherd and wife Dr. Bartley Gorin and wife, Col. Joseph Johnson and wife, Charlotte Turpin, and Mrs. Harrold, none of whom are now living.

The following have served this church in the ministry: Joseph Hostetler, John W. Tyler, George A. Patterson, James Fanning, B. W. Henry, Robert Foster, J. P. Lancaster, Hughey Bowles, Walter P. Bovles, Wm. Harrow, Tobias Grider, A. J. Kane, W. B. Happy, Wm. Ebert, Dr. John Hughes, Wm. C. Dawson, P. D. Vermillion, Ira Mitchell, Lucius Ames, A. D. Northcutt, and the present pastor, F. S. Haynes.

The present membership is 225. Its Sunday school was organized in 1855, by E. M. Nabb, who was its first superintendent. Ransom Wright, W. E. Nelson, W. W. Shockey, W. E. Brigham, L. B. C. Leffingwell, N. S. Haynes and W. L. Hammer have succeeded to the superintendency. The present enrollment of this school is 154. The value of church property is $10,000.

THE UNITED BRETHREN CHURCH.

The first sermon preached in this county by a U. B. preacher was by Rev. James Parks, in the spring of 1848, at the house of Rev. M. T. Chew, five miles southwest of Decatur. The first class consisted of these two persons and Mrs. M. T. Chew. In the fall they petitioned to the annual conference to send them a preacher. James Parks was licensed by the conference and returned to act as minister of this small class. There were but three families in the community, and often there were but two or three present at the meetings.

The first church in Decatur of this denomination was organized in 1856, by the Rev. M. Ambrose, in the old Masonic Hall. The charter members were, S. B. McClelland, J. E. McClelland, Rachel McClelland, S. W. Hamsher, Sarah Hamsher, Jacob Bohn and Mary Bohn. The next year they succeeded in erecting a church house on Cerro Gordo and North Main streets.

The following are the names of the ministers who have had charge of this congregation: M. Ambrose, A. Winsett, T. A. Tawney, S. P. Hay, L. M. Bennett, H. H. Hilbish, A. A. Shesler, S. Levick, H. Elwell, L. Fields, and Isaac Kretzinger, the present pastor. In 1873 the church purchased two lots at a cost of $2350, and erected a new house at a cost of $5000. This is located on the corner of Broadway and Edwards streets. The present membership is 85, and a Sunday school of 115 scholars.

The following are the statistics of the county:

Number of church houses, 10.

Members in county, 500.

Number of Sunday schools, 11.

Total number of scholars, 620.

Total value of church property, $19,600.

Joseph Stevens.

THE FIRST SETTLER OF MACON COUNTY.

[NOW LIVING.]

BAPTIST DENOMINATIONS.

The Decatur Baptist church (United Baptist) was organized on the 14th of September, 1843, in the house of David L. Allen.

It was composed in its first organization of the following members of the United Baptist church of Springfield: David L. Allen, Julia E. Allen, Thomas H. Read, Elizabeth Read, David Brett, Margaret Brett, Henry Rigs, Malinda Rigs, Lemuel Allen, Robert Allen, Margaret Pratt, and S. C. Allen. It was organized by Elder H. W. Dodge.

The first house of worship, on the northeast corner of Water and William streets, was dedicated Dec. 27, 1857. They have now a much more commodious and elegant building on North street, between Water and Franklin streets. The successive pastors have been, H. W. Dodge, Moses Lemon, B. Carpenter, C. H. Gates, N. Alvord, J. N. Tolman, B. F. Thomas, S. G. Miner, F. M. Ellis, F. G. Thearle, S. F. Holt, J. C. Banham, and W. G. Inman. The present number of members is about 175. It has also a flourishing Sabbath School of over 200 members.

THE ROLLING MILL CHAPEL

Was erected by the Baptist church in 1871, at a cost of $2500. It has a Sabbath school of 150 members.

ANTIOCH, AFRICAN.

This was organized in the year 1858, with 14 members. House of worship on South Main street, near Brambles' Grove.

There is also a new church of this denomination at Oreana.

SALEM CHURCH (SEPARATE BAPTIST.)

This church is located five miles southwest of Decatur. It was organized in 1846, with the following members: John Burke, Micajah Burke, L. B. Ward, Elizabeth Ward, Coleman Brown, Elizabeth Brown, Ephriam Cox, Nancy Cox and Amos Walker. The successive pastors have been, Robert Henson, J. W. Vaughan, John Turner, F. S. Randolph, S. B. N. Vaughan, and others. The membership at present numbers about 40. It has a Sunday school of about 40 members.

The cemetery at this church, perhaps the oldest in the county, was commenced in the year 1829 or 1830. A Mr. Mangrin and wife were the first buried there.

OLD SCHOOL OR PRESBYTERIAN BAPTIST.

This church never had a regular church organization in this county, though there have been ministers and preaching since a very early day in different localities throughout the county. There is a membership of about 50 persons, who belong to the different societies throughout the Sangamon Association, which extends throughout Central Illinois. The first minister of this denomination who preached in this county was William Shields, who was the contractor for the old court house. The next was Michael Mann, from Logan county. John B. Moore, C. B. Stafford, John Alsbury, Charles Alsbury, Stephen Hugle, Chester Carpenter, Richard Newport, Daniel Parker, P. McCary, Lemuel Davis, William A. Thompson, Joseph Richardson, Edmund T. Morris, William L. Campbell, A. W. Murray, James H. Ring, and John H. Myers have successively preached to the people of this denomination throughout the county. Mr. Myers, who is one of our oldest native born citizens, is now preaching regularly in the city of Decatur, and expects to organize a church during the spring of 1877.

UNIVERSALIST CHURCH.

This society was organized in 1854, by Rev. D. P. Bunn. The early members of the organization were Joseph Spangler, sr.; Joseph Spangler, jr.; Jacob Spangler, J. B. Hanks and wife, John Rickets and wife, John Capps and wife. The present membership is about 75. The successive pastors of the church have been, D. P. Bunn, (14 years,) S. S. Hebberd, S. F. Gibb, and M. W. Tabor. The present value of the church property is $10,000.

A Sunday school was organized in connection with the church in 1854, and has continued uninterruptedly since, with a present membership of 50.

CHURCH OF GOD.

DECATUR CHURCH.—This church was organized in May, 1857, by Elder A. J. Fenton, with 11 members, viz: Jackson Fisher and wife, Mrs. Howenstine, Mrs. David Givler, David Hamsher, John Hamsher and wife, J. Fenton and wife, Mrs. Fisher, and Jacob Knisely. The successive pastors have been, A. J. Fenton, David Kyle, J. H. Hurley, James Worner, —— Connelly, Thomas

DeSherry, R. White, J. B. Soule, S. M. Newcomer, Henry L. Soule, O. V. Kennison, and W. B. Allin.

Present membership, 75.

There is a Sunday school under the control of the church of about 75 scholars.

Value of church property, $4,000.

There are churches of this denomination at Boiling Springs, Hickory township; Fairview, in same township; Warrensburg and near Macon.

CATHOLIC CHURCH.

ST. PATRICK'S Church was organized in 1854, and the present church building erected in 1863, which, at the time, was the most costly church edifice in the county. There is a membership of something over three hundred families, and a large Sunday school in connection with the church. The present pastor is the Rev. Mr. Hickey.

PROTESTANT EPISCOPAL CHURCH.

ST. JOHNS, of Decatur.—This church was organized in 1856, with the following members: Wm. Prather, C. H. Fuller, M. S. Fuller, Cyril Fuller, Maurice Fuller, Chas. B. Smythe, Elam Rust, M. E. F. Rust, Chas. M. Smythe, J. W. Richardson, Jas. Simpson, Sarah Simpson, Emma Lutrell, S. D. Macy, A. S. Halbert. The successive Rectors of the church have been, Rev. S. R. Child, Rev. W. L. Bostwick, Rev. E. P. Wright, Rev. Wm. M. Steel, Rev. Silas Totten, D. D., Rev. S. D. Pulford, Rev. P. McKim, Rev. W. W. DeWolf, and Rev. Stephen H. Granberry. The latter is the present rector.

NOTE.—We notice the different churches of Maroa, Macon, etc., in connection with the history of those towns found in Chap. VIII.

MASONIC ORGANIZATIONS.

MACON LODGE NO. 8, A. F. & A. M.

This Lodge was chartered Oct. 5, 1841, by the Grand Lodge of the State. Its charter members were George A. Patterson, Joseph King, William Laforgee, Henry Prather, Elijah League, Leonard Ashton, and James Ashton. The officers were—

Geo. A. Patterson......W. M. | Joseph King...........S. W.
            Wm. Laforgee........J. W.

The present officers are—

W. W. Foster..........W. M. | W. L. Hammer............T.
F. M. Cox.............S. W. | J. S. Carter..................S.
A. C. Corman.........J. W. | James L. Peake.........Tyler.

This Lodge is, as will be seen by its number, one of the oldest Lodges in the State, and is the owner of considerable property in Decatur.

IONIC LODGE NO. 312, A. F. & A. M.

Ionic Lodge was chartered in Oct. 1859—the following named persons constituting the charter members: A. B. Bunn, Geo. R. Moffitt, D. W. C. Hardy, S. S. Goode, Joseph Lowenstein, J. M. Lowry, and George Goodman. It has at present a membership of 96. The following are the present officers—

J. N. Baker ..........W.M. | A. A. Murry..........Treas.
W. H. Stoer ..........S.W. | John O. Barnes........Sec'y.
Wm. Young...........J.W. | Wm. Towling..........Tiler.

MACON CHAPTER NO. 51, R. A. M.

This Chapter was organized Sept. 29, 1855, by the Grand Chapter of the State of Illinois, with the following named persons as officers:

D. P. Bunn...........H. P. | W. W. Oglesby........P. S.
J. R. Gorin...........King. | Jos. King............R.A.C.
Henry Prather........Scribe. | J. C. Weaver......M. 3d V.
Josiah Hunt..........C. H. | J. J. Peddecord.....M. 2d V.
            W. H. Ennis ......M. 1st V.

Present officers—

A. A. Murry	H. P.	W. H. Starr	G. M. 3 V.
J. S. King	K.	J. N. Baker	G. M. 2 V.
E. D. Carter	S.	A. L. Roberts	G. M. 1 V.
R. C. Crocker	C. H.	W. L. Hammer	Treasurer.
W. H. Gipson	P. S.	W. H. Wilson	Secretary.
A. C. Corman	R. A. C.	Wm. Towling	Tiler.

BEAUMANOIR COMMANDERY NO. 9, K. T.

This Commandery was organized Nov. 3, 1859, by the Grand Commandery of Illinois, with the following named persons as charter members: Robert Green, S. T. Greer, I. C. Pugh, C. H. Fuller, John N. Fuller, Geo. W. Bright, Jerome R. Gorin, Henry Hummell, Wm. Dewees, Wm. Martin.

The following persons are the present officers:

A. A. Murray	E. C.	W. L. Hammer	T.
D. P. Elwood	Gen'l'mo.	J. S. Hand	Recorder.
W. M. Camp	C. G.	J. T. Barnett	St'd. Bearer.
J. H. Babbitt	S. W.	W. J. Wayne	Sw'd Bearer.
J. N. Baker	J. W.	C. M. Imboden	Warden.
	Wm. Towling	C. of G.	

ODD FELLOWS' ORGANIZATIONS.

DECATUR LODGE NO. 65, I. O. OF O. F.

This lodge was organized in July, 1850, with the following named persons as charter members: S. K. Thompson, H. Hummell, J. R. Turner, B. F. Oglesby and John W. Koehler. This is the oldest lodge of this order in Decatur, and has considerable property.

The present officers are:

Wm. Ragan	N. G.	P. D. Kline	P. S.
Bruce Woodruff	V. G. R.	John Ulrich	T.
Rev. Inman	R. S.	J. W. Rockway	D. D. G. M.

CELESTIAL LODGE NO. 186, I. O. OF O. F.

This lodge was organized Oct. 12, 1855, with the following named persons as charter members: W. W. Oglesby, P. D. Kline, S. K. Thompson, Henry P. Elliott, R. F. Jones, Joseph King, Jas. Shoaff, J. L. Peake, A. J. Wolf, C. H. Fuller, Geo. W. Baker, B. H. Cassell, and John J. Ballentine.

The present officers are:

John Armstrong	N. G.	Joseph Gates	P. S.
Samuel Funk	V. G.	I. W. Ehrman	T.
John Mark	R. S.	G. W. Patterson	D. D. G. M.

ENCAMPMENT NO. 37, I. O. OF O. F.

This encampment was organized Dec., 1856, with the following persons as charter members: G. A. Smith, H. Kain, B. F. McCoy, Hamilton McCoy, William T. Peake, Stephen Grimes, Peter Terrell and Alonzo Pierce.

The present officers are:

Henry Bower	C. P.	George Cole	J. W.
John G. Cloyd	H. P.	Wm. Towling	Scribe.
P. D. Kline	S. W.	Geo. W. Patterson	T.
	F. G. Richmond	D. D. G. M.	

DAUGHTERS OF REBEKAH.

BENEVOLENT LODGE NO. 61, I. O. OF O. F.

This lodge was organized October 14, 1873, with the following persons as charter members: I. N. Martin, P. L. Kline, Wm. Towling, G. W. Baker, Newton Edwards, B. J. Schock, Joseph Mills, Wm. McDonald, B. Stine, John Ulrich, M. Forstmeyer, E. Swartz, O. F. McKim, Mrs. I. N. Martin, Miss Kate Towling, Mrs. Kate Baker, H. Swartz, Mrs. R. Jones, Mrs. Ballentine.

The present officers are:

W. Patterson	N. G.	Mrs. E. P. Tuttle	R. S.
Mrs. Wm. Young	V. G.	Mrs. H. H. Stafford	F. S.
Mrs. L. L. Haworth	T.	Geo. Patterson	D. D. G. M.

I. O. G. T.

Decatur Lodge No. 568, of the Independent Order of Good Templars, was chartered on the 23d day of February, 1874. The following named persons are among the 60 charter members who assisted in the organization and who still reside in the county: D. L. Bunn, Jesse Lefargee, Aurilla Culver, S. A. Jones, Jennie Young, S. H. Corman, Sallie Blair, Mattie Hanks (Righter), Theo. Coleman, J. J. H. Young, W. H. Hubbard, M. Y. Givler, Casper Bazou, Mary Bazou, and Ben. H. Righter.

The present officers are:

D. L. Bunn ....L. D. | Theo. Coleman ....W. C. T.
W. G. Inman......P. W. C. T. | Ruth Culver........W. V. T.
John House........W. S.

DECATUR PUBLIC LIBRARY.

This library was the result of the labors of the Ladies' Library Association, which was organized some eight years ago. The library was collected and managed by that association until Sept. 9, 1875, when all the books and furniture were transferred to the city of Decatur, and is is now under the auspices of the city council. There were in the library when control was assumed by the city 1692 volumes and at the end of the first half year there were 1300 borrowers. During this period 17,572 books had been loaned, or an average of 117 per day, and 28,345 persons had visited the rooms. At the end of the first year 24,933 books had been loaned, or 3130 per month, and 40,138 persons had visited the library and recorded their names, which the librarian estimates is not more than half the actual visitors, as many visitors do not record their names. At present the number of volumes in the library is in excess of 2000 and is being increased as the funds under the control of the library board will justify. The library is supported by a tax levied upon the city property under the law of the state. There is in connection with the library a reading room, on the files of which are kept all the leading newspapers, journals, magazines, etc., of the United States. Fifty different newspapers alone are on file. The books in the library have been selected with care and judgment, and it is useless to add anything more than the above exhibit of the number of readers to show the benefit being derived by the public through this small library. It is hoped that the number of books will soon be increased so as to meet the public demand, as it is felt that the present facilities are entirely inadequate. The interest the community takes in reading and general information derived from a general library and reading rooms, is a matter of education to a large extent. The aggregate value to be attached to this channel of information cannot be estimated. Many young persons are found daily at the library and reading rooms, engaged in reading useful books or papers who otherwise would be denied any privileges in that direction for want of means. Others are there who have cultivated a taste for the study and perusal of useful books, who otherwise might be cultivating a taste for vice in some one of its thousand enticing forms.

The following constitute the present members of the library management:

W. A. Barnes, President.

Mrs. S. F. Greer, Secretary.

R. L. Evans, Librarian.

DIRECTORS.—W. A. Barnes, J. L. Peake. W. L. Hammer, Mrs. S. F. Greer, Mrs. B. F. Sibley, Mrs. C. A. Ewing, W. W. Foster, Fred. Kuney, W. T. Wells.

STANDING COMMITTEES.

Administration.—W. L. Hammer, W. T. Wells, Mrs. B. F. Sibley.

Finance.—J. L. Peake, W. L. Hammer, Mrs. C. A. Ewing.

Buildings and Grounds.—Fred. Kuney, J. L. Peake, Mrs. C. A. Ewing.

By-Laws and Regulations.—W. W. Foster, Fred. Kuney, Mrs. B. F. Sibley.

Library and Reading Room.—W. T. Wells, W. W. Foster, Mrs. S. F. Greer.

CHAPTER VII.

OUR MANUFACTORIES.

We give below a few brief sketches of some of our principal manufacturing institutions, though we fail to notice all, for want of space, what we have to say is not in the way of laudation or fulsome praise of any of the institutions mentioned, nor as an advertisement to either of them;* but to illustrate as best we can the present condition of the county in this department of wealth and progress. We have aimed thus far in this work to treat of facts as we find them, without undue praise or partiality. Of the importance to be attached to manufacture in adding to the prosperity of a city or locality, nothing need be said. We only need point to places having equal facilities—one with manufacturing institutions, and the other with none. The one is alive with energy and activity, the other is dead; the streets of one city are noisy and bustling with business and trade, and those of the other are lifeless and inactive; the one grows rapidly, and soon has its buildings, its churches, its schools and colleges of superior merit and magnificence, the other has its old tumble-down, rickety rookeries, and its grog-shops are the principal places where the people congregate.

Among the early manufacturing institutions of the county was the "old ox mill," erected just east of the old Revere house site, in the year 1839. This was erected by J. J. Peddecord, Ninian Peddecord and E. O. Smith. The motive power was obtained by placing three or four cows upon an inclined wheel, their heads being

---

* No institutien mentioned in this chapter has contributed one cent for the notice given it, and some of them not even subscribed for this work.

secured to a cross beam. Much difficulty was experienced for some time after this mill was set in operation, in getting the machinery so regulated as to be under the control of the person in charge. The gearing apparatus was not perfect, and occasionally a cog slipped, or the connections between the wheel and the mill machinery became detached, and then there was a runaway. The cows would become frightened and commence running, which gave the revolutions of the wheel more velocity, and then a scene of general consternation spread throughout the village. All kind-hearted citizens would rush to the rescue, and assist "Uncle Henry" in stopping his mill, by throwing rails and logs under the wheel. Some of the cows on the wheel being larger unable to keep up with it, its revolutions were so rapid, would be found dragging by the head. The bellowing of the cows, the screaking of the machinery, the smashing of the rails; the quick, excited and shrill voice of "Uncle Henry," in giving orders, are remembered by many of the old settlers, and related with wonderful minuteness. When it was announced that the mill was running away with itself, then there was running to and fro like there was at Belgium's capital, on a certain noted occasion.

The principal product of this mill was corn meal, and the tolls derived glutted the market, and there being no demand except the home demand, the mill soon proved an unprofitable investment, and was sold to Joseph Stickel. He sought to make it a paying investment by grinding corn for Allen's distillery. As soon, however, as it was known that he was, in this indirect way, giving "aid and comfort," as it were, to the production of whisky, he was brought before the church, of which he was a member, and required to produce the "thus saith the Lord," for his iniquitous and nefarious traffic, or be expelled from the church. What the result was of the indictment of Bro. Joe, we do not know, but so it was, however, in a short time the mill ceased to run, and was purchased by a man from Clinton, by the name of Ward, and was converted into a carding factory, and run as such for a great many years.

It may not be known to many that lime was ever manufactured in this county, but such is the fact. Capt. D. L. Allen, at an early day erected a lime kiln on the river, a short distance southwest of the city of Decatur, at what is still known as the "old lime kiln ford." He manufactured a considerable quantity of lime from limestone obtained in that vicinity, sufficient, at least, to meet the wants of our people. The lime produced is said to have been of a very fine grade, and was purchased by builders in Springfield on account of the superior finishing qualities it possessed.

Senator R. J. Oglesby was imbued, in his early days, with the idea that rope making would be a success, and started a rope factory. Hemp was raised and ropes were actually made and placed in the market by Mr. O., but the remuneration not being adequate to meet his expectations, the rope works, after a year or so, were abandoned.

THE DECATUR FURNITURE COMPANY.

This is one of our largest manufacturing establishments. It was commenced in 1866, under the firm name of Wm. Lintner & Co. Mr. L. sold his interest in 1875 to his co-partners, Messrs. Peddecord & Burrows, who are now the owners of the entire establishment. This firm is engaged in the manufacture of all kinds of furniture, and has a capital invested in the business of about one hundred thousand dollars. The furniture manufactured by this firm is shipped to all parts of Illinois, Missouri, Iowa, and Indiana; the sales of which amount, in the aggregate, to one hundred and fifty thousand dollars annually. The lumber used by the company is obtained from southern Illinois, Indiana, and Tennessee, and is required to be selected with great care, as none but the best is suitable for the grades of furniture manufactured by this company. The yearly pay-roll will average about 100 men, to whom is paid annually about $50,000. It is a matter of verification that the number of persons deriving a support from this factory alone, will equal in numbers, if not exceed, the entire population of Decatur prior to the building of our railroads.

The company is also engaged in the manufacture of wood pumps, which are sold largely throughout the northwest. The business was commenced by the manufacture of this article in 1863, by Messrs. Barnes & Lintner, who employed, at the commencement, not to exceed a half dozen men. As the business increased, new buildings were erected and machinery purchased, until at present the main building used by the company is 108x36 feet, five stories high, with two additional buildings 100x32 and 99x92, each three stories high, besides other out houses used for the drying and storage of lumber.

The railroad facilities at this point enables this firm to compete successfully with the older and larger establishments of Cincinnati and eastern cities.

The established reputation and capital of the Decatur Furniture Co., will continue to render it one of the manufacturing institutions which Decatur and Macon county may justly be proud of.

UNION IRON WORKS.

These works are among the most important of our manufacturing institutions. They were commenced in 1864 by Burroughs & Co., upon a limited scale, intending at the time only to start a first-class repair shop for machinery. Like all institutions of the kind, however, that are backed by capital and industry, their work increased as its character became known. Additions have been made to the buildings, machinery facilities, etc., from time to time, to the extent of $75,000. The company is at present engaged in the manufacture of steam engines, mill and elevator machinery, the Western Corn-Sheller and Cleaner, and general repairing. Their facilities are such that engines of the most powerful construction, as well as of the most intricate nature, are being made here and shipped to all parts of the west, and east as far as Ohio, and south as far as Tennessee.

About one hundred thousand dollars worth of work is annually turned out by the firm, requiring a working force of at least thirty-five men—the most of whom are skilled mechanics. The chief characteristics of the engines manufactured are, durability, simplicity and symmetry. In the construction of the various parts they avoid clumsiness and weight, except where absolutely necessary for strength. From all the information we have been able to obtain from persons who have used engines manufactured by the Union Iron Works, we do not hesitate to say that their work is entitled to be classed as equal to any other product of western skill. The work of manufacturing engines is divided into separate and distinct departments, and each department has a superintendent who has attained his position by years of practical experience.

Another branch of the business of this firm is devoted to furnishing plans and specifications, and superintending the construction of flour mills and elevators. Millwrights are constantly kept employed in this department.

Within the last two years, the manufacture of the "Western Corn Sheller" and the "Western Corn Cleaner" has been engaged in. These machines are the inventions of C. C. Burroughs, one of the members of the firm, and are meeting with a success scarcely anticipated by the inventor. They are supplanting the old machines that have been in popular favor for years, and are destined to be of material benefit to the whole agricultural west. Three of the principal articles of manufacture of Macon county are Macon county inventions, and are designed to supply the wants of our agricultural community. The one above mentioned, while we have no space to devote to a description of its merits, we doubt not will become, when properly before the public, an article of remuneration to its inventor and manufacturers, as well as a valuable machine in the speedy preparation of our immense crops of corn for the market.

The Union Iron Works are owned by C. C. Burroughs, James Millikin, John M. Flood and Charles Gradweld, the latter two having become members of the firm in 1873.

DECATUR BAGGING CO.

During the summer of 1875, the Decatur Bagging Co. was formed, composed of the following parties: Moses Jerome, A. W. Conklin and D. S. Shellaboyer. Immediately after the organization of the company very large and extensive buildings were erected on the Toledo, Wabash and Western Railroad, in the city of Decatur, for the purpose of carrying on the business in. These buildings, together with the necessary machinery, engines and fixtures, were erected at a cost of over $50,000. The business of the company is the manufacture of but a single article, viz: "bagging," which is used only for covering cotton bales. The market for this article of manufacture is all points south devoted to the culture of cotton.

In connection with this manufactory, and belonging to the company, are four tow-mills, located as follows: Paxton, Buckley, Rantoul and Onarga, which cost about $35,000. The flax lint is manufactured into tow in these mills and shipped in bales to the factory here, where it is spun and wove into cloth and shipped south.

This manufactory requires the labor of 160 hands, who are employed winter and summer alike, one-half of whom are females, and the average pay of all is $1 per day. We were pained to learn that five-sixths of the raw material used by this company in the manufacture of its goods is raised in other counties than our own, so that, while the location of the manufactory is here and the most of the employees are residents, which are of great benefit to Decatur and the county, it might be made to contribute far more to our material worth, if the farmers of the county were to devote attention to the cultivation of flax and hemp, so as to supply the demands of the factory. If the culture of the raw material be a source of income to the farmers of Ford and Champaign counties, why may it not be to our own people, especially when the cost of transportation must of necesssity be taken from the price paid in those foreign counties. Besides, it is a well attested fact that our soil, climate, etc., are equally if not better suited for the successful cultivation of this article. This, together with the fact that hemp and flax are articles of easy culture, very prolific, and will meet with a home market, ought to stimulate some of our farmers to devote some attention to this article of agriculture. We are disposed to assert, from an examination given to this subject, that if our farmers would devote some part of their farms to the culture of hemp and flax, so as to supply the demands of the factory, it would save to the people of the county thousands of dollars that are annually expended elsewhere, and induce the bringing to this county the tow mills now erected in other counties, besides being a source of revenue and profit to our own people.

The bagging factory is now owned entirely by Messrs. A. W. and C. A. Conklin, who are men of capital, energy and perseverance, and who are now thoroughly initiated in the business. We have no doubt they will, with their business qualifications, soon make this, to us, new branch of industry one of the best paying institutions located in our midst. The class of persons furnished employment in the factory though not what are termed skilled mechanics, yet they are of that industrious and peaceable sort who otherwise might have difficulty in obtaining employment or means of support for themselves and their families, and whose earnings are devoted to that purpose rather than indulgence and vice, as we see among employees of other manufacturing institutions. We have no hesitancy whatever in saying that the Decatur Bagging factory is now one of our most important manufacturing institutions, and one of which Macon county ought to be proud, and is destined to be of far greater importance to us.

It asks no bonus or support from us other than what is to the interest and profit of our people to give, in the way of material furnished, for which a market is made. Its owners are our own citizens and of us and expect to remain with us.

HAWORTH & SONS.

"To save time is to lengthen life,"

Is an old saying, and as true as it is old. The object sought to be obtained in almost all of our modern inventions is time and labor. So with Haworth's Check-Rower. Its main object is to save the time and labor of the farmer in the corn-planting season, when every minute of time saved is almost as precious as minutes of gold. When he is ready for planting his corn, every hour lost is a proportionate loss in bushels at the ensuing autumn. The check-rower is the invention of George D. Haworth, one of the members of the firm, and was completed and a patent obtained therefor in the year 1869. Valuable improvements have been added to it from time to time since as experience has dictated, so that farmers who understand and have had the use of this machine attach to it a value next in importance to the corn-planter itself. Upon level western prairies, where the soil is such that the weeds grow as rapidly as the corn, and sprout and commence growing as soon as the ground is broken up, it is found very desirable that the corn should be planted in rows each way, and planted as soon as possible after the soil is turned over, so that the corn will have an equal chance with the weeds and grass. Without the use of the check-rower it is necessary that the entire piece of land, ten or twenty acres as the case may be, shall be broken up, then it must be marked off with a marker so as to make the cross rows, by which it is found that by the time the entire piece of land is broken up and crossed off the weeds are beginning to show themselves above ground in the part first plowed. But with the check-rower this difficulty is obviated, and that too, even if the farmer has but one team to use.

But it is useless to dilate upon the merits of this machine; as such it is an invention of the county, and of which the people will yet more thoroughly appreciate. The firm engaged in the manufacture of this implement are M. Haworth, L. L. Haworth, J. W. Haworth, and George D. Haworth—father and sons. They were formerly from Clinton county, Ohio, and removed to Illinois in 1852, and to Macon county in 1857. They are all men of energy and thorough business qualifications. They took hold of this invention a few years since, and by industry and perseverance have overcome the natural prejudice existing among the people against all new inventions; so that now increasing demands are coming from Illinois, Iowa, Missouri, Kansas, Nebraska and Texas, for it.

During the past year the original shops, machinery and facilities for manufacture, have been increased to more than four times their original capacity. The value of the real estate, shops, machinery, warerooms, of the firm does not probably vary far from $150,000. Thirty-five men are employed by the firm. One feature connected with the manufacture of the check-rower is that every part of the machine is made here in the shops, so that there is but a very small outlay of money by the firm that Macon county does not receive the benefit of. The value of the manufactures of this firm for the year 1876 will not vary far from $200,000.

ROBERTS, LYTLE & CO.

This firm has been in business but three years, and is composed of the following named gentlemen: T. T. Roberts, R. P. Lytle and O. Z. Green. While the articles manufactured by this firm, viz: wooden burial cases and caskets, are not pleasant to contemplate, and never purchased except when painful necessity requires, yet in these pre-cremation days the demands therefor is steady and constant, and unaffected by the fluctuating influences operating upon other articles of manufacture. $40,000 worth of burial cases are annually manufactured by this firm, and shipped throughout Illinois, Missouri, Kansas, Iowa and other States. The lumber used is obtained from southern Illinois, Michigan and Tennessee. Twenty men are employed by the firm the year round.

The members of this firm are all young men of energy and business qualifications, and their growing business will soon create a demand for much larger works and a greater investment of capital. Their present grounds, buildings and machinery cost in the neighborhood of $20,000.

H. W. HILL & CO.,

Manufacturers of Hardware Specialties and Hog Rings and Ringers.

This firm is composed of H. W. Hill and C. P. Housum, and commenced business in 1872. They were first engaged in the manufacture of H. W. Hill's hog ringer and rings; and by perseverance and energy have established a business in that line of work exceeding all others combined. With their present machinery they have a capacity of manufacturing 140,000 rings daily, and have placed upon the market in four years 30,000,000 rings, consuming 900 miles of wire. The market for this article of commerce extends from Maine to California and Texas, and some goods have been exported to Europe. The demand for this device, manufactured by this firm, is increasing as its merits become known by the farming community. Over nine millions and a half of rings have been sold during the past year, which is fifty per cent. in excess of the sales the year previous.

The firm commenced business on a limited capital, and under disadvantages arising from imperfect machinery, or rather no machinery at all; from prejudices naturally existing against all new and valuable improvements, and have been harrassed by litigations in reference to patents, almost without number. But notwithstanding these obstacles, they have by business tact and energy overcome them, and now constitute one of the substantial and securely established manufacturing institutions of which we may well feel proud, and have a capital of $30,000 invested. They also manufacture, to a considerable extent, corn-huskers, ladles, etc., which are inventions of the firm. They also have in connection with their business a printing office, by which they are enabled to do all their own printing and advertising.

H. W. Hill, the senior member of the firm, is a native of North Carolina, and has been a resident of Macon county about 11 years.

Charles P. Housum, the junior member, is a native of Ohio, and has been a resident of Macon county about 11 years.

The reputation of Decatur as a manufacturing city and railroad center has been largely increased through the extensive advertising done by the firm. About three tons of advertising matter are annually distributed to all parts of the United States by them.

CHAMBERS, BEHRING & QUINLAN.

Manufacturers of Champion Hog Ringer, Rings and Holder, Eaglebill Corn Husker, and Barnes' Wire Check-Rower.

The firm of Chambers & Quinlan was formed in the spring of 1875, for the purpose of manufacturing the Champion Hog Ringer, Rings and Holder. By their perseverance and devotion to the manufacture of their articles, they have succeeded in building up a business that is growing and permanent; so that they in Dec. 1876, associated with them Mr. J. Ed. Behring, as a partner, and extended the list of articles manufactured by them, and are now manufacturing the Eagle-bill Corn-Husker, Barnes' Wire Check-Rower, and Brown's Hog Ringer and Rings.

We have no space to enter into an examination of the merits of the various articles manufactured by the firm. It will be seen that all the articles are intended to meet the demands of our farming community. The Champion hog ringer and rings made by the firm is the only invention of the kind in use. The ring is a double ring and is said to have advantages over the single ring. It is sufficient to say that this article is found upon the shelves of hardware dealers throughout the United States, and is being introduced in Europe.

The Barnes' check-rower, made by this firm, has only been upon the market for a short time, and its merits not fully understood. The advantages claimed for it are, durability; that it will not contract or extend; no side draft; convenience in use, and adaptability to all planters.

The firm employs on an average about 14 hands, and occupies the old agricultural shops.

The members of this firm are thorough business men. Mr. Chambers is now (1876) mayor of the city of Decatur, and Mr. Quinlan is an old and respected citizen of the county.

W. & B. SAWYER.

Linseed Oil and Oil Cake.

The oil mill of this firm was put in operation in 1867, and with the additions made since, including machinery, is valued at $30,000, There are $75,000 worth of oil and cake annually manufactured, the principal markets for which are St. Louis and New York. A large proportion of the oil cake is exported to Europe. They also have a retail trade extending throughout Illinois, Indiana and Missouri. The number of men employed by the firm is 13. The flax seed consumed by the mill averages about 50 thousand bushels per annum, and is principally raised in Southern Illinois, for which $1,40 to $1,50 per bushel is paid.

The firm is composed of William Sawyer and Benjamin Sawyer. The latter has been a resident of Macon County since 1836, and the former since 1867. Of the business qualifications of the firm nothing need be said. It is a straightforward business firm; energetic and responsible.

BOYD, HASKELL & CO.

"*Decatur Woolen Mills.*"

This is among the oldest existing manufacturing institutions of the County, having been established in 1859, by the present firm composed of the following persons, viz: Wm. H. Boyd, L. C. Haskell and W. J. Myers. The principal goods manufactured are flannels, yarns, blankets, jeans, and, also, card and spin. The wool used by the firm is procured from Macon and adjoining counties entirely, and the products of the factory are sold throughout Illinois, Wisconsin, Iowa, Michigan and Indiana; amounting annually to about $75,000 in value.

In 1868 the mills were destroyed by fire, but were immediately rebuilt. The value of mills, including machinery, is not far from $30,000. The firm are thoroughly initiated in all the details of the business, and are sound business men, and have in their employ about 25 persons the year round.

Prior to their engaging in this business here in 1859, Mr. Boyd was a resident of Maryland, Mr. Haskell of New York, and Mr. Myers of Pennsylvania. The latter has been an influential member of the city council.

This firm, but with little attempt at show or display, has been, and continues to be, engaged in a department of manufacture that Macon County could illy afford to be without.

PETER LOEB.

Manufacturer of Agricultural and Gray Iron Castings.

Mr. L. erected his shops and foundry in the summer of 1876, and is a man of twenty years experience in his line of business. He has on an average ten men in his employment since ready for business. He says with the patronage thus far received, and the facilities he has, he will in a short time more than double his present amount of business, which he estimates for 1876 at $15,000. The necessity for a foundry of the character of Mr. L's., of course can not be denied. Our farmers annually expend thousands of dollars for the repairs of machinery ordered at Cincinnati, Pittsburg and elsewhere, which might just as well be expended at home. Loss of time and the freights in the shipment should be considered and would be no small items in the aggregate.

H. MUELLER & CO.

Manufacturers of Water Main Tappers, Toy Pistols, Gunsmithing and General Repairing of Machinery.

This firm has been in business since April, 1874, the senior member having carried on a gunsmith and general repairing shop for a great many years. He is thoroughly conversant with his business in all of its branches, and the firm is wide awake and thoroughly energetic in all things pertaining to their line of work. Their annual manufactures will run from twelve to fifteen thousand dollars per annum, and the monthly pay-roll will not fall short of nine men. Their business is increasing, and their shops, machinery, etc., speak well for the present and future. The water main tapper made by the firm is an ingenious and very simple invention, perfected and patented by H. Mueller.

KRAMER & McCLELLAND.

Manufacturers of Road, Spring and Lumber Wagons Carriages and Buggies.

This is one of the oldest firms, if not the oldest in the county, having been established in 1854. Each member of the firm has been a resident of the county since 1853. The firm has a capital invested of $10,000, and their annual manufacture aggregates in the neighborhood of that amount. Their wagons, etc., find a market in this and adjoining counties, and some are shipped to Indiana and New Mexico. Their work, as thousands of their customers can verify, is of the most substantial character, as well as ornamental, and needs no commendation. They make a specialty of "Jump seats and Greencastle bodies."

WAYNE BROS.

This firm is engaged in the manufacture of carriages, buggies and spring wagons, and also do a large repairing business. The members of the firm are, John B. and Wm. J. Wayne. They are natives of Pennsylvania, but have been residents of Illinois for about 25 years, and of Macon county four years. Each of the firm is thoroughly conversant with all the minutiæ of the business. Their average annual manufacture of vehicles of various kinds aggregate $20,000, the most of which is sold to home customers; some goods, however, are shipped to Iowa, Kansas and Texas. The material used by the firm is obtained in the eastern markets, and is selected with the greatest of care. The carriages and buggies made are substantial and well built, and this firm has turned out some of the finest work in Central Illinois. They have in their employ about 20 of the most skillful mechanics, in the different departments of their work.

D. S. SHELLABARGER.

Flour Mills.

This firm commenced business in Decatur in 1862, and is composed of D. S. Shellabarger, John B. Shellabarger and Wm. Bowers, though we believe some changes have been made in the firm in that time. Each member of the firm is thoroughly acquainted with the flouring business in all its departments. The senior member of the firm has been mayor of the city, as well as alderman. They have a capital invested in the milling business, consisting of real estate, machinery, etc., of $35,000. The average annual value of manufactures will run from $175,000 to $200,000. They have in their employ eight men, and their principal market is Macon county and surrounding country.

—26

GEO. PRIEST & CO.

Flour Mills.

One of the oldest flour mills in the county is that of Geo. Priest & Co. The firm is now composed of Geo. Priest and A. N. Deal, both of whom are thoroughly initiated in all the departments of their business. They have a capital invested in the business of about $33,000, and the annual product of flour, etc., manufactured amounting to $150,000, requiring the labor of eight men. Their business extends throughout the county and along the railroad lines leading from Decatur.

GREENFIELD, BELL & CO.

Flour Mills.

This mill has been in operation about eight years, and has an investment of $20,000 in real estate, buildings and machinery, with a capacity of producing annually 11,000 barrels of flour, employing six men, and has a trade extending in almost every direction within a radius of thirty to forty miles from Decatur. The members of this firm are old residents of Macon county, Mr. Bell having been born here, and Mr. Greenfield came at a very early day.

HARPSTRITE & SCHLANDEMAN.

Manufacturers of Beer.

This firm began business in 1862, in Decatur. The members of the firm are Edward Harpstrite, who came from Clinton county in 1855, and Henry Schlandeman, who came from Logansport, Ind., in 1856. They have an investment of $60,000 in their business, and their annual manufactures amount to about $40,000, which finds a market in Macon and adjoining counties. They annually consume about 10,000 bushels of barley, for which they pay on an average ninety cents per bushel, which is shipped to them from Kansas, Nebraska and Minnesota. Their hops are obtained from New York. Ten men are in the employ of the firm.

FERRIS & EMMONS.

Manufacturers of and Dealers in Lubricating and Illuminating Oils and Axle Grease, and Dealers in Animal Oils.

This firm was organized in 1875. The members of the firm are W. P. Ferris, who came to Macon county in 1871, and was engaged until 1875 as conductor on the T., W. and W. R. R. G. W. Emmons came to Macon county in 1870, and was conductor on the above road until 1874. Mr. F. is a native of New York, and Mr. E. of New Hampshire. The annual sales of goods manufactured and on sale, are $100,000 per annum. Number of men employed by firm, six. Principle market for goods, Illinois, and some have been shipped to Kansas. The carbon oil used by this firm is shipped in large iron tanks made expressly for the purpose, and transferred directly from the tanks by means of siphons to the tanks of the firm, which have a capacity of 8,000 gallons. From these tanks the oil is transferred to the barrels for distribution.

ELWOOD & CO.

Manufacturers of Doors, Sash, Blinds, etc.

This firm was organized in 1865; the Messrs. Elwood having been residents of the county for 22 years. They have a cash capital invested in this county of about $40,000, and have been doing a large and increasing business in their line since they came to Decatur. They own large pineries in Michigan, which are under the charge of D. Elwood, one of the members of the firm, from which they obtain the principal part of their lumber. The annual average manufactures of the firm amount to $40,000, and from 23 to 25 men are employed by them. The firm manufactures and sells about two million feet of lumber per annum, which finds a market in Macon and adjoining counties.

RAILROADS.*

A history of the railroad interests of the State, would be a volume of itself, and not devoid of interest.

From the introduction of railroads in this country, Illinois has been destined to be a railroad State. The foresight of Hon. Ste-

---

NOTE.—The first successful locomotive steam engine in the world was invented by George Stephenson, and is still preserved at Darlington, England. Prior to its invention Mr. S. was regarded as "the craziest man in all England," but after its successful operation, on its trial trip he was regarded as "the smartest man in all England and in all the world." The first railroad and upon which this engine ran, was completed from Stockton to Darlington, England, Sept. 27, 1825. The project of Stephenson was ridiculed in parliament, and a large concourse of people gathered upon the occasion of the trial to ridicule the "insane" Stephenson. The engine was attached to a train of 34 coal wagons and coaches, which were about the size of an ordinary old-fashioned stage coach. The passengers took their places in the coaches, and a man on horseback took his position in front of the engine to herald the approach of the coming train! The signal for starting was given, and the engine started off with the cars like a "thing of life." The gentleman who was to ride on horseback in front of the train to announce its coming, soon found it convenient to "look out for the cars," and left the track in disgust! The ridiculing spectators who were left behind, were in a ridiculous state of mind at the unexpected successful working of the crazy man's engine. The journey was completed at the speed of 15 miles an hour, and from that time since the name of George Stephenson has been written high upon the scale of the world's benefactors.

In 1831 a railroad was completed from Albany to Schenectady, New York, a distance of 16 miles, which was among the first roads upon which a train of cars were propelled by steam in America, and took place the year the road was finished. The trains upon this road, however, ran very slowly The road ran over hills and down into the valleys, so that it was necessary to draw the trains up acclivities, in places, by stationary engines. The first engine upon this road was the "John Bull," which was made in England, and weighed four tons. The venerable Thurlow Weed was among the 15 passengers upon the first train of passenger cars propelled by steam. But little did he suspect on the morning of that excursion that in much less than half a century he would behold trains running through that Mohawk valley at the rate of 40 and 50 miles an hour, and still others bearing freight sufficient in value to have paid for the entire Mohawk & Hudson Railroad, with its equipment. One of Stephenson's engines was put upon a road constructed by the Delaware and Hudson Canal Co., from their coal mines to Honesdale, in 1829, but it was not used for passenger traffic to any great extent, if at all.

phen A. Douglas in getting the Illinois Central Railroad constructed from Cairo to Chicago and Dunleith, has resulted in incalculable benefit in opening up the fertile prairies of Illinois to cultivation. He lived long enough to see his expectations more than realized, and his predictions fully met. The early railway legislation of this State fully manifests the popular feeling as to the necessity of some means for the transportation of our grain and herds of cattle and hogs. The means of attaining the requisite railways, however, were matters of serious consideration, and of no well-defined opinion. One crude idea that seems to have pervaded the entire legislature in 1835-6-7, was that these great highways of commerce might be legislated into existence; hence it was that in those years there were enacted that gigantic enterprise that has since been known as the internal improvement scheme. It had for its object the construction of canals and railways, branching out to almost all parts of the country; all to be built and owned by the State; the construction of one-half of which would have bankrupted Illinois beyond all hopes of recovery.

It was a gigantic undertaking without any means of accomplishing. It was a brilliant idea, without any sort of conception as to the requisite amount of capital to give it practical shape and direction. It was akin to that other idea, and had about as much consistency in it, by which the fellow undertook to jump across the Mississippi by taking hold of his boot straps. The whole internal improvement scheme collapsed with the financial panic of 1837. Several millions of dollars were appropriated from the treasury and expended with scarcely a dollar to show therefor except a few embankments in different parts of the State. Among the projected lines of railway under which work was commenced under the improvement system was that of the Northern Cross Railroad, chartered in 1837, running from Quincy to Danville and the State line. The first locomotive engine that ever ran in Illinois was placed upon this road, and ran through from Meredosia to Jacksonville, perhaps in the winter of 1838-9.

The above road was completed through to Springfield from Jacksonville in 1842, and the cars made three trips to the Illinois river every week; which feat is spoken of by the journals of that day as wonderful! This road was constructed by nailing flat pieces of iron upon long pieces of timber, running lengthwise with the road. The road, however, had not been in use long before the track became uneven and rough, and the engine was so out of repair that it had to be taken off the road, and the cars were then propelled by mules! This process of locomotion finally became unendurable, and the whole road was sold by the State for a mere nominal consideration. We mention these facts, as they constitute the first railroad experience of Illinois; and also for the reason that the Northern Cross Railroad formed a part of the line, which, after various consolidations, became the

TOLEDO, WABASH & WESTERN RAILWAY.*

This, though built under a different name, was the first railroad that was constructed through the county of Macon. From the time its cars ran into Decatur in April, 1854, commences the rapid improvement and almost unexampled prosperity of our county. At that date commences the real history of our agricultural and commercial advancement. Then all the stock in trade of all the merchants in the county would have made but a few dray loads. From that period hog drovers became scarce. Thenceforward those old-fashioned, broad-tyred Virginia wagons, with their inevitable accompaniments—the two dogs and a tar bucket—ceased to be vehicles transporting our dry-goods and groceries from St. Louis and Chicago. Their owners, who had hitherto made the principal part of their living by "wagoning," looked upon the construction of the railroads with an eye of suspicion, and regarded it as an interference, to some extent at least, with "vested rights." Other objections were urged against the construction of railroads, that to us in this day would seem laughable indeed; among others it was urged that the whistling of the engines and noise of the cars would drive away all the game! Others said the ranges would all be destroyed, and poor people would have to keep their cattle and hogs enclosed.

The T., W. & W. R. R. has been one of the two roads that has been largely instrumental in making our county what it is. To our merchants and our farmers who ship stock and grain east, this road has been of incalculable value.

---

* We understand that after January, 1877, the name of this road is to be changed to the Wabash Railway.

The length of the road is as follows:

Main line from Toledo to Quincy	473	miles.
St. Louis Division (from Decatur to E. St. Louis)	110	"
Keokuk Branch	41	"
Naples Branch	3	"
Total	627	"

Of these 627 miles there are in Illinois 386 miles.

The annual shipments forwarded by this line will average from 350 to 400 thousand dollars, and the annual receipts are about one hundred and twenty thousand dollars from Decatur station, as shown by the books of the company. The passenger traffic from Decatur varies between 90 and 100 thousand dollars. The payroll for men employed in Decatur, runs between five and six thousand dollars per month.

THE ILLINOIS CENTRAL RAILROAD.

In September, 1850, an act of Congress was passed granting lands to the State of Illinois for the purpose of constructing a railroad through Central Illinois. The legislature of Illinois in 1851 incorporated the Illinois Central Railroad, and the lands held in trust by the State were transferred to the company upon a compliance with the conditions of the charter. The road was completed through Macon county in 1854, from the north, and the entire line soon thereafter opened to the public.

The procurement of aid from the general government, by the donation of lands, was a subject that the people of the county had taken an interest in for several years prior to the passage of the act. It became a question in the election of representatives to the legislature, and was made one of the issues of the campaign of 1848. It is said that a senator from Macon county was the first to introduce and secure the passage of a resolution by the legislature requesting and urging our senators and representatives in congress to secure the desired aid from the general government. As elsewhere remarked, Senator Douglas, who was always alive to anything that had for its object the improvement of the State, and the benefit of our people; acting upon the resolution, secured the passage of the law, donating to the State for the use of the railroad, every alternate section for the distance of six miles upon each side of the proposed line.

There was some little apprehension existing for a while in reference to the location of the road through the county. An effort was made to locate the road six miles west of Decatur, crossing the river at what was, in early days, known as the "cut-off," and a survey upon this line was made, but through the exertions of Hon. E. O. Smith and other citizens of Decatur, the "cut-off route" was abandoned, and the present route selected, though said by the engineer, Chas. A. Tuttle, to be more expensive.

This road, by judicious management, and the capital derived from the sale of its lands, has always been upon a sound financial basis. Its treatment of its patrons has been such as to call for no great amount of complaint, for want of equipment or means and proper facilities for transportation. Its management has been such that but rarely are suits brought for the recovery of damages for negligence on the part of its agents.

The passenger cars upon the road have never been remarkable for their costliness or splendor of their appointments; yet are usually substantial, safe, and have all the necessaries for ease and comfort. Its employees have been well paid and selected with reference to their qualifications and abilities. Engineers, conductors and agents, who were in the employment of the company in 1854, still hold their positions.

There are 705 miles of road in Illinois, under the management of this company, distributed as follows:

Main line (Cairo to Dunleith)...................... 455 miles.
Chicago branch (Centralia to Chicago)............ .. 250 "

By an arrangement recently consummated this company has now the control of a road extending to New Orleans, from Cairo, making an entire line from either Sioux City or Chicago to New Orleans.

The average annual shipment forwarded by this road from Decatur, amounts to $25,000; and the receipts will double that amount, as shown by the books of the company. The ticket sales at the Decatur office do not vary far from $20,000 annually.

HISTORY OF MACON COUNTY.

DECATUR AND EAST ST. LOUIS RAILROAD.

This road was chartered in 1867 and built in 1868, under the management of the T., W. & W. R. R., and has since been under the control of that road. It runs to East St. Louis, a distance of 108 miles, and since the construction of the great bridge across the Mississippi its trains run into the city of St. Louis. This road is regarded as one of our best and most important roads, and should it be extended to Chicago, as it was intended that it should be, it will be second to none as a means of furnishing transportation to the markets for our producing people. When we have a direct outlet to both Chicago and St. Louis—the great cities of the southwest—then our railroad facilities will be most ample and complete. We sought to accomplish this by means of the

DECATUR AND STATE LINE RAILROAD,

the charter for which was more than once defeated by the Chicago & Alton Co. It is asserted by some of our best informed citizens that the construction of this road after the charter had been obtained was defeated through manipulations originating from the same source. We do not know where the blame lies for the loss to the people of this county of this very important road, but whoever was instrumental in it has a conscience inimical to the public interests of Macon county. The road was important; the subscriptions along the line were sufficient for its construction; it was under contract and partially built; and Decatur six years ago anticipated soon being the principal city on the shortest line of road through the most fertile portions of the state, between *the* cities of the northwest, but awoke one morning and found the work suspended and the people along the entire line dumbfounded, like the workmen at the tower of Babel. But why, the author is unable to state.

PEKIN, LINCOLN AND DECATUR RAILROAD.

This road was chartered in 1861, and the charter amended in 1865, and constructed in 1871. It is 67 miles in length, and was leased by the T., W. & W. R. R. Co. at its completion, and has been under its management until 1876. It extends from Decatur to Pekin on the Illinois river, but its trains run through to Peoria.

THE DECATUR, MONTICELLO AND CHAMPAIGN R. R.

This road was constructed in the year 1873, and extends to Champaign, Ill., where it connects with the branch of the I. C. R. R., north, and the I., B. & W. R. R., east. It is now consolidated with the latter road, and is known as the Decatur branch of the Indianapolis, Bloomington & Western. It secures to us competition for eastern transportation.

DECATUR, SULLIVAN AND MATTOON R. R.

This road was chartered in 1861, and constructed in 1872, and extends to Mattoon, Ill. It was intended that this road should be extended through to Grayville, on the Ohio river, securing to us a southeastern travel and transportation but financial embarrassments have prevented its construction farther than Mattoon.

ILLINOIS MIDLAND R. R.

This is a consolidation of the Peoria, Atlanta & Decatur and Paris & Decatur Railroads. The road was constructed in 1872. Its line extends from Terre Haute, Ind., to Peoria, Ill.

Entire length .... 176 miles.
Entire length in Illinois .... 168 miles.

INDIANAPOLIS, DECATUR AND SPRINGFIELD R. R.

This road was chartered in 1850 as the Indiana & Illinois Central R. R., but was not constructed until 1872, and then finished only to Montezuma, on the Wabash. It is thought that it will shortly be constructed through to Indianapolis, and when done will be one of our most important roads. The name was changed in 1876.

AGRICULTURE.

This is the oldest branch of industry. It needs no words of commendation. Those who engage in tilling the soil form a large and very important element in society—a necessary element, and one just as dignified, when duly appreciated, as any of the others. In character, influence and relative position the agricultural class is what its members make it. It is high or low, as its masses are energetic, educated and skilled. In some localities the sun seems to be always shining. The farmers are busy the year round. Their farms are neat and well fenced. Their barns and outhouses are painted and in perfect repair. They have reapers, mowers, corn planters and all the modern improvements in the art. The dwellings are neat and comfortable, and their occupants seem always cheerful, and are intelligent, refined, social, industrious, and are always glad to have you come and see them. This is what people call "a good neighborhood to live in," "a good farming community," etc., etc.

There is another community, sometimes but a few miles distant, occupying a position at the other extreme. There seems to be always a cloud over it. It is hedged in and about with *ennui* and lassitude and laziness of the most reckless sort. The fields are haggard and torn and lacerated, and seem to have been cultivated in a haphazard sort of a way without reference to the points of the compass. The fences are racked and partially down, and where standing seem to cling to the shrubs and trees for support. The plows, reapers and mowers stand in the field, as they were left when last used. The farm house is in the last stages of decay, and ready to tumble down upon the slightest provocation. Its doors are old and weatherbeaten and fasten with a latch and string. The windows are dilapidated and pretty well filled up with hats of ancient date or pillows sable and dusky hued. The inmates are living specimens of inertia, dejected and downhearted, whose whole travel seems to have been over stony roads. They have a corduroy look about them, as though they had spent many weary nights in pondering over Mark Twain's Roughing It. The head of the household trudges about with one boot and one shoe and a single suspender, as though he was continually weighing in his mind the question whether he ought or ought not to. His "old woman" —that is his wife—poor soul, does as well as she can, endures all, works hard and dies young, an object of pity and neglect. The children, a half dozen or more, grow up in rags and penury, half starved, half clothed, half educated and sore-eyed, and are continually knocked and buffeted about in the world, and pricked and stung by the ragged edges of poverty. The barn is a cross between a rail pen and a "straw-stack," and is "fearfully and wonderfully made." The team of "critters" is a bona-fide spectacle pitiful to look at, lame and often blind. The yellow dogs that lie in the front door yard have scarcely sufficient energy to recognize a stranger or bark a good square bark. They look as though they wanted something and did not know where to get it.

Such are pictures of the two classes of farmers. The latter class is becoming rare in this age of steam and progress. They have been rooted out and gone off " where it aint so thickly settled."

There is a most perfect harmony existing between the agriculturalist and the manufacturer, the mechanic and professional man. There is no agency at work, when their relations are properly understood, that tears the one down to build the other up. They each have a work to perform and a sphere to fill. Our whole industrial system is like a perfect machine. Some parts may be more powerful and exert a greater influence than others, yet all the parts are of equal utility. The farmer is not independent, nor is the mechanic, the laborer, the lawyer, the doctor, nor any one who labors with muscle or brain.

We do not deem it material to devote space to notice the different agricultural and horticultural products of the county. They are substantially the same throughout Central Illinois. Corn is now, and no doubt will remain our staple product. As our prairies were being opened up for cultivation, and when the soil was very rich, a very large acreage of wheat was sown. But of late years the wheat crop has been on the decline so that now it is fequently the case that we do not raise enough of this cereal for home consumption.* This is owing to several reasons; the decline in price since the war, the destruction of late years by chinch-bugs, rust, severe winters, etc., the labor required to produce it, as compared with corn, and other products. If the amount of labor that is bestowed upon wheat culture in St. Clair and other wheat-growing counties, was expended here, our wheat crops would double their present yield. The timber soil of this county is better adapted to wheat raising than that of the prairie; which, no doubt, is owing to the protection the wheat receives from the snow lying upon the ground more evenly upon timber fields, and also owing to the fact of there being more clay in the timber soil, which seems to be better adapted to prevent the injury arising from constant freezing and thawing. The soil is more compact, and seems to protect the roots better.

But little spring wheat is sowed, and very little rye and barley—though good crops are raised of both the latter. Of late years a great deal more attention is being given to pasturage. Formerly but a small proportion of our farms was devoted to meadows, but now many of our farmers devote more space to grass than to grain. Our soil and climate are admirably adapted to the culture of timothy and clover, and the labor required for the preservation of these crops is insignificant when compared to that required for corn and wheat. Oats are raised in sufficient amount for home use, but not largely for foreign market.

A great deal of attention is now being given to the raising of hogs and cattle. No doubt much more attention will be given to this as our country grows older, than to the raising of grain for the market. The stock of hogs now in the county is far superior to that which we had in our early history; while our beef cattle have improved equally as much. One of our oldest butchers states that our cattle now upon the market for home consumption will average at least one-third better than they did twenty years ago. The "scrubs" and "hazle-splitters" of the last quarter of a century are growing scarcer day by day. It costs no more to raise a good cow or a good hog than a poor one, if indeed as much. Better stock—thanks to our Pickrells, Taylors, Barbers, and a host of other names we might mention—is upon exhibition now at our county fairs than

---

* It is estimated that three-fourths of the wheat consumed by our mills in 1875 and 1876, is foreign wheat.

could be found at our State fairs a few years since. As a breeder of stock, especially short-horns, James H. Pickrell of Harristown, is known among stock men throughout North America and Great Britain. He holds the position of President of the North American Short-horn Association. In the fall of 1875 he visited England and Scotland, and collected a herd of cattle perhaps not excelled in the United States or Canada.

There are now but few sheep in the county—11,349 in 1870, and 6,538 in 1876.

We close this chapter with the following brief table, compiled from the assessor's books for the years 1860, 1870, 1875 and 1876, though the valuations affixed, of course, are much below the real value:

1860.

ARTICLES.	NO.	VALUE.
Horses	5,079	$213,300
Neat Cattle	11,601	125,737
Mules and Asses	482	23,265
Sheep	3,783	4,007
Hogs	13,728	35,109
Improved lands (acres)	305,558	2,315,909
Improvements on land		698,792
Acres in corn	49,410	
Acres in wheat	16,322	
Acres other field products	7,611	

1870.

Horses	10,888	295,765
Neat Cattle	15,623	160,754
Mules and Asses	1,480	45,684
Sheep	11,549	5,453
Hogs	30,102	58,862
Improved lands (acres)	305,558	2,315,909
Improvements on land		648,792
Acres in corn	91,929	
Acres in wheat	30,145	
Acres other field products	25,085	

1875.

Horses	12,568	659,603
Cattle	19,617	404,128
Mules and Asses	2,287	161,014
Hogs	45,750	195,242
Improved lands (acres)	344,621	8,881,791

1875.

ARTICLES.	NO.	VALUE.
Unimproved lands	23,321	$390,679
Acres in corn	156,673	
Acres in wheat	13,718	
Acres in oats	24,163	
Acres in meadow	18,171	
Acres other field products	9,279	
Acres in pasture	47,209	

1876.

Horses	12,607	608,111
Cattle	18,931	360,569
Mules and Asses	2,438	156,748
Sheep	6,538	11,737
Hogs	38,886	179,001
Improved lands (acres)	340,218	8,718,936
Unimproved lands	21,021	412,953
Acres in corn	146,244	
Acres in wheat	6,733	
Acres in oats	24,817	
Acres in meadow	20,385	
Acres other field products	5,905	
Acres in pasture	49,986	

CHAPTER VIII.

Our Cities, Towns and Villages.

THE CITY OF DECATUR.*

The history of a county and that of its county seat are so intimately connected that it is difficult to speak of them separately; their interests are the same; that which advances one advances the other; that which retards the one retards alike the other. But we deem it necessary to devote a short space to the history of the city proper. We sometimes observe the town advance more rapidly

---

*NOTE.—STEPHEN DECATUR—This city was named after that gallant commander Stephen Decatur, of whom it is proper in this connection to give a short sketch of his brilliant history, successes, triumphs and the unfortunate termination of his earthly career. This "Bayard of the seas" was born in Worcester county, Maryland, Jan. 5, 1779. At the age of nine years young Stephen made a sea voyage with his father, from which, no doubt, he received the impressions that determined his course of life. His early education was received in Philadelphia, where he returned soon after the evacuation of that city by the British. He was a leader in all the amusements at school, and was called "Capt. Dick." He next was sent to Pennsylvania University, where he remained but a short time.

We next find him assisting in the construction of the frigate "United States," which he afterwards commanded, and which became famous in our country's naval history. He went with Commodore Barry on board the United States on a cruise through the west Indies, to suppress the depredations of the French privateers. On this voyage several successful encounters were had with French vessels in the vicinity of Martinique, in all of which Decatur, then but twenty years of age, manifested the bold, daring disposition of his future life, and ren-

than the surrounding country, and *vice versa;* but that has not been the case with Macon county and the city of Decatur. They have kept step by step in their advancement in wealth, improvements, population and general prosperity. Political demagogues are sometimes, for their own selfish purposes, disposed to array the city against the country or the country against the city, as the case may be; but to the true observer their interests are one and inseparable, as a moment's reflection will demonstrate. The man that takes no interest in his county town and its advancement is an

---

dered signal services for which he was made lieutenant. He was next engaged in cruising along the coast from Georgia to Cape Cod, protecting our commercial interests. He then made two voyages across the ocean, after which a treaty of peace was declared between the United States and France, which put an end to the naval prospects of Decatur for the time being.

The United States soon after sent a squadron to the Mediterranean to stop the depredations of the Tripolines and Algerines upon our commerce. Decatur was commissioned first lieutenant under Capt. Bainbridge, on board the Essex, which was stationed to guard the coasts and port of Tripoli, where he remained until 1802, when the Essex was relieved by the Chesapeake, under Com. Morris, when he returned home. After spending a few weeks at home his restless spirit induced him to join the New York, under Capt. James Barrow, with whom he again set sail for the Mediterranean in Sept., 1802. He remained but a short time and returned home, where he was put in charge of the Argus, on which he sailed to Gibraltar, where he assumed command of the schooner Enterprise, with which, on the 23d of October, 1803, he captured the Tripoline craft Mostico, with 70 prisoners. In the early part of 1804, Captain Bainbridge, being a prisoner in the City of Tripoli, and the gallant old ship Philadelphia having been captured, which, with its forty guns, well manned, effectually guarded the harbor of Tripoli, it was determined that this ship should be burned, but who was to undertake the hazardous experiment? Decatur volunteered his services. With his little schooner Intrepid, with but a few guns, assisted by the Siren, he set sail for Tripoli, where he arrived July 4, 1804. They cautiously approached the harbor where the Philadelphia lay anchored, and on a dark night the Intrepid, with Decatur at the helm, came up to within a few yards of their coveted prize before being discovered. They lashed the Intrepid to the towering form of the Philadelphia and Decatur and his brave men jumped on deck of the latter, drew their swords and rushed upon the panic stricken crew, and in five minutes killed and drove them pell-mell into the water. The cables of the Philadelphia were cut and she was set on fire, floating at the mercy of the winds. "As the streaming flame circled around mast and boom, flinging its lurid glare over the waste of water, the old vessel floated along until her final explosion. The exultant shouts of her captors penetrated the prison walls of Tripoli and proclaimed speedy liberation."

enemy of his county; and the resident of the town that likewise disregards the interests of the surrounding county, has studied but little of the relative demands of each, and fails to see their mutual interests, or his own interest even.

The land on which the original *Town of Decatur* was located was entered by Parmenius Smallwood, Easton Whitton and Chas. Prentice, for which, at the time of the location of the town, they had received no patent from the government. On the 20th day of June, 1829, they entered into bond with the then county commis-

---

A short time afterwards he commanded a division of gunboats at the bombardment of Tripoli, in which he was engaged in several hand-to-hand encounters and was wounded with a pike in the hands of the captain, who had assassinated his brother but a few minutes before. Decatur was now made post-captain, and received a sword for his gallantry displayed. At 25 he was in command of the Constitution, one of the finest vessels in the service. With this he proceeded to Malta, and in a short time peace was declared and Decatur returned home, where he was met with demonstrations of honor and esteem.

Soon after the close of the Tripoline war, England and France began their system of spoliation on our commerce, and Decatur was placed in command of a squadron on the Chesapeake. When the American embargo was declared, Decatur was placed in command of the frigate Chesapeake. More elaborate preparations were authorized by Congress. Among the vessels then put in preparation was the United States, the vessel he had assisted in constructing, and on which he started in his naval career. He was transferred to the squadron of Com. Rogers on June 21, 1811, and started on a cruise with a view of attacking a British fleet bound for Jamaica. The fleet captured six vessels and returned to Boston. On the 25th, he met, near the Island of Madeira, the English ship Macedonian, commanded by the experienced and highly accomplished Capt. Corden. After a hard engagement, the latter surrendered, with 104 killed and wounded and the whole crew prisoners. Decatur lost 12 killed and wounded. He then returned home. Great applause heralded his arrival. Resolutions and medals from Congress and state legislatures were voted, and he was everywhere proclaimed the champion of the American navy.

The Macedonian and Hornet were now added to Decatur's command, and he placed his squadron in Long Island Sound. In 1814 he was again placed in command of the President. In January, 1815, he fell in with the British squadron, about fifty miles east of Long Island, and after a bloody engagement was, for the first time in his career, compelled to surrender. He was sent to Bermuda, and thence home. In the meantime peace was declared.

He was not content with peace, however. The piratical Algerines had been creating havoc with our commerce, and Decatur was soon in command of a squadron en-route for Gibraltar, on arriving at which place the whereabouts of the Algerine fleet was ascertained, and he immediately started in pursuit and

sioners, that after they should receive a patent they would convey to the commissioners a deed of gift for 20 acres of land, on which the town had been located on the 10th day of April, previous.

On the 1st day of June, 1829, at a meeting of the county commissioners' court an order was made as follows:

"*Ordered*, That Benj. R. Austin, county surveyor for the county of Macon, be and he is hereby required to lay off the town of Decatur, in said county, after the form of Shelbyville, and make and return to one of the commissioners of this court a complete plat of the same, on or before the first day of July next."

Under this order the survey was made and acknowledged on the 7th day of July following. At the same term of court the following order was also made by the commissioners:

---

soon overtook and captured a part of the squadron. He pushed on to Algiers and dictated peace to the frightened inhabitants, which closed forever the Algerine war and Algerine piratical thefts.

Notwithstanding the treaty made with the Tripolitans, ensuing the war with that power above referred to, they continued to harrass our commerce in connection with the pirates of Tunis. Decatur left Algiers without authority from his government, and proceeded to Tunis and forced an indemnity. Thence he proceeded to Tripoli, and the Bashaw, not willing again to meet the gallant Decatur, likewise agreed upon terms.

Decatur then returned home, where he met the same enthusiastic reception as before. He was appointed Commissioner of the Navy, which post he filled with credit, which concluded his brilliant naval career, which will be honored and respected as long as our flag floats over the seas.

The gallant commander's life was now shortly to close. We would gladly drop the pen at this period in this wonderful man's career. Unfortunately, at that period, the "code of honor," that relic of barbarism was still tolerated. On the 22d of March, 1820, he fell, mortally wounded in a duel with Com. Barrow, at Bladensburg. He fell saying: "I am mortally wounded, and I wish that I had fallen in defense of my country." He sank rapidly, beseeching his friends to look after his wife, whom he tenderly loved, and not to him.

The following notice heralded to the world the unfortunate occurrence: "A hero has fallen. Com. Decatur, one of the first officers of our navy, the pride of his country; the gallant, noble-hearted gentleman is no more. Mourn Columbia, for one of thy brightest stars is set—a son without fear, without reproach, in the fullness of his fame, in the prime of his usefulness, has descended to his tomb." His remains repose on a beautiful site overlooking Washington and the potomac.

A worthy name for a rising young city of the west to assume.

"*Ordered*, That a sale of lots take place in the town of Decatur, in this county, on the 10th day of July next, on the following terms, to-wit: a credit of twelve months will be given, and note with approved security will be required, and that the clerk of this court is required to advertise the sale in the paper printed in Vandalia until the day of the sale."

At the next term of court we find that D. McCall was allowed $500 "for money paid to R. Blackwell, for warrants and advertising the sale of lots in the town of Decatur."

At the sale on the 10th day of July, the first lot sold was lot No. 2, in block 3, where Priest's Hotel now stands, which being a "corner lot," was bid in by John Manly, for $53.50. The second lot sold was lot 6, in block 1, where Armstrong's drug store now is, which was bid in for $12.00.

The first house erected in town was by James Renshaw—"Uncle Jimmy Renshaw," he was called—on lot 3, block 3, just north of Priest's Hotel. The second house erected was by Philip D. Williams, on lot 4, block 1, where the store of Close & Griswold now stands. "Philip" kept a livery stable in those early days—or rather a place for the "entertainment of beasts." There was a very large log lying in north Water street, nearly opposite the entrance to the present court room. Upon this log boxes had been nailed or trenches cut in which the horses were fed. There was also a log lying in front of Renshaw's house, which we omitted to mention was a tavern—the first in Decatur—upon this log, in early days, card playing was carried on. It was the card table, and rather conspicuous, we should say. Whether any fortunes were lost and won, we are unable to say; but, judging from the court records, and the number of entries of "indictments for gaming," entered thereon, it appears that gaming was a very common pass-time, and the number of "convictions" would indicate that there was also playing "for money," and the names of the parties charged, would further indicate that the "heads of town" were accessories, if not principals, in the enchanting games.

The officers of the town, and afterwards city of Decatur, since its organization, are as follows:

HISTORY OF MACON COUNTY.

BOARD OF TRUSTEES.

1836.—Richard Oglesby, President. Trustees: Wm. T. Crissey, G. R. White, *Wm. Webb, Thomas Cowan, †H. M. Gorin, Henry Butler, Landy Harrall. †Andrew Love, Clerk; James Carter and Wm. Webb, Constables.

1838.—†Joseph Williams, Henry Snyder, Presidents. Trustees: James Renshaw, James F. Montgomery, George R. White, Henry Prather. Edmund McClellan, Clerk; Richard Oglesby, J. P. Hickcok, Treasurer; John S. Adamson, Assessor; William Radcliff and Thomas Cowan, Supervisors; J. H. Elliott, Constable.

1839.—Trustees: William T. Crissey, S. B. Dewees, J. M. Fordice, ‡James F. Montgomery.

1839.—Kirby Benedict, President. Trustees: John S. Adamson, Thomas Cowan, Samuel B. Dewees, Jesse H. Elliott, William T. Crissey, Thomas H. Read. H. M. Gorin, Clerk; George R. White, Treasurer; H. Prather, Assessor and Collector; G. W. Gilbrath, Zebulon Cantrall and William Webb, Constables.

1840.—Joseph King, President. Trustees: Henry Goodman, William Cantrill, B. F. Oglesby, David Wright, John G. Speer, David E. Ralls. H. M. Gorin, Clerk; G. R. White, Treasurer; I. C. Pugh, Collector; William Webb, Constable.

‖ 1841.—Thomas P. Rodgers, President. Trustees: J. H. Elliott, D. E. Ralls, G. R. White, Henry Goodman, Benjamin R. Austin, J. D. Tait. J. S. Post, Clerk; J. H. Read, Treasurer; Joseph Stevens, Assessor and Collector; Wm. Webb, Constable.

1846.—David Crone, President. Trustees: Elijah Krone, Joseph Kauffman, Michael Elson, Thomas H. Read. E. B. Hale, Clerk; G. A. Smith, Constable.

1847.—D. Crone, President. Trustees; J. H. Read, M. Elson, Joseph Kauffman. Nathan P. West, Clerk; E. McClellan, Constable; B. H. Cassell, Assessor.

* Died. † Resigned. ‡ It does not appear from the record that these last named trustees ever met, but that there was an election held on the 6th day of May, 1839, under a special act incorporating the town of Decatur, at which election another board was chosen.

‖ This was the last meeting of the Trustees of the town of Decatur for five years.

1848.—J. H. Elliott, President. Trustees: H. Prather, H. Armstrong, E. O. Smith, Jos. King. N. P. West, Clerk; E. McClellan, Constable; B. H. Cassell, Assessor and Treasurer.

1849.—Joseph Kauffman, President. Trustees: H. J. Armstrong, J. H. Elliott, Jos. King, W. S. Crissey. N. P. West, Clerk; B. H. Cassell, Assessor and Treasurer; H. Goodman, Constable.

1850.—Joseph King, President. Trustees: W. J. Stamper, Wm. Prather, C. H. Pringle, Wm. Wheeler. B. H. Cassell, Clerk; Wm. Wheeler, Constable; B. H. Cassell, Assessor and Treasurer.

1851.—Wm. S. Crissey, President. Trustees: Wm. Prather, C. H. Pringle, Joseph King, W. J. Stamper. B. H. Cassell, Clerk, Treasurer and Assessor.

1852.—W. J. Stamper, President. Trustees: W. S. Crissey, Wm. Prather, C. H. Pringle, Jos. King. B. H. Cassell, Clerk, Treasurer and Assessor.

1853.—Wm. Prather, President. Trustees: W. S. Crissey, W. J. Stamper, Joseph King, John Ricketts. B. H. Cassell, Clerk, Treasurer and Assessor.

1854.—William Prather, President. Trustees: William J. Stamper, William S. Crissey, Joseph King, Thomas H. Wingate. B. H. Cassell, Clerk.

1854.—Thomas H. Wingate, President. Trustees: William S. Crissey, Willam Martin, Elias Tanner, John Ricketts. B. H. Cassell, Clerk; H. Churchman, Constable.

1855.—Thomas H. Wingate, President. Trustees: A. L. Kellar, J. R. Gorin, William S. Crissey, William Martin. B. H. Cassell, Clerk.

CITY COUNCIL.

*1856.—John P. Post, Mayor. Aldermen: Frank Priest, 1st ward; E. O. Smith, 2d ward; J. R. Gorin, S. P. Ohr, 3d ward; J. J. Ballentine, H. Taylor, 4th ward. C. C. Post, Clerk and Attorney.

* An election was held for city officers, under a special charter, on the 7th of January, 1856.

1857.—William A. Barnes, Mayor. Aldermen: George Goodman, Joseph Mills, 1st ward; H. B. Durfee, George Dempsey, 2d ward; A. T. Hill, John P. Post, 3d ward; Israel B. Gring, Geo. Wessels, 4th ward. J. P. Boyd, Clerk and Attorney.

1858.—James Shoaff, Mayor. Aldermen: Joseph Mills, J. B. Trull, 1st ward; H. B. Durfee, Isaac D. Jennings, 5d ward; John P. Post, Samuel F. Greer, 3d ward; George Wessels, O. Powers, 4th ward. S. S. Goode, Clerk and Attorney.

1859.—A. T. Hill, Mayor. Aldermen: James Simpson, J. L. Mansfield, 1st ward; John W. Bear, M. Haworth, 2d ward; Samuel F. Greer, William Lintner, 3d ward; O. Powers, J. C. Benton, 4th ward. S. S. Goode, Clerk and Attorney.

1860.—Sheridan Wait, Mayor. Aldermen: James Simpson, S. S. Hale, 1st ward; E. McNabb, William J. Scanlan, 2d ward; Wm. Lintner, Peter M. Wykoff, 3d ward; J. C. Benton, John L. Peake, 4th ward. J. R. Gorin, Clerk and Attorney.

1861.—E. O. Smith, Mayor. Aldermen: F. Priest, long term, Chas. A. Tuttle, short term, 1st ward; James Millikin, William J. Scanlan, 2d ward; W. H. Bramble, P. M. Wykoff, 3d ward; Joel C. Benton, long term, William A. Barnes, short term, 4th ward. J. R. Gorin, Clerk and Attorney.

1862.—Thomas O. Smith, Mayor. Aldermen: F. Priest, D. H. Elwood, 1st ward; James Millikin, Lowber Burrows, 2d ward; Henry Goodman, W. H. Bramble, 3d ward; Joel C. Benton, Benson Henkle, 4th ward. J. R. Gorin, Clerk and Attorney.

1863.—J. J. Peddecord, Mayor. Aldermen: D. H. Elwood, David S. Hughes, 1st ward; James Millikin, Lowber Burrows, 2d ward; William H. Bramble, Henry Goodman, 3d ward; John Ullerich, Benson Henkle, 4th ward. J. R. Gorin, Clerk and Attorney.

1864.—J. J. Peddecord, Mayor. Aldermen: C. A. Tuttle, D. L. Hughes, 1st ward; M. Y. Givler, James Millikin, 2d ward; M. Forstmeyer, J. G. Starr, 3d ward; Benson Henkle, long term, T. B. Albert, short term, 4th ward. K. H. Roby, Clerk and Attorney.

† Resigned.   * To fill vacancy.

1865.—Franklin Priest, Mayor. Aldermen: Charles A. Tuttle, Charles H. Fuller, 1st ward; M. Y. Givler, William J. Usrey, 2d ward; M. Forstmeyer, E. A. Barnwell, 3d ward; †Benson Henkle S. T. Trowbridge, 4th ward. K. H. Roby, Clerk and Attorney.

1866.—Franklin Priest, Mayor. †Charles H. Fuller, S. F. Hawley, 1st ward; W. J. Usrey, E. McNabb, 2d ward; E. A. Barnwell, M. Forstmeyer, 3d ward; G. Howell, short term, H. Muller, long term, 4th ward. †A. B. Bunn, Clerk and Attorney.

1867.—John K. Warren, Mayor. Aldermen: S. F. Hawley, Joseph Mills, 1st ward; E. McNabb, 2d ward; M. Forstmeyer, J. R. Gorin, 3d ward; H. Muller, B. F. Dodson, 4th ward. C. H. Fuller, Register.

1868.—Isaac C. Pugh, Mayor. Aldermen: D. P. Elwood, Joseph Mills, 1st ward; L. L. Haworth, S. Burrows, 2d ward; M. Forstmeyer, J. R. Gorin, 3d ward; B. F. Dodson, H. Prather, 4th ward. C. H. Fuller, Register.

1869.—Wm. L. Hammer, Mayor. Aldermen: D. P. Elwood, D. S. Shellabarger, 1st ward; L. L. Haworth, J. L. Libby, 2d ward; M. Forstmeyer, G. S. Simpson, 3d ward; H. Prather, W. F. Busher, 4th ward. C. H. Fuller, Register.

1870.—F. Priest, Mayor. Aldermen: †E. M. Misner, D. S. Shellabarger, 1st ward; Benj. Dill, *E. McNabb, 2d ward; G. S. Simpson, M. Forstmeyer, 3d ward; W. F. Busher, E. Harpstrite, 4th ward. C. H. Fuller, Register.

1871.—E. M. Misner, Mayor. Aldermen: Joseph Mills, *Wm. J. Myers, 1st ward; Benj. Dill, E. McNabb, 2d ward; M. Forstmeyer, Wm. H. Bramble, 3d ward; E. Harpstrite, Wm. Gabbler, 4th ward. C. H. Fuller, Register.

1872.—D. S. Shellabarger, Mayor. Aldermen: Joseph Mills, W. J. Myers, 1st ward; F. Hardy, E. McNabb, 2d ward; A. T. Hill, Wm. H. Bramble, 3d ward; Wm. Gabbler, B. B. Richards, 4th ward. George P. Hardy, Register; Thomas Lee, Attorney ; M. K. Hatch, Treasurer; G. V. Loring, City Engineer; John W. Haworth, Marshal.

1873.—Martin Forstmeyer, Mayor. Aldermen: Geo. Stare, W. J. Myers, 1st ward; Frank Hardy, L. F. Muzzy, 2d ward; A. T. Hill, T. J. Able, 3d ward; James Peake, B. B. Richards, 4th ward;

Joseph Leake, A. Shoemaker, 5th ward. Geo. Hardy, Register; I. A. Buckingham, Attorney; G. V. Loring, City Engineer; M. K. Hatch, Treasurer; John W. Haworth, Marshal.

1874.—F. Priest, Mayor. Aldermen: H. W. Waggoner, Geo. Stare, 1st ward; E. McNabb, L. F. Muzzy, 2d ward; J. T. Able, Isaac Ehrman, 3d ward; James Peake, J. W. Butman, 4th ward; Joseph Leake, R. N. Mills, 5th ward. Geo. P. Hardy, Register; I. A. Buckingham, Attorney; M. K. Hatch, Treasurer; Geo. V. Loring, City Engineer; John W. Haworth, Marshal.

1875.—R. H. Merriweather, Mayor. Aldermen: H. W. Waggoner, W. J. Myers, 1st ward; Wm. M. Boyd, H. B. Durfee, 2d ward; Isaac Ehrman, B. F. Stephens, 3d ward; James Peake, J. W. Butman, 4th ward; Joseph Leake, R. N. Mills, 5th ward. George P. Hardy, Register; M. K. Hatch, Treasurer; I. A. Buckingham, Attorney; John W. Haworth, Marshal; S. Burgess, City Engineer.

1876.—W. B. Chambers, Mayor. Aldermen: W. J. Myers, W. J. Wayne, 1st ward; H. B. Durfee, L. F. Muzzy, 2d ward; I. W. Ehrman, B. F. Stephens, 3d ward; James Peake, Edward Harpstrite, 4th ward; Joseph Leake, Kilburn Harwood, 5th ward. Geo. P. Hardy, Register; I. A. Buckingham, Attorney; M. K. Hatch, Treasurer; S. Burgess, City Engineer; John W. Haworth, Marshal.

ITS WATER WORKS.

The Sangamon river furnishes ample facilities to the city of Decatur for fire protection and water privileges. It runs within a short distance of the southern limits of the city. At the most available point on the river, just above the crossing of the Illinois Central Railroad, and above the drainage and sewerage from the city, is located the city water-works. There has probably been no acquisition to the city, since the construction of the railroads, that has added more to its advancement and permanent improvement than the water-works. At the time of their construction there were a few grumblers opposed to their construction, for reasons they no doubt thought were plausible, but at the present time it is safe to say that there is not any enemy to them. It is a remark often made that for fire protection alone more property, in value, has been saved by means of the water-works than the entire cost of their construction and operation. They were constructed under the direction of the city council, in 1871, at a cost of $35,000, and the additional mains, machinery, and other incidental expenditures up to the present time amount in the aggregate to $130,000, which has been paid with the exception of the original debt. The works are constructed upon the holly system; the engines being located at the river, and the water forced from that point to all parts of the city. Hydrants are placed at different points upon all the principal streets, so that by the attachment of hose to them, we have what is equal to a steam fire engine at the corner of almost every block in the city. The mains are tapped by persons desiring the use of the water for domestic, manufacturing and other purposes, and the revenues derived from this source are now about equal to the expenses of running the works, including labor, repairs, fuel, etc. There are about 8½ miles of pipes laid, and 81 fire plugs, which are being extended from time to time, as necessity requires. The capacity of the works is about eight hundred thousand gallons per day, which will be sufficient to meet the demand for years. The water furnished being filtered, is pure, and suitable for all domestic purposes, in fact is very much preferable to that obtained from the wells in the business part of town. The water is not impregnated to any considerable extent with lime deposits, which renders it suitable for manufacturing purposes.

FIRE DEPARTMENT.

In connection with the water works, it is proper to notice the Decatur Fire Department. It is, as at present organized, perhaps as efficient as any similar organization in the State. The companies, though unpaid, are prompt and energetic. The fire apparatus of the various companies is excellent, and kept in good condition, and is controlled by the companies with almost as much skill as is displayed by the regular paid companies in our large cities.

The Hook and Ladder Company was first organized, which was in June, 1868. Some of the members of this company are among our most wealthy merchants and business men. At present it has a membership of fifty men, and is well uniformed, and has all the implements pertaining to such companies. Homes Cloyd, foreman; Enos Kepler, 1st assistant; Chas. Fletcher, 2d assistant.

Rescue Hose Company, No. 1, was organized in 1871; W. W. Foster is foreman; George Craft, 1st assistant; N. Pringle, 2d assistant.

Eldorado Hose Company No. 2, was organized in 1871; Andrew Shoemaker is foreman; John Sutler, 1st assistant; .... 2d assistant.

Neptune Hose Company No. 3, was organized in 1875; W. J. Wayne is foreman; Samuel Funk, 1st assistant; James Hughes, 2d assistant.

The department is under the control of a chief and two assistants, viz: H. B. Durfee, chief; William Dodson, 1st assistant; John Ulrich, 2d assistant.

MAROA, ILLINOIS.

This is the largest and most important town, except Decatur, within the limits of Macon county, and is located 13 miles north of the latter city. It is situated at the junction of the Illinois Central and Illinois Midland Railroads. The original plat of the town was jointly laid out by the "Associated Land Company" and the "I. C. R. R. Co." The Illinois Central Railroad was opened to the public in 1854, and that may be stated as the commencement of the town of Maroa. Mr. John Crocker was appointed the first agent of the road, which position he held until 1866.

The first house built in Maroa was in the fall of 1855, by G. J. Schenck, which was then, and still is used by him as a dwelling; part of it, however, has been used as a store-room.

The second house erected was also by Mr. Schenck, but was for Mr. Barndt, in 1856; and Mr. Friedman erected the next two—a dwelling and a store-house. He started the first regular store in Maroa, and he has continued in business to the present, and is the oldest store-keeper in Maroa.

In 1858 Wm. Greer erected the "Prairie Hotel," which was the first hotel, though prior, and even since that time, Mr. Schenck's hospitable home has alwas been a place open to the weary traveler. In the same year the first school house was erected in Maroa, and Robert Collins was the first school teacher. The present Maroa school house was erected in 1866, at a cost of $7,000, and furnishes accommodations for 200 pupils.

Maroa Lodge No. 314, I. O. O. F., was organized May 3, 1865, and the following officers installed: Thomas Hunter, N. G.; M. Friedman, V. G.; O. J. Harlow, S.; James Huff, P. S.; Jonah Lingle, Treasurer. The lodge now numbers about 75 members.

Maroa Lodge No. 454, A. F. A. M., was organized July 4, 1865, and the first officers installed were: John H. Crocker, W. M.; R. C. Crocker, S. W.; O. J. Harlow, J. W.; G. W. Conover, T.; A. C. Keever, S. D.; Jacob Cooper, J. D., and W. L. Webb, Tyler.

Maroa Lodge, No. 102, Order of Patrons of Husbandry, was organized January, 1873, with 27 members, with the following officers: J. B. Garvin, M.; Henry Jones, Overseer; J. B. Gardner, Lecturer; John Longstreet, Steward; A. Wykoff, Assistant; J. B. Parkhurst, Chaplain; W. P. Funk, Treasurer; Joseph Jones, Secretary; W. O. Williams, G. K.; Mrs. Emma Williams, Ceres; Miss Mary A. Garvin, Flora; Mrs. K. Cooper, Poma.

The Maroa Library Association was organized August 27, 1870, through the instrumentality of the Rev. J. A. Hood, and is at present organized under the State law. The library, though quite small, has been a source of improvement to its patrons, and no doubt will, in the course of a few years, become the nucleus of a library that will be an honor to its founders and the citizens of Maroa.— Among the liberal donors to this institution, as to all others that have the improvement of his fellow-citizens as their object and aim, we mention, specially, Elder John Crocker.

The Maroa Steam Flouring Mills were erected in 1866, by Conover Bros., at a cost of from fifteen to twenty thousand dollars. It has a capacity of about fifty thousand bushels per year, and is regarded as one of the best mills in Central Illinois. It is at present under the management of W. J. Compton.

The Maroa Steam Elevator was erected in 1867, by J. W. Richards & Co., of Chicago, but is now under the management of Messrs. Crocker & Co., and has a capacity for storage of 14,400 bushels, and can shell and load five hundred bushels per hour. We might mention still other business houses of Maroa, but space forbids.— We can truthfully say, however, that the business men of this town, as a class, are energetic and successful. In fact, the tact of the business men of Maroa has made the town what it is to-day. As a town, it has had no more natural advantages than many others in

Central Illinois that it has outstripped and quadrupled in population and advancement. As a shipping point, there are few, if any other places along the entire line of the I. C. R. R., that excel it. There has been shipped from this point, in a single year, as high as 650,000 bushels of grain. It is the second town in size in the county—the population at present being about 1,500—and has reached that point in business and commercial importance, which assures it a steady and onward progress. The town of Maroa was incorporated by special act of the legislature, March 7, 1867. Job A. Race, John B. Cary, Henry Stauffer, Joseph Wilson and Henry Jones, being the incorporators. Mr. Race was the first President of the Town Board, and Mr. Cary, Secretary. Maroa has four churches, viz: Presbyterian, Methodist-Episcopal, Methodist-Protestant, and Christian. The former was organized January 30, 1850, by the Rev. A. J. Norton, and its church edifice erected in 1867. It has a regular pastor, a large membership, Sunday school, etc. The Christian church was organized by Elder A. N. Page, May 4, 1868, and the present church edifice was erected the following year. The membership is large, and the Sunday school well attended.

The Methodist-Episcopal and Methodist-Protestant churches are in a good condition, so far as membership and progress are concerned. Their church edifices are ample in size, and meet the demands of respective congregations.

Maroa and surrounding community has supported a weekly newspaper for several years. The first paper published was the *Times*, in 1867; T. J. Sharp, editor. This was succeeded by the *Tablet*, and that in turn by the *Tribune*, in 1868; A. H. Corman, editor. This paper was removed in 1872, to Decatur, and was succeeded by the *News*, which is at present owned by Mr. Corman, and is an eight-page, forty-column sheet.

THE CITY OF MACON.

This place was incorporated as a city on the 19th of April, 1869. The first house built was commenced by Esquire A. J. Harris, one Sunday Morning in the spring of 1860. The first store-house was built by Charles Williams and James Seamens, in the year 1859. The first hotel was kept by the station agent, Mr. Ruby. After the incorporation of the town, the first officers were J. H. Matthews, Mayor; T. C. Drinkall, Clerk; and C. A. Turner, M. Dunlap, Charles Van Horn and Jacob Frick, Aldermen. Its present officers are C. A. Turner, Mayor; J. W. Harrah, Clerk; and James L. Hight, Daniel Kalips, J. D. Peters and William Whitaker, Aldermen.

In 1865, the present school house was erected at a cost of about $4,000. It has a capacity for about 250 pupils.

Macon Lodge, No. 467, A. F. A. M., was organized in 1865, and is in a flourishing condition.

There is also a Lodge of the I. O. G. T., No. 884, that has been in existence several years.

There are two large grain elevators in the town; one owned by W. Harbert & Co., and the other by N. Failing. The former was erected in 1874, and has a storage capacity of about thirty thousand bushels, and with its facilities can shell and load two thousand bushels of grain per day, and in the shipping season employs four or five men. The firm owning this elevator are W. Harbert and C. Dunkel; the former has been a resident of Illinois since 1874, and the latter since 1876. The "Macon" elevator was erected in 1867, by John Hatfield, Fletcher Miller, N. Failing and D. C. Webb, and is at present owned by Mr. Failing. This elevator has a storage capacity of twenty thousand bushels, and can shell and load five thousand bushels per day. This elevator and machinery cost in the neighborhood of twelve thousand dollars, and furnishes employment for four men. Mr. Failing came to Macon from Rock Island in 1863, and has represented his town in the board of supervisors for several years. He is a thorough and safe business man, and has done a great deal for the advancement of the interests of his town. Macon formerly was one of the best shipping points for grain on the I. C. Railroad, but the building of the town of Blue Mound, on the St. Louis branch of the T. W. & W., has taken from it one-third at least of its original shipping interest. The population at present is in the neighborhood of 650. The business men of Macon compare favorably with those of all our inland towns. It has four churches, viz: Methodist-Episcopal, Presbyterian, Catholic, and Lutheran—all of which are well sustained. The church edifice of the former was erected in 1865; the Presbyterian and Catholic in 1867, and the Lutheran in 1871.

BLUE MOUND.

Soon after the construction of the Decatur and East St. Louis Railroad, in 1868, this town sprung into existence, and has continued to increase in population and a commercial point of view from that time since. It has some residences and store-houses that would be a credit to a much larger place, and its streets often present a scene of activity and business astonishing to one not acquainted with the thriving, go-ahead character of its merchants and business men. There is more business transacted in some of our railroad towns in one day than there is in a week in towns of double their size in some of our eastern states; and Blue Mound is a fair illustration of the truthfulness of this remark. The town was laid out through the influence of Doctor Goltra, who owned at the time of the location of the railroad, the land upon which the town plat was laid out.

This town has its churches and school—all of which are in successful operation. It derived its name from two large mounds, situated not far distant. These mounds have been objects of speculation and curiosity to our citizens from the time of the first visit of white men to this vicinity. Whether they are of natural or artificial origin, will, in all probability, remain matters of conjecture, and upon which the writer, in this connection, does not deem it proper to add suggestions.

NIANTIC,

Is situated on the main line of the Wabash Railroad, west of Decatur, and is an energetic, lively town. It is surrounded by an excellent agricultural country, which was practically donated to Macon county, as elsewhere noticed, because it was thought to be absolutely worthless. Niantic and Niantic township present a marvelous outgrowth of the swampy appearance it presented in early days. It is affirmed by some of our early settlers that the swamp land commissioner could not have disposed of the whole township for ten cents per acre in the first settlement of the county. Now it is one of our best townships, and its town is one of our most thriving and energetic.

Niantic is the home of the erratic poetical genius, Captain Joab Wilkinson, who worships at the shrine of the muses, and whose daily conversation bubbles up with poetical gems from Milton and Burns.

HARRISTOWN,

Though situated too near Decatur to ever become large, deserves special mention as a shipping point for the surrounding country. It is the home of J. H. Pickrell, our famous breeder of short-horns, elsewhere noticed; also of M. G. Camron, who, as a member of our board of supervisors, has been faithful and vigilant in guarding the interests of the county.

WARRENSBURG,

In Illini township, has grown up within the last few years, since the construction of the Pekin, Lincoln & Decatur Railroad. As a point for the shipment of grain and stock it is destined to be of very considerable commercial importance.

MOUNT ZION,

Though until the construction of the P. & D. (now I. M.) Railroad, was without railroad facilities, has been known for a quarter of a century as the location of the Mt. Zion Seminary, which at one time, was a flourishing school. The village is located near the junction of the I. M. and M. S. & D. Railroad, and is in one of the oldest, wealthiest and earliest settled neighborhoods of the county.

FORSYTH,

Is situated on the I. C. Railroad; has an elevator, and is one of the best grain markets in the county.

ARGENTA AND OREANA,

On the I. B. & W. Railroad, are towns growing in importance and will, in a few years, become points of considerable commercial interest.

OAKLEY, SANGAMON, WHEATLAND, BOODY,

Are villages of local interest to their surrounding neighborhoods, and all have stores, and some of them elevators and other conveniences for shipping.

CHAPTER IX.

THE COMMON SCHOOLS.

A history of the county without noticing the educational interests, would be incomplete, and yet we are unable to give much valuable information in regard to the early school system of the county. The fact is the early schools of the county were like angel's visits are said to be, few and far between; and the whole educational system—if system it may be called—of Macon county, in common with the state, was almost without order or management. There were good schools taught, but as compared with the present system, and its advantages, they were far inferior. There were some good "school masters" in those days, who were very successful in rearing the tender minds and teaching the young ideas how to shoot; but the majority were but poorly qualified for the duties of instructors. The popular standard of education was low, owing to the peculiar incidents and surroundings of pioneer life. The country was sparsely settled, and the people generally poor; and however anxious they may have been for good educational advantages, it was utterly impossible to obtain them. But few who had qualified themselves for the profession of teaching wandered so far west. The school master was generally some unfortunate, poverty-stricken wretch that had been wafted to the outskirts of civilization, and had become snow-bound, water-bound, or frost-bitten, and was compelled to "take up a school" to keep soul and body together until a favorable opportunity presented itself, for him to get to his destination, or back to his home in the east. Not infrequently did it happen that a man was to be found who was too lazy, in the popular estimation, for anything else than a school teacher, who was induced to pass around his "subscription for signers," and "take up" a school! Some people seemed to have entertained the idea that laziness was one of the qualifications of a school teacher! The Biblical camel could about as well accomplish the needle's eye feat as one of these living specimens of inertia could properly manage and "keep a school," in those days, when the big boys were boiling over with mischief, and had no great respect for the restraint of the school room, any how. The teachers were, of necessity, poorly paid, and, all things considered, perhaps, rendered as much instruction in proportion to the compensation, as those of the present day. It was certainly no pleasant task in those days the teacher had to perform. He usually "boarded round" with the scholars, and in this respect was like a stray dog, having no fixed place of abode. He was compelled to make long and laborious journeys to and from his temporary stopping places; which, taken in connection with the fact that the poor fellow was often poorly clad, and possessed no great amount of vitality, at any rate, rendered him an object of mingled commiseration and pity. He was likewise made the target at which was hurled all the knotty questions of theology, mathematics, science and politics, that had descended down to the different households from generation to generation.

These knotty problems were piled on the poor pedagogue promiscuously, and in pell-mell order, as though he were a creature of infinite power, and had the ability to solve them, *seriatim*, by some magical power to the populace unknown. The teacher and big boys of the neighboring district poured in on the poor fellow all sorts of mathematical questions that would have puzzled the arithmetic makers themselves, and it was a forfeiture of his standing in the community if he did not furnish a solution and prove his demonstration by the rules of Smiley or Adams. It was not infrequent in later days that the school-master was put through a most critical examination on Kirkham or Smith, by *pater familias*, to determine his fitness to teach Sarah Jane the rudiments of English Grammar, and woe betide the unfortunate pedagogue if by chance he happened to transgress the *ipse dixit* of the inquisitor's favorite author. He was, also, the neighborhood calculator of interest on all the paid and unpaid notes of the community, and was also expected to furnish each family with the mathematical data as to the required number of hogs, at a given price, to purchase the adjoining forty acres at the next sale, at the land office. He was also expected to furnish to order reasonable and satisfactory arguments for combatting the heretical dogmas of preacher so-and-so, who had a short time previous came near capturing the whole neighborhood with his " new light" doctrines, or anti-total-depravity-theories.

He had, also, divers other difficulties to meet and overcome. He was usually compelled to court the good graces of the young men who were his pupils. They sometimes were disposed, on slight provocation, to plot treason against the government, which sometimes ripened into overt acts. It often happened that open rebellion existed, and the poor teacher was subjected to a pummeling at the hands of the refractory members of his school. At other times the parents themselves, for grievances they supposed justifiable, took the law into their own hands, and inflicted upon the offending master, a punishment entirely too serious for a well-regulated community to tolerate. An instance is related of one poor fellow who had offended his patrons, being compelled to make the best record known in the community, in the shape of a foot-race, being urged on and on, in front of a pair of brutal stogas which were propelled by an irate father. His coat-tails are said to have ever and anon floated high in air, at the touch of the swearing, raging, pursuing ursine. Whether, henceforth, the offending teacher became a wanderer, disconsolate and heart-broken, like Ichabod Crane, is not stated.

Other instances might be given where ye pedagogue was bound hand and foot by his pupils, taken by force of arms from his castle, as it were, and ducked in the creek or frog-pond, and that, too, when the temperature was almost as frigid as it is supposed to be on the north side of the icebergs in Iceland. There was, also, a habit in early days of baring the teacher out of the school-house on Christmas if he would not treat the school to apples, candy, or something of that nature equally as insignificant. It is even said that the demands of the elder portion of the male pupils were often for a jug of something stronger and more exhilarating. This was a custom originating no one knows where, at one time rigidly adhered to, but now passed away with many other aforetime usages.

The teacher had his pleasures and enjoyments as well. It was not all thorns and thistles that grew along his pathway. A few flowers—puny, sickly blossoms of the morning-glory order, to us they might seem but flowers, nevertheless—also grew among them. He was one of the lords of creation, as he boarded around from house to house. There was nothing too good in the eating line, from the dried pumpkins that hung in strings on the wall, to honey and venison and wild turkey, that was not placed before him. There was nothing but the dyspepsia that prevented the revolving teacher from fareing sumptuously every day; and few remember of having seen a school-teacher in those days of long walks, airy school-houses, who was dyspeptic. The general experience of the good old house-wives of those days is, that a school-teacher who had eaten a cold dinner, or no dinner at all, and then after school "was out" had walked from two to five miles to his evening domicile, and had his appetite whetted by the appetising aroma that rose from the semicircle of cooking victuals in front of the old-fashioned fire-places, could come as near reading his title clear, to earthly enjoyment, as any one. He was generally able to do ample and complete justice to the repast, so to speak. There was enjoyment in it. He was *ipso-facto*, for the time being, lord of all he surveyed, and he surveyed with a kind of *otium cum dignitate* grace that would make a hungry mortal feel glorious.

If he had any knack at all in story-telling, he was undoubtedly highly edified in sitting around the firesides during the long winter evenings, and dealing out to the listening household those startling stories that have descended down for generations, and have accumulated in size and horror at almost each repetition. Old grandma, too, was often on hand with her stories of goblins and ghosts, that made the little folks, and teacher as well, feel shaky and down-hearted, and almost afraid to move. There were in those early days when most people had nothing to read, except, perhaps, the Testament, Peep of Day, Life of Boone, or Marion, much real enjoyment in story-telling, and the teacher was always expected to do his duty in this regard, or else be voted an uncommon bore. And then he was the generalissimo at all the parties and gatherings, from the "apple-pealings" up to the wedding. At the latter place he was regarded as but little lower than the parson himself, and was expected to furnish the fun necessary for the occasion—and it was usually a very cheap order of fun required, for on such occasions the whole assembly was easily set wild with mirth and laughter on the slightest of provocations. An old-fashioned wedding with the teacher left out, was not regarded as altogether a success. The materials were all there, but it lacked a free and easy sort of a fellow, such as the teacher usually was, to set the giggling machinery a-going.

But it was in the school room of those early days that the teacher showed his powers to the greatest advantage. There he was the supreme autocrat, and ruled, usually, with a kind of sledge-hammer bravado that was a terror to little urchins. The moment he called "books" there was a mingled expression of sternness and gravity that settled on his austere brow, as though he was born to rule the storm. That very moment he become transposed from Philip drunk, to Philip sober, as it were; and he gathered up all the hilarious faculties about him, and drowned them out as if thenceforth and forever he expected to remain an iceberg of despair and solemnity. When he spoke, he spoke as one having authority; and his orders were peremtory and absolute. There was no look of compromise in his appearance, and the black flag was kept continually unfurled from his ramparts. On the morning school commenced he read a string of rules as long as the code Napoleon, and altogether more stringent. These rules he carried in his hat, read once a day, by way of warning, and in the enforcing of which he directed more energy, mental and physical, than to imparting instruction. There stood in the corner, or lay concealed in the desk, a weapon of daily use, of hickory or hazel origin. This he used as a war measure, both offensive and defensive. It was not used as a dernier resort, but as a first resort, and that, too, often quite vigorously. When the offending urchin had passed the line prescribed by the oft repeated rules, no matter whether intentional or not, down came the rod, if for no other reason than to show the inexorable quality of the aforesaid rules. Order was the first law of heaven, and the keeping of order was the keeping of the rules. If, for instance, the rules said, "No laughing out in school allowed," and by the merest accident, and wholly unintentional, the most innocent little titter was heard above the surrounding din, the dogs of war were let loose, and the offender dragged to justice. Who that has ever been in school with a lot of little, mirth-loving brats, all bubbling over with fun, and does not know that there are little incidents occuring in the school-room daily, that it would be worse than death itself if the little fellows could not laugh. Just as well try to dam up the Niagara at the rapids, as suppress one of these involuntary laughs in a child full of spirit and life. "It won't down." Yet the teacher had his rules, and these rules were absolutely without provisos; and he enforced them without an if or a but. He regarded it as a kind of dot-your-*i*-and-cross-your-*t* transaction. The act was sure to bring on the penalty, without regard to intention or any other element of crime.

The method of teaching was also quite different from that of the present day. It is hardly susceptible of accurate description. It is one of those things that ought to be seen to be duly appreciated. The school books were very few. Webster's spelling book was the book used by beginners, usually; though, perhaps, not used in the first schools of the county. There was the old English reader, that succeeded next in order, after the spelling book; but few, however, were able to obtain it. There was no uniformity in the school books. Almost every family of children had a different kind of book, which their parents had used in their school days, and had handed down usually in a good state of preservation. It was not unusual that the children learned their a, b, c's from a shingle, upon which the letters were cut or made with chalk or charcoal. The New Testament was often used as a reader for all grades of advancement. It answered the purpose of a first, second, third, fourth or fifth reader. It was in arithmetic, however, that the defects of the early system of educational training were the most apparent. In this there was absolutely no order or system. There were no classes, and each pupil, provided with an arithmetic, slate and pencil, "ciphered" on at his own pleasure, without explanation or verification. He was required to commit the rules to memory, or so much of them as was printed in *italics*. This done, he launched out into the solution of the problems, having but one object in view, and that was to obtain the answer given. The whys and wherefores of the different steps taken in procuring the answer were matters of no concern whatever. The "sum" stated, and the thus saith the rule, were all the pupil desired, and all that the teacher required. It was a kind of mechanical process that he went through with without being able to give a single reason for a single step taken, except the mere fact that the rule said so and so. When the pupil came to an example, which, after a trial or two, he failed to obtain the given answer, he reported the fact to the teacher, and the solution was given on the slate, often without explanation, and the pupil returned to his place in the school-room satisfied; not because he understood the *modus operandi*, but because he had the answer required. This process was kept up until the pupil had progressed as far as the "single," or, perhaps, the "double rule of three," which was generally regarded as the *ultima thule* in mathematical education; and that, too, quite often from an inability on the part of the teacher to conduct—if conduct it may be called—his pupil farther. All that lay beyond that, as a usual thing, was as a sealed book—a frozen sea on which the pupil dared not, or considered it useless to venture. The arithmetics of the early days were far inferior and less suitable for pupils than those of to-day. The old dry pages of Daball, with their pounds, shillings and pence, would make a fit subject for comparison with the old bar-shear plow of fifty years ago. If these two articles of the past were not on exhibition at the Centennial of 1876; they should have been, as mementos of the past, to mark our onward steps of progress.

English grammar was a study seldom pursued. It was considered as rather too effeminate in its nature for the hardy sons who grew up in the early days of the county. It was sometimes studied, however, by the girls, as being more suitable to their natures and mental characteristics. It was not until within the last few years that anatomy, physiology and hygene, were made a part of the common school curriculum. The laws of life and health were singularly omitted in the education of the children under the old system of education. It was considered, however, as highly proper that the children should spend nine-tenths of their school-days in learning to spell the contents of Webster's Elementary from asperity to the pictures, without for once learning the simplest rudiments pertaining to the preservation of health and life.

The methods of recitations and teaching were different from those of to-day; and the modes of study and deportment of the pupils were also very different. It was quite common during school hours for all the pupils to study aloud; some reading, some spelling, some reciting; some in one tone of voice, and some in another, and all striving, seemingly, to make a bedlam equal to Babel. There were swells in the general racket when it seemed impossible to distinguish, in the din, one idea of human origin or sense. The noise and confusion were worse confounded than the jabbering of an army of monkeys in Africa. This would gradually die out until some little urchin, alone, would be heard unconsciously coming over his b-a-k-e-r baker, s-h-a-d-y shady—the only audible sound to be heard in the whole room. He, too, when nudged in the side by some seat-mate, would see the ridiculousness of the situation, and relapse into profound silence. Then the condition of affairs would fitly illustrate the saying, that "after a storm the sea grows calm."

The school-houses were likewise worthy of mention. They were almost invariably built of logs, and were "chinked and daubed." Some of them had no floors, and those that did have the floors were made of puncheons hewed upon one side, and not altogether as smooth as marble floors. The school-house was heated from a large fire-place at one end of the room. These fire-places were of capacious dimensions. Huge logs were often rolled in or carried in by the teacher and scholars, that, except in length, would have made good saw logs. The chimneys were made of wood and clay, of sufficient size to have permitted a good sized yearling elephant to have been thrown down them. Of course most of the heat from the fire-places below passed up the chimney, instead of being thrown out into the room. The windows were usually made by cutting out a log upon one side of the school-house, making the windows rather wide but not very high. Glass, they had none, for the first school-houses, and these "openings in the wall," that have been described, were covered over with greased paper! The effect of greasing the paper, in this glazing process, was to make it more transparent, and also tougher, so as to withstand the storms of wind and rain. It must have been a mellow-tinted light, that which was admitted through those tallow-dipped window panes! However, whether good or bad, it was the only make-shift they had until glass became accessible. The seats in those old school-houses would be a terror to this generation. They, too, like the floors, were made of slabs, hewed upon one side, and, of course, had no backs to them. The little fellows were placed side by side on them rough benches, six, eight or ten in a row, and scarcely any of these could reach the floor with their feet, the benches were so high. Legs were driven into the slabs from the lower side, and it was not always that they were of the same length, so that, at times, the benches would rock from side to side, greatly to the terror of the little boys or girls perched on the top, as the equilibrium was changed.

It must not be inferred, however, from what has been said, that there were no good results growing up from the educational facilities I have mentioned, defective though they were. Men have graced the presidential chair, and earned national and world-wide reputations, whose minds received their first impulses in development from just such school-rooms and educational advantages as I have mentioned. Bud Means' are quite common in this western country. And it may be debatable ground to-day whether Oxford and Harvard have made more great men than the stinging, urging necessities to self-improvement and self-education, growing out of the defects and wants of educational facilities of these pioneer colleges. Perhaps the want of education, and the feeling of that want, has built as many school-houses as the possession of education, coupled with a consciousness of its advantages. "Wittles" were what the hungry Sam Weller wanted most.

The writing desks were made of split logs, and in later days of planks, which were ranged around the sides of the room, usually under the windows. Pins were driven into the wall, and the slabs or planks laid on them, and this constituted the writing desks for a great many years. They were not of that gilt-edged and varnished sort of to-day, but were quite as substantial. These are the desks that the boys took such a vicious delight in defacing with their jack-knives. They cut upon them all sorts of hieroglyphical characters, checker-boards, and representations of beings human and not human, some of which, no doubt, would have made Th. Nast ashamed of himself. The larger boys and girls were privileged to set at these desks, not only while writing, but while "doing their sums." Blackboards and charts were unknown in those days, and in fact, were not needed in the method of teaching then prevailing. A good many young men remember when the new-fangled idea of a blackboard was looked upon with a little bit of distrust by some of the kind-hearted conservative old fellows. It was the same old chaps who also winked a kind of knowing wink at each other when the corn-planter was introduced.

Such as I have mentioned were the school-houses, school furniture and schools of fifty, forty, and even thirty years ago. They were the best that could then be afforded. It may seem, and it does seem to many who have witnessed the educational facilities above detailed, that the present generation of children do not duly appreciate the advantages that surround them. They do not, perhaps, duly appreciate their advantages for the same reason that the person reared in wealth and luxury poorly understands the condition of the poverty-stricken wretch, that ekes out a miserable existence, always on the verge of want and starvation.

Now, then, a few words in reference to the present condition of our educational interests. In 1855 the legislature of the State of Illinois passed what is known as the free-school law. Like all laws designed to reach innumerable evils, and embracing a subject comprehensive and complicated, it was in many respects defective. Frequent amendments and modifications of the law have been, and will continue to be made, as wisdom and experience may suggest. One great object attained, partially, has been to bring order and system in place of the chaotic and disjointed school machinery previously existing. That our school system is perfect, no one will assume. That it will be perfect while our young men and women employed as teachers, as a usual thing, engage therein as a temporary avocation and stepping-stone to something higher, of course, is impossible. It is not the fault of the teachers that this is so. It ought to be and will be so, that teaching will be a profession the same as law and medicine. The requirements and qualifications of a teacher should be just as exacting, and a course of preparation and study for the one should be just as imperative as in the others. No person can teach a six-months' school, properly, with the thoughts and expectations of assuming another and different avocation or employment at the end of that period. It is not now so in our cities to any considerable extent, but there are but few teachers in our country schools that follow teaching as a business or profession. It is seldom they could do so if they desired; for the average country school is perhaps not more than five months in length, and no teacher can live properly and support a family upon five months' wages. And then the management under our district system is such, that even though a teacher qualify himself properly, and teaches a good school for his patrons, he is liable to be thrown out of his position by some nondescript that happens along who can afford to underbid him, and does so. A cheap shoe is not always the cheapest. It may answer the purposes for the time being, even though the material is poor and the fit is bad; but nine chances to one, you will have corns, and it may be, bunyons, when it is done with. Our school system is not yet perfect, when a change of residence from one district to another, involves the purchase of a new set of school-books for the whole family of school-going children. It is not perfect when there are placed together in one school, perhaps forty pupils, all under the charge of one teacher, and pursuing studies ranging from the lowest to the highest permitted to be taught. None will receive the attention they require. This difficulty, of course, will be remedied as our population becomes more compact, and graded schools are established.

Again, our school system is not and cannot be perfect, when there are in the state forty-four thousand officers charged with the duty of engineering and operating our school machinery. We have in the state about twelve thousand school districts, and thirty-six thousand school directors, and these thirty-six thousand directors, each possessing his individual ideas as to the management, etc., of the schools.* Each board is empowered with the authority to determine the kind of text books to be used, the methods of instruction, the discipline and government required, and the kind of teacher, mentally and morally, to be employed. Is it possible, under this army of school officers, each board managing and controlling its affairs in its own way, that there will be much uniformity or system in our schools. No good results are accomplished, except by system and order. When a hundred men are charged with a duty which six, or even three, can perform, the probability is it will not be done, or if done, the work will not be very satisfactory, and especially so, if each performs his part in his own way, not knowing or caring how or in what manner the others are doing their part.

Again, suppose a teacher, by twenty years' teaching and practice, had qualified himself for the duties of his profession, and understood human nature, as displayed in the school-room, in all its phases, so that by looking over the school-room, he could, by a glance, pick out all the little "inglorious Miltons," the sulky Johnies, and the stubborn Sarah Janes, and knew at once the sauce for each, so to speak; and suppose he knew, by careful examination, the merits and demerits of the whole list of school-books that have passed

---

* We have in Macon county 119 districts.

through the ten-cylinder presses of Hinkle & Wilson, what sort of propriety would there be in allowing a board of directors who, however well versed in hogs and cattle, and their peculiarities, in plows and cultivators and their advantages, to say, "teach Ray's series, Green's rudiments, McGuffey's readers; or, if the pupils don't obey, flog 'em, its the only thing that will answer in this deestrict, or you do thus and so, or don't you do thus and so?" So it is, however.

Of course, there are still defects in our present educational system. Nothing devised by man can be perfect. And still it is astonishing to see the rapid strides we are making in the direction of perfection. Ask our Superintendent of Public Instruction how many schools and school houses and school teachers—male and female—and the average salary paid them, and total number of school children between certain ages, and the entire cost of the education, and the average cost to each pupil in the state; and he can tell you. Ask our County Superintendent how many there are in the county between the ages of 6 and 21, how many of these go to school, and how many do not; how many of them can neither read or write; the actual standing of each teacher in educational qualifications; how much money is expended in the county for schools, school-houses, school furniture, etc.; and he can tell you. Every teacher, no matter if he pretends to have been a college professor, must have a certificate in order to teach. If a board of directors, for lack of funds, or otherwise, desire a teacher who "passes muster" as a "second grade," it can have its wants, and *vice versa*.

We conclude this chapter upon the schools of Macon county, by giving the following table of statistics, compiled from the report for the year ending Sept. 30, 1876, of S. P. Micky, our County Superintendent of Schools:

Total No. of schools in county, (free public)............... 127
"   "   " school-houses.............................. 127
"   "   " graded schools............................. 13
"   "   " teachers—male............................. 144
"   "   "   female................................ 111

    Total No. of teachers................................ 255

Average wages paid male teachers $54 86
  " " " female " 38 41
  " No. of months taught........................ 7.9
Total No. of children in county between 6 and 21......... 10,279
  " " " pupils enrolled 7,714
  " " bet. 12 and 21 who can neither read nor write.. 18
  " amount of money raised for school purposes from all sources, year ending Sept. 30, 1876......... $122,008 38
  " amount of money expended for all school purposes for year ending Sept. 30, 1876............. 99,565 24

In this connection it is proper to mention the Mount Zion Academy, which was erected in 1856, through the instrumentality of John Smith and other leading citizens of the village of Mt. Zion. The first officers were: Rev. Daniel Troughber, President; Geo. A. Smith, Secretary; and Hon. Charles Emerson, J. D. Campbell, W. C. Moyers and John Smith, Trustees. The trustees secured the services of Rev. P. H. Crider as first principal. He was succeeded by Rev. G. W. Kensolving, and he, in turn, by A. J. McGlumphy, D. D., now President of Lincoln University, Lincoln, Illinois. The school was prosperous until the establishment of the latter school, soon after which the Mt. Zion Academy went down, and is beyond all hopes of resuscitation.

CHAPTER X.

BIOGRAPLICAL SKETCHES OF EARLY SETTLERS.

BENJ. R. AUSTIN was born in Virginia, March 26, 1802, and removed to Macon county in the fall of 1825. He was a surveyor, and laid out the original town plat of Decatur, and was for a great many years justice of the peace. He married Margaret Warnick, who was born in Tennessee, February 22, 1806. Of their children—

JANE was born May 27, 1826; WILLIAM was born Dec. 22, 1828; NANCY C. was born Sept. 15, 1830; PERLINA was born Sept. 5, 1832; died May 3, 1870; LUCINDA was born Sept. 10, 1834; died. SUSAN was born Nov. 28, 1836; died March 5, 1837. MARGARET A. was born Feb. 23, 1837; EDMISTON was born Sept. 25, 1839; GEO. W. was born August 21, 1851.

WM. A. AUSTIN was born in Virginia, April 26, 1806, and removed to Macon county in 1828, where he married Eleanor Warnick, who was born in Tennessee, January 23, 1810. She was a daughter of Wm. Wornick, and came to Macon county in 1825; died Nov. 16, 1853. Of their children—

HENRIETTA was born Nov. 18, 1832. LETTECIA J. was born July 3, 1834; died Sept. 20, 1835. MAY E. was born May 3, 1836; died June 13, 1840. JOSEPH was born Oct. 31, 1837. BENJ. L. was born Nov. 26, 1839. GEO. W. was born Aug. 21, 1841; died May 15, 1860. WM. C. was born Jan. 1, 1843. LOUISA M. was born Aug.

11, 1845; died August 21, 1845. JOHN A. was born July 19, 1846. NANCY J. was born April 22, 1849. LEWIS N. was born Feb. 25, 1851. THOMAS J. was born Nov. 5, 1853.

Mr. A. was married a second time, August 12, 1853. Children by last wife—

KATE was born Jan. 12, 1861. ALVIN W. was born Sept. 13, 1863. MARY E. was born Sept. 4, 1867. INFANT SON was born Sept. 19, 1869; died Sept. 19, 1870. JAMES M. was born May 4, 1873.

JESSE AUSTIN was born May 3, 1818, in Rutherford county, Tenn., and moved to Macon county in 1831; was married in 1847 to Catharine Faris. Of their seven children—

NANCY E. was born July 2, 1848; died 1853. JOSEPH H. was born Feb. 16, 1850. ROSETTA A. was born Sept. 14, 1851, and was married to Wm. Getts, March 24, 1870. WILLIAM I. was born July 16, 1853. MELLISSA E. was born August 25, 1862. ELIZABETH was born April 2, 1865. MARY J. was born Oct. 3, 1857.

JOSIAH ABRAMS was born in Ohio; moved to Sangamon county in 1822, and to Macon county in 1829; married Nancy Davis. Of their children—

LEVI was born July 25, 1808; married Mayon Moore. ELIZABETH was born in 1810; married Dan. Howell. HENRY A. was born Oct. 12, 1812; married Elizabeth Primm. MARIA J. married Burdine Church (dead). DELILA married A. J. Sinclair. JEMMIMA married S. R. Wheeler. JAMES married Louisa Johnson. SUSAN married Felix Butler. FRANCIS M.

CAPT. DAVID L. ALLIN was born in Loudon county, Va., March 14, 1806, and came to Macon county in the fall of 1828, and located where James C. Lake now resides, on North Water street. There was at that time a small cabin, which had been built by Hubbell Sprague, standing near Mr. Lake's present residence, which was regarded as a country residence. Mr. Allin entered from the government the east half, northwest, section 14, town 16, 2 east, which now embraces about one-fourth of the city of Decatur, and of which North Water street was the western line. Mr. A. built the second water mill that was ever built in the county, in 1831-2, which was afterwards sold by him to Robert Maffit, and known for many years as Maffitt's Mill. Mr. Allin also made the first lime ever manufactured in Macon county, at the "old lime kiln," a short distance southwest of Decatur, on the river. The lime was said to be of a very superior quality, and a great deal of it was hauled to Springfield, and used for finishing purposes, owing to its superior quality. In September, 1830, Capt. Allin married, in Rutherford county, Tenn, Miss Julia E. Read, who was born in Charlotte county, Va.

SAMUEL C. ALLEN was born in Loudon county, Va., Oct. 3, 1810; left Virginia in the fall of 1831; came on horseback through Pennsylvania, Ohio, Kentucky, and spent the winter in Rutherford county, Tenn., and came to Illinois the next spring; lived the first year in Sangamon county; moved to Decatur the next fall, and has made that and the vicinity his home ever since. Was married to Jane E. Reid, Dec. 7, 1858, (widow of Miner Reid, and daughter of Enos Gore, of Adams county, Ohio.) She was born in Loudon county, Va., July 27, 1827. Of their children—

EDWIN GORE was born May 27, 1860. WM. LEE was born Oct. 21, 1861. MILTON JAMES was born Feb. 14, 1864; died November 26, 1866. ORVILLE REID was born October 11, 1865. FRANK D. was born Jan. 24, 1868.

Mr. Allen has been school treasurer, county and township assessor, and has been postmaster since his removal to this county. He has been engaged as a farmer most of the time, but was in the mercantile business several years.

ALEXANDER W. BELL was born in East Tennessee in 1812, and came to Macon county in 1829, and located in what is now Mt. Zion township; was married to Mary Montgomery, who was born in 1816, in Tennessee. Mr. Bell was a member of the company from Macon county that enlisted in the Black Hawk war. Of their children—

JAMES M. was born April 17, 1848. MAGGIE L. was born April, 1851; married to Geo. T. Outten. MATTIE A. was born April 21, 1854; married to J. Edgar Davis.

SAMUEL BRADEN was born November 5th, 1769, in Ireland, and emigrated to America the year peace was declared; after remaining in Philadelphia a short time he located in —— county, South Carolina, where he married Nancy Young, who was born in the latter state, near Charleston, during the Revolutionary war, (date unknown). They removed from South Carolina to Kentucky, and thence to Tennessee, and from the latter state to Macon county, Ill., in September, 1828. Mr. B. died in 1833, and Mrs. B. in 1842. Of their three children—

SIDNEY R., was born November 4th, 1814, in Tennessee; removed to Illinois with his father, and returned to Tennessee the following year, where he died in 1830.

JOHN Y., was born March 22, 1818, in Tennessee; was married January 23d, 1840, to LAURA A. HUNTING, who was born in Vermont, December 24, 1819, and came to Macon county in 1840. Of their nine children, Sidney R. Braden was born November 15, 1840, and married Jane E. Cox, May 23, 1861, and died January 11, 1875, of wounds received at Vicksburg during the late war. John E. Braden was born September 26, 1842; married Mary E. Bear, October 21, 1875. Alzina P. Braden, born December 3, 1844; married Charles Nichols, December 25, 1861; died September 13, 1863. Jerome O. Braden was born February 13, 1847; married Ella Howerton, December 15, 1873. Thos. J. Braden, born August 25, 1849. Maryette A. Braden, born September 13, 1851; married William Biven, April 27, 1871; died April 11, 1872. Flora A. Braden, born August 26, 1853; married William L. Bear, December 30, 1874. George A. Braden, born September 29, 1855. Cora A. Braden was born November 8, 1857.

GEORGE M., was born in 1816 in Tennessee, and removed to Illinois with his father. He died in 1852. Mary Y.—(See Miller.)

JOHN F. BLANKENSHIP was born in Virginia in 1801; married to HANNAH WILSON who was born in North Carolina, in 1805, and is now living in this county. Mr. B. died a few years ago. Of their children—

FRANCIS I., was born March 6, 1827. P. W., was born January 9, 1832. J. T., was born March 25, 1834. WM. F., was born August 15, 1837. GEORGE A., was born January 4, 1840. NANCY W., was born June 27, 1843. ROBERT L., was born September 28, 1874; died 1873.

NEWTON N. BAKER was born in Lincoln county, North Carolina, February 28, 1803; moved to Rutherford county, Tenn., when he was eleven years old, and moved to Macon county in

1830 and settled 5 miles east of Decatur; was married to Tabitha J. Hodge in 1835, and died May 27, 1872. His wife was born in Orange county, North Carolina, in 1814, who came to Illinois in 1829, and settled in Sangamon county, remained one year and then removed to Macon county; she is still living in Decatur. Of their children—

AMZI H., was born in 1836; was married to Anna White, in 1867, and is now living in Decatur. MARY C., was born in 1839; was married to S. C. Davis, in 1857, and is still living in this county. JOSEPH N., was born ——, and is now living in Decatur. JAMES W., was born ——, also living in Decatur.

WILLIAM D. BAKER was born in Lincoln county, North Carolina, on the 12th of September, 1800, and came to Macon county in the fall of 1828, and settled in what is now Long Creek township. Mr. Baker was a member of the first grand jury of the county; he married in Tennessee, Marrila Martin. Their children are Matilda L., wife of Andrew Dennis, Jas. T. Baker, Rev. Wm. P. Baker of Grayville in White county, Mrs. Elizabeth Smith and Rev. N. M. Baker. Mr. Baker was one of the few men of whom in a long life no one can say ought against.

JAMES M. BAKER was born September 19, 1811, in North Carolina, and came to Macon county in 1830; was married to ARRAANNA H. HODGE, who was born in North Carolina, May 15, 1816, and removed to Macon county in the winter of 1830-31. Of their children—

ROBERT was born September 10, 1830. S. A. E., was born March 7, 1848; married to JAMES GREGORY, and died in March, 1873.

KIRBY BENEDICT was born November 25, 1810, at Kent, Connecticut, and was married to CHARLOTTE C. CURTIS, October 23, 1834, who was born September 20, 1810, in Newton, Connecticut; they removed to Sangamon county, Illinois, in 1835, and to Macon county in March, 1836, where he engaged in the practice of law, and remained here until 1849, when he removed to Paris, Illinois; in the fall of 1853 he was appointed by President Pierce as one of the associate justices of the territory of New Mexico, in which capacity he served for three years, when he was appointed chief justice of the same territory, which position he held until his removal by Andrew Johnson in the winter of 1866. After this he again engaged in the practice of law and was editor and proprietor of the New Mexico Union, until he died on the 28th day of February, 1874. Mr. B. held the office of probate justice of the peace of Macon county from 1838 to 1842 and was the third resident practicing lawyer of Macon county; he received a common school education, and afterwards became proficient in the French and Spanish languages; he studied law with Judge Quitman in Natches, Mississippi, where he was admitted to the bar. Of their children—

OPHELIA C, and LAURA K., died when young. WORTHINE C., married JAMES SMITH and resides near Moweaqua, Illinois and KIRBY S., resides at Tuscola, Illinois.

RICHARD H. BRETT was born in Prince Williams county, Va., November 1st, 1772; was married to Margaret Lee, November 22, 1798, who was born May 6, 1779. They moved to Macon county in 1835. Of their 14 children—

MARGARET was born Sept. 17, 1799; died 1860. FRANCES was born March 31, 1801; was married to Jacob Munch. JOHN was born May 17, 1802; was married to Sarah Fergerson. JANE was born March 29, 1804; was married to Reuben Rogers; she is now dead. MILDRED was born December 14, 1805; married to George Montgomery in January, 1837, and has since died. PENELOPE was born October 14, 1808; married to Franklin Montgomery in 1836. SARAH was born July 13, 1811. GEORGE E. was born February 4, 1813, and died in November, 1835. JAMES E. was born October 11, 1814; died July 3, 1833. MARY E. was born March 21, 1816; was married to John Gulick in April, 1848; she is now dead. DANIEL was born December 21, 1817; was married to Elizabeth Wheeler, February 4, 1847. ANN M. was born June 24, 1819; died in September, 1836. ALEXANDER was born March 2, 1822; was married to Rebecca Hays, who afterwards died; he then was married to Martha Cox. FREDERICK S. was born January 3, 1825; and was married to Martha Montgomery.

Mr. B. died ——; Mrs. B. died ——.

DAVID BARNWELL was born in South Carolina in 1802, and moved thence to Davidson county, Tenn., where he married Elizabeth Haddick, who was about the same age, and born in

Tennessee. They removed to Illinois in 1833, and first settled in what is now Long Creek township. Mr. B. died in 1836 or 7, in Fayette county. Mrs. B. died about 1840, in Macon county. Of their six children—

ALFRED A. was born January 30, 1823, in Tennessee; died 1871. EDWARD A. was born August 30, 1824, in Tennessee; now resides in Cerro Gordo. RICHARD G. was born April 31, 1828, in Tennessee; resides in Idaho Territory. ALMIRA C. was born September 3, 1829, in Tennessee; married Orrin Foster, and now resides in LaBette county Kansas. JOHN B. was born May 19, 1832, in Tennessee; resides in Macon county. NANCY E. was born about 1834; died in infancy.

MICAJAH M. BURKE was born in Kentucky, April 6, 1804 and came to this county in 1834, and married Lucy A. Pasly, who was born in Kentucky, April 21, 1814. Mr. B. died May 26, 1863. Of their children—

JOHN H. was born March 29, 1835. JAMES W. was born November 21, 1837. ROBERT Y. was born May 5, 1840. THOMAS was born April 3, 1843. DELPHA was born August 9, 1845. JOSEPH was born February 20, 1848. LEWIS B. was born January 8, 1851.

WILLIAM CANTRALL was born in Green county, Ky., January 17, 1800; came to Sangamon county, Ill., in 1825, and to Macon county in 1833. The first part of his life in Illinois was spent in selling goods. He has held several offices of trust since his connection with Macon county. Was married on the 14th of February, 1828, to Elizabeth Hall, who was born in 1809, and died in 1868. Of their children—

THOMAS was born in November, 1829; died in Washington Territory. JANE was born in 1831; married Dr. Kellar, who now lives in Sullivan. MARY was born in 1835; married Dr. Dillon in 1854; they now reside in Adams county. SUSAN was born in 1844; married Harl P. Christie; they are now living in Decatur.

Mr. Cantrall was married a second time, August 19, 1869, to Mrs. Han, who was born in the State of Kentucky.

EPHRAIM COX was among the early settlers who came here about 1828 or 9. We have no record of the family complete.

GEORGE M. COX was born April 6, 1830, in Macon county,

and married Ellen Downs, who was born in Ohio, March 15, 1832. Of their children—

Nancy C. was born October 24, 1852; married John Woods, December 17, 1873. Mary A. was born February 27, 1854; married John A. W. Bell, October 19, 1876. William H. was born March 8, 1856. John C. was born April 5, 1858; died February 23, 1862. M. J. was born August 16, 1860. L. A. was born December 24, 1863; died August 15, 1864. Ida F. was born April 16, 1865. George E. was born November 15, 1867. Eda A. was born February 22, 1870; died February 26, 1870. S. C. was born July 26, 1871.

MARGARET E. was born March 14, 1832; married Cornelius Morris in 1848, who was born November 6th, 1825. Of their children—

Nancy A. was born February 28, 1849; died December 9, 1861. Mary E. was born September 27, 1850; married November 19, 1872, to C. W. Frew. Margaret M. was born February 22, 1853. Lewis J. was born July 17, 1856; died November 12, 1875. Thos. F. was born April 23, 1861. Amanda E. was born April 7, 1864. George W. was born July 1, 1867. Ada A. was born June 27, 1870. Elmer O. was born May 8, 1872.

REV. WM. S. CRISSEY was born in Connecticut, April 21, 1811, and came to Macon county in 1831, on a visit, and removed here in 1834. In 1831-2, Mr. C. was upon the Tazewell Circuit, which included a very large territory, viz: Peoria, Pekin, Bloomington, etc. In 1832-3, he was assigned to the Jacksonville Circuit, which was as extensive as his former field of labors. Of the experiences of circuit rider among the pioneers of Illinois, Father Crissey relates some very amusing instances. He has been a close observer of men and events, and has a mind well stored with facts gathered from a long life and varied experiences.

COL. E. D. CARTER, was born February 2, 1814, in Logan county, Ky., and removed thence to Shelbyville in 1833, and thence to Springfield in 1836, and thence to Decatur in 1838, where he now resides. He married Christina Smick, who was born in Kentucky in 1812.

JAMES D. CAMPBELL was born June 26, 1803, in North Carolina; removed thence to Caldwell county, Kentucky, and thence to Wayne county, Illinois, in 1826; thence to Sangamon county in 1828, and to Macon county in 1830. He married in Kentucky Lavina Travis, who is still living. Mr. C. was a member of the county commissioners' court, and for many years a justice of the peace. He died in 1864. Their children are—

Matilda, John T., Margaret, (married Thomas Warfield,) David, Louisa, (married Wm. Foly,) and Mary, (married Geo. Schroll.)

WILLIAM COX was born in the State of Maryland, December 19, 1803; was married to Martha ———, July 3, 1832, who was born April 14, 1806, in the state of Virginia; died December 18, 1867. Of their children—

MARY ELIZABETH was born August 24, 1833; was married to Harvey Travis; died February 6, 1862. MARTHA ANN was born December 17, 1834. ALMEDA VIRGINIA was born May 7, 1837; was married to Gilbert McDaniel; died November 5, 1861. WILLIAM EPHRAIM was born July 15, 1838; was married to Ellen Traughber, now Hunt; died December 18, 1861. TRIPHENA was born November 5, 1840; was married to Thomas Price; died February 24, 1862. EMILY was born March 12, 1843; died December 27, 1861. CHARLOTTE was born September 9, 1845; was married to John Miller, and now resides in this county. LUCETTA was born January 14, 1848; was married to Harvey Epling, and now resides in Kansas.

DR. IRA B. CURTIS, the 17th county treasurer of Macon county, was born October 23, 1823, in Delaware county, Ohio, and moved to Sangamon county, Ill., in 1835, and has been a resident of this county since 1844, excepting seven years of which time he was a resident of Christian county. He was a physician in active practice from 1846 until 1862, when he received a stroke of paralysis in his lower limbs, and has been unable to walk since, which, of course, destroyed largely his usefulness in his profession. In 1863 he was elected county treasurer, which position he held until 1869.

JACOB CAULK was born November 5, 1802; was married to Mary ———, January 7, 1830, who was born January 22, 1804. Of their children—

JAMES was born October 26, 1830; died September 5, 1833. MARTHA was born February 19, 1832. JOHN was born October 12, 1833; married Malinda Pound. They are now residents of

Decatur. ALBERT was born June 20. 1837; supposed to have died in the army. MARY was born November 19, 1839. SARAH was born December 23, 1841. Jacob Caulk and wife were among the first settlers of this county; neither of them is now living.

DAVID DAVIS was born in Lincoln county, North Carolina, May 2, 1798. At the age of 17 he emigrated to Rutherford county, Tennessee. In 1828 he came to Illinois and settled in this county. At the age of 23 he had the misfortune to become paralyzed in his lower extremities, and throughout his long life he walked with great difficulty. Notwithstanding this, he was ever energetic, and gathered a handsome competence for himself, and provided liberal means for beneficent charities. He died August 19, 1875. He was once county treasurer and one of the judges of the first election held in Macon county. He was married to Mary Martin September 28, 1825, who was born in Rutherford county, Tennessee, November 15, 1806. Of their children—

ISABELLA C. was born August 17, 1826; was married to Michael C. Rozzell, November 4, 1845. WILLIAM M. was born January 14, 1831; was married to S. J. Nicholson March 23, 1854. SYLVESTER C. was born June 8, 1834; married to Mary C. Baker, September 3, 1857. MILTON Z. was born August 29, 1835; married to Emma Eichinger, September 3, 1865. MARY P. was born January 11, 1838; married to Hiram G. Wheeler, October 11, 1855. ELIZABETH E. was born September 6, 1841; married to John Rucker, December 28, 1858; died January 24, 1862. JOHN L. was born December 22, 1842; died April 26, 1865. TRAUGHBER L. was born March 2, 1845; was married to Mendosia Houseman, September 25, 1873. MARILLA A. was born January 2, 1847; was married to Thomas J. Odor, September 28, 1869.

WILLIAM DICKEY, SR., was born May 6, 1764, in Virginia, and removed thence to South Carolina, and was in the revolutionary war; was married about 1790 to Mary Stephenson, in North Carolina, who was born March 26, 1774. Of their children—

SARAH was born February 3, 1792; died same year. JOHN was born January 4, 1793; died in 1847. MARTHA was born September 9, 1795; died in 1837. JAMES was born December 23, 1797; died ———. EDA was born June 6, 1800; married M. Davis; died 1826. MARY was born November 14, 1802; married James Cain.

WILLIAM was born March 9, 1805. SARAH was born January 5, 1807; died in infancy. JESSE was born December 11, 1809, married Mary Brown. MATHIAS was born April 2, 1812; died 1816. ANDREW was born November 15, 1814; married Ely Russell.

JOHN DICKEY was born in 1793, and came to Macon county in 1829; married Martha Stevenson; was killed by a run-a-way team in 1846 or '7.

WM. DICKEY, JR., was born in Kentucky, Oct. 11, 1814, and married Isabella Foster, Nov. 30, 1837, who was born in Tennessee. Mrs. D. died May 30, 1852. Of their children—

JOHN B. was born October 26, 1838. DAVID A. was born August 28, 1840; died July 22, 1864. MARTHA A. was born March 20, 1843; married J. W. Welton. ABNER L. was born March 5, 1846; married E. Mendenhall. W. M. was born January 14, 1849. MARY C. was born May 8, 1851; died May 27, 1851.

Mr. Dickey married to his second wife, Mrs. Sarah A. Warner, October 19, 1852, who was born in Canada, August 25, 1828. Mr. D. died January 17, 1875. Of their children—

CLARETTA was born Feb. 19, 1855. SARAH J. was born Dec. 27, 1856. HENRY E. was born January 13, 1859. ELIZA A. was born February 17, 1861; died August 30, 1862. GEO. B. was born September 20, 1862; died September 6, 1863. CHAS. A. was born July 21, 1864. MARGARET C. was born November 21, 1866. NANCY B. was born February 15, 1869. JAMES H. was born July 22, 1873.

ALEXANDER C. DICKEY was born February 22, 1818; married Nancy Foster.

HARVEY DICKEY was born February 23, 1837; married R. Dowling.

DAVID DICKEY was born March 19, 1817, in Lovington county, Ky.; came to Macon county in 1829; was married to Mary Chambers, Feb. 2, 1844, who was born February 27, 1821; died November 10, 1865. Of their children—

MARY was born December 16, 1844; died October 1, 1859. NANCY was born February 26, 1847; died September 16, 1847. JAMES was born April 12, 1851; died October 18, 1859.

Mr. Dickey was married a second time to Nancy J. Dike, December 22, 1870. Their only child, MAGGIE, was born Sept. 17, 1871.

SAMUEL DAVIDSON was born in South Carolina, in 1774. From South Carolina he came to Southern Illinois; thence to Macon county in 1830; was married in South Carolina to Elizabeth Mays, who was born in the latter State in 1776. Mr. D. died in 1843, and Mrs. D. died in 1844. Of their children—

JOHN was born in 1796; died in 1844. POLLY was born in 1798; died in 1840. ANDREW was born in 1806; died in 1871. NANCY was born in 1808. ELLA J. was born in 1810. ELIZABETH was born in 1813; died in 1833. CYNTHA was born in 1816; died in 1835. BAXTER was born in 1817; was married to Elizabeth Harbaugh in 1842, who was born in 1817; died in 1867. Of their children—

D. L. was born in 1843; married in 1867 to Virginia ———. John A. was born in 1845; married in 1871 to Maula ———. M. R. was born in 1848; married in 1874 to Emma Reeme, who was born in 1851. Arminda A. was born in 1850. Naoma A. was born in 1856. Mariah F. was born in 1859.

Mr. Davidson was married the second time, in 1869, to Lovina ———, who was born in 1835.

JAMES EDWARDS was born in 1806, near Raleigh, North Carolina. When a young man he came to Tennessee, and remained there a few months; then removed to Illinois, arriving in Macon county in the fall of 1827, when there was but 160 acres of land entered upon the south side of the river. He was accompanied to this county by Dempsey Pope and Jones Edwards—the latter a brother of his, who remained 12 or 15 years, and removed to Iowa, where he died. James E. worked the first year after he came to Illinois for John Ward. During that time the Indians made some threats against the Wards, and Edwards was one of a company of 12 to assist in driving them away. A few more Indians made their appearance in the vicinity in 1828, but soon left, and were followed and overtaken in the prairie, a short distance east of Mt. Zion. There were twelve in number, besides the squaws. A gun was taken from one of them, after a severe struggle, by Smith Mounce, of the Ward company. It was returned, however, by order of John Ward, who had command of the expedition, and the Indians were then ordered to move on, which they did. This was the last appearance of the Kickapoos, or other Indians, in Macon county. James E. was married to Nancy L. Hill, in the winter of 1830-31. She was born in Mecklinburg county, Virginia, June 22, 1806; moved to Rutherford county, Tenn.; removed to Illinois in 1829, and has ever since resided in this county. Of their children—

MARTHA E. was born March 31, 1834, and married Abraham Lynch, and died. NANCY E. was born January 26, 1836; married John D. Smith, and died on the 11th of August, 1869. JEROME was born March 22, 1837, and married Mary J. Stingly. JOHN was born September 9, 1838, and died in Indiana on the 12th of September, 1862. FRANK was born January 4, 1840, and was married to Mrs. Henry Edwards, March 16, 1874. SARAH J. was born August 4, 1841, and died March 20. 1854. RUFUS was born January 1, 1843. SAMUEL S. was born June 22, 1844; married to Isabel Allen, December 24, 1873. ANN was born August 13, 1846; was married to Richard Whitley, in October, 1862, and now resides in Vernon county, Mo. HENRY was born April 6, 1848; married to Elizabeth Brown in 1869, and died on the 7th of November, 1872.

HON. CHARLES EMERSON was born in North Haverhill, Grafton county, New Hampshire, April 15, 1811; he came to this state in the year 1833 and located at Jacksonville, where he spent one term in Illinois College; he removed thence to Springfield, Illinois, and studied law under the instruction of Judge Keys; on his being admitted to practice law he came to Decatur and entered upon the practice of his profession in the spring of 1834; in 1841 he married NANCY HARRELL who died December 16, 1866; he remained here until 1847 and then went to Paris, Edgar county, where he remained three years, returning in 1850; on his return he was elected to the legislature and was re-elected in 1851; in June, 1853, he was elected judge of the circuit court, which position he filled until 1867, when he ran for judge of the supreme court but was defeated by a small majority by Judge Walker now of the supreme bench; he then resumed practice and was elected to the constitutional convention in 1869. He attended the early part of that convention but was suffering with a severe cold and cough which terminated his earthly career, on----day of April 1870. As to his judicial career his memory needs no comment; his mind was evenly balanced and he held the scales of justice so impartially that few dared to question the correctness of his adjudications; he seemed to be absolutely unbiased. Though he was a man of strong convictions predjudice was never attributed to him in the discharge of his judicial duty. Meanness he absolutely detested, yet no man was brought before him, however serious his crime, but received a fair and impartial trial. He was a strong party man, yet, when on the bench his opponents never had occasion to utter one word against him as to predjudice, bias or partiality. His mind was broad and grasping; the intricacies of the law he could comprehend readily, and solve the most difficult and perplexing questions of law and fact with scarcely a moment's reflection. He had the power of presenting his views succinctly and in such a way that those who heard him, in making a decision, at once acknowledged the justness and correctness of his position in the matter in question. He was charitable, his hands being open on all occasions to succor distress, to encourage enterprise, and support good institutions. He was modest and unaffected and possessed not one particle of personal vanity; "he had no desire for display, and no ambition for admiration." He made no effort to win attention in conversation or argument, beyond what the occasion absolutely required; what he said was always well said, because it was always from a full mind accustomed to deep reflection. He never obtruded his opinions upon others, but brought them out only as they were sought, and then with clearness and earnestness. To the casual observer, or on first introduction he was thought to be cold and reserved; but he was neither the one or the other. He had great simplicity of manner, dress and deportment, but his simplicity was never accompanied with want of perception of what was right and fit for the occasion. The first impression of a stranger was that of disappointment; it hardly seemed credible that such simplicity should be accompanied with his known position and reputation in life. The consciousness of power was not there; "there was no play of lights and shades of rank; no study of effect in tone or bearing." He never thought of himself and the air of office was not there. What was said of the great Marshall may with equal truth be said of Judge Emerson: "after all what may be said of his fame in the eyes of the world, that which in a just sense was his highest glory, was the purity, affectionateness, liberality and devotedness of his domestic life. At home he indulged himself in what he most loved, the duties and blessings of the family circle. There his heart had full play. There the sunshine of his soul diffused its soft radiance and cheered and soothed and tranquilized the passing hours." The writer has seen him in the family circle surrounded by his children, so completely absorbed in their childish pranks, that he seemed almost oblivious to all passing events; to them he was kind and affectionate, and indulgent to a fault, almost. In his public character he was upright and conscientious. He would not do what he thought to be wrong no matter how popular or pressing was the public clamor; he would not shrink from what he thought right though he might stand alone in his position. In this he was as firm as a rock. On one occasion, having made a decision, he was reminded that the supreme court had decided directly the contrary doctrine: "I know that," he replied, "but they are wrong and I am right, and I will give them one more chance to correct their error." He loved the law, not as a trade, but as science; he disdained to mislead the court, the jury or his client; the practice of law was to him the enforcement of the principles of right and justice, rather than the temporary success his knowledge of the rules of practice might give him. He resorted to no technicalities for success. His treatment of his brethren at the bar was kind and courteous, whether practicing with them or while on the bench. To the younger members of the bar he was a friend indeed, and was never known to take advantage of their inexperience that he might show his own strength and knowledge, as some petty judges delight to do. He was studious, and his judicial learning was above the ordinary judges of our courts, yet the original bias as well as choice of his mind was to general principles and comprehensive views, rather than technical and recondite learning. In his character, in his family circle, in his practice, in his judicial career, in all the varied stations in life, he was a model worthy of emulation, not perfect and without blemish, but his better characteristics so far exceeding the imperfections and blemishes, that the latter were almost unobserved. Of their children—

ALBERT was born February 5, 1842, and is now residing in Monticello, Piatt county, Illinois. JEROME was born December

25, 1846, and is now living at Clarinda, Iowa. JOSEPH was born September 21, 1850; is now living in Lake City, Moultrie county, Illinois. ELIZABETH was born November 3, 1852, and married S. H. RECORD, of Charleston, Illinois, where she now resides. LAURA M. was born February 11, 1855, and died January 13, 1876. LEORA M. was born April 11, 1857, and now resides in Decatur. LUCY A. was born April 13, 1859, and now resides in Charleston, Illinois.

GEORGE W. FALCONER was born in 1777, in Frederick county, Maryland, and came to this county in 1839, and died January 6, 1856. His children were—

JEREMIAH, ANNA, ELIZA, ENOCH G. and MARY.

JOHN FALCONER was born January 21, 1830, in Frederick county Maryland, and came to Macon county in 1839.

JEROME R. GORIN was born in Hopkinsville, Kentucky, October 12, 1817, and came to Illinois in 1828 and settled at Vandalia, Illinois; he removed thence to Macon county in 1833; he married in Decatur, April 1, 1845, Miss ELEANOR E. D. FAWCETT who was born February 18, 1824. in Jefferson county, Virginia. Mr. G. was admitted to the bar in 1843, but has been engaged for several years past in the banking business in the firm of J. Milliken & Co.

DR. B. W. GORIN was born in Christian county, Kentucky, in 1838, and came from there to Vandalia, in this state, where he remained until 1831, when he removed to Shelbyville and thence to Decatur, and was engaged in the practice of medicine. He remained here but two years, and then went to Louisiana, Mo., where he died in 1874.

HENRY M. GORIN was born in Christian county, Kentucky in 1812, and removed thence to Vandalia, Illinois; he came to Decatur, Illinois, in 1832, and remained until the year 1841; he was at one time circuit clerk and county clerk of Macon county; after removing to Missouri he engaged in farming, and has held the office of clerk of the circuit court in his county; his records kept by him bear evidence of his carefulness and pains taking.

JACOB HOSTETTER was born in Shelby county, Kentucky, July 6, 1810; married TABITHA CRUM in March, 1835, and came to

Macon county in 1835, where he died in 1873 of smallpox. Mrs. H. was born in Oldham county, Kentucky, November 4, 1816. Of their children—

FRANCIS M. was born in Clark county, Indiana, February 3, 1835; married ELIZABETH WYKEL, 1857. MARY J. was born October 15, 1836 and married JANE C. CAMPBELL, March 8, 1865. MALINDA E. was born August 31, 1838; married CHARLES E. HUNSLEY, October 25, 1865.

JAMES HERREL was born in Grayson county, Kentucky, August 29, 1813, where he remained until 1834, when he removed to Macon county and remained two years; returned to Kentucky, thence to New Orleans; thence to Florida, as teamster in the war against the Seminole Indians; returned to Macon county in 1839, where he married Mary Miller, November 26, 1840. Of their children—

ALBERT G. was born January 6, 1843; married S. J. Miller. TABITHA was born July 6, 1844; died February, 1845. ELIZABETH A. was born October 18, 1845; died June, 1846. GEORGE W. was born October 8, 1847. FRANCIS M. was born June 14, 1850; dead. JAMES C. was born January 27, 1852; dead.

JOHN HANKS, once the old friend and associate of Mr. Lincoln, was born in Kentucky about 1802, and come to Illinois in 1826 or '27, and settled on Stevens' creek; he married in Kentucky, Susan Wilson, who was about the same age as Mr. H., and who died in 1861. Of their children—

WILLIAM, who lives in Piatt county, and LEWIS, who lives in Oregon, were both born in Kentucky. JANE was born January 15, 1831, in Illinois, and married to A. T. Metlin, who was born in 1830, in Pa. EMILY, born in 1833, in Illinois, married to ——Lomis, and resides at Minonk. PHELIX, dead. GRASON, resides in Missouri. LEVI resides in Macon county.

JAMES HOWELL was born in 1802, in Galleo county, Ohio, and removed to Macon county in 1831, having been in the state five years. His wife was born in Virginia in 1803.

Their children were Mary, William T., Emily, Nancy, Charles D., Brice A., John, Elizabeth.

WILLIAM HOWELL, DANIEL, JOSEPH and ISAAC, were brothers of James, and came to Macon county early.

DOLLISTON HEFTON was among the very early settlers of the county. He was one of the old "forty gallon Baptist" preachers, and had a sing-song tone to his preaching that was truly wonderful. From the recollection of one of his hearers, we are enabled to give a small extract from a sermon delivered by Mr. H. over 40 years ago, which illustrates the peculiar ah's and ideas of which his sermons abounded. " My respected brethren-ah, hell-ah is like takin' a pillow-slip of corn-ah and wadin' the snow-ah and rain-ah, and goin' to Jim Wheeler's mill-ah, and gettin' it ground-ah to make mush-ah! You grind and grind and grind-ah! Brethren-ah, that is hell-ah. But, my hearers-ah, there is another good place-ah, which we all expect to go to-ah, and when we get there-ah, will feast forever-ah on spare-ribs, biscuits and coffee-ah, and that's the place we call heaven-ah." Mr. Hefton kept store at Mt. Gillead for a while, and had his family, household goods and merchandise all in one room. His stock of goods consisted of a barrel of pale whisky, that would freeze up in winter, a small quantity of tin-ware, and a few dollar's worth of sugar and coffee. One day some one offered to buy his entire stock of tin-ware at a given price, but he refused to sell, because it would "break his stock."

JAMES HERREL was born in Grayson county, Ky., in 1813; came to Illinois in 1833 or '4, and settled in Decatur; remained there until 1840, when he removed to the place where he now lives, about 4 miles west of town. He was married to Mary Miller in 1840, who was born April 22, 1811.

ALBERT G., son of J. and M. Herrel, was born in 1843, and now resides in this county.

JOSEPH HOSTETLER was born in Shelby county, Ky., February 27, 1797. His father and grandfather were natives of Pennsylvania. His great-grandfather was born in Germany, near the river Rhine.

Joseph's mother, Agnes, was the daughter of Anthony Hardman, of whose ancestry nothing is known. Mr. Hostetler commenced preaching according to the "Yunker Doctrine," about the year 1815. In 1816 he was married, and the same year authorized to preach by the Yunker church. In 1817 he moved to Washington county, Ind., and remained there two years. He then moved to Orange county, in the same State, remaining there until 1832, when he moved to Illinois, settling in this county, not far from Decatur.

In 1828, he, with others, renounced all "creeds," "confessions of faith," and took his stand with the Church of Christ, or Christian church. After he came to Illinois he performed much hard labor as a pioneer minister, as well as a pioneer farmer.

In October, 1832, he organized a church in his neighborhood, of fourteen members. The same church is still in existence, having at present over one hundred members. In 1833 he organized in Decatur the Church of Christ, which exists to-day. In the following year he moved to Decatur, and commenced the practice of medicine, in connection with his preaching. In 1836 he returned to Indiana, and settled on an unimproved farm near Bedford, Lawrence county. In 1843 he moved to Sheboyagan county, Wisconsin, where he opened a farm in heavy timber land, and here, too, he continued to preach and practice medicine. In 1855 he removed to Salem, Washington county, Ind. Here he was engaged principally in the practice of medicine. In 1861 he moved to Lovington, Moultrie county, Illinois. During all this time he was incessantly engaged in preaching or practicing medicine. On the 27th day of August, 1870, he died, at his residence, near Lovington. His disease was a functional derangement of the heart. He was a heavy built man, weighing about two hundred pounds; was five feet eight inches high, and seemed to bear the weight of years with remarkable firmness and strength.

ANDREW HAMILTON was born May 31, 1806; came to Macon county in 1830; married Margaret Hall in 1829. Of their children—

JOHN W. was born December 9, 1830; married to Amelia Clements. ROBERT G. was born January 20, 1832; died February 21, 1832. MARTHA F. was born February 21, 1833; died January 21, 1837. ALFRED C. was born June 5, 1835; died April 27, 1876. MARGARET S. was born January 12, 1838; died December 18, 1860. MARY S. was born October 20, 1840; died November 20, 1840. EMILY H. was born April 17, 1842; married N. Boles. A. L. was born January 4, 1844; died December 4, 1844. MARY J. was born May 9, 1849; died February 12, 1873.

ULYSSES HUSTON was born August 25, 1824, in Pickaway county, Ohio; came to Macon county in the month of November,

1836; married to Matilda McCoy, Feb. 25, 1847, who was born May 19, 1825, in Montgomery county, Indiana, and came to Macon county in 1840. Of their children—

PHEBE was born January 5, 1848; was married to Robert M. McCoy, November 5, 1866. JOHN was born October 13, 1849; died April 14, 1856. ROBERT was born August 22, 1852. ORUS B. was born January 3, 1856. MARTHA M. was born February 18, 1859. EMILY J. was born January 7, 1862. WILLIAM N. was born March 2, 1865. MARY E. was born December 12, 1868. All of which now reside in Macon county.

SAMUEL HORNBACK was born May 8, 1808, in Bath county, Ky., and was married September 2, 1830, to Margaret Johnson, who was born February 24, 1811, in the same county and State. They removed to Macon county in September, 1830. Of their nine children—

ABRAHAM was born February 5, 1835. LETHA ANN was born December 16, 1835; was married December 17, 1856, to Geo. W. Schroll. ISAAC was born July 26, 1838; married to Martha Hide, December 20, 1858. NANCY J. was born October 23, 1841; married to Wm. Gepford, August 22, 1865. SAMUEL C. was born January 1, 1844; married to Margaret Vice, May 6, 1866. MARGARET was born December 12, 1846; married to George Houser, November 23, 1865. ELIZA A. and LOU ANN, twins, were born February 5, 1850. JNO. W. was born August 15, 1853.

ROBERT JOHNSON was born in Bath county, Ky., March 3, 1807. Was married to Lou Ann Church April 5, 1831, who was born July 13, 1813. They moved to Macon county in October, 1831. They have no children.

DR. JOSEPH KING was born in 1810, and came to Macon county in 1839, and married —— Packard. At that time there were but two or three physicians in the county, Drs. Read and Spear. Dr. Rogers came here in 1840, and remained a few years. Dr. K. received his medical education in Cincinnati, O., and soon after his arrival had an extensive practice, and was often called upon to ride 25 or 30 miles to see a patient. The Doctor relates some very amusing incidents connected with the early practice in the county, and some that were not so amusing to the participants;

such as being lost on the large prairies, and riding all night in the cold, when the wolves were uncomfortably thick. The Doctor says he was always afraid of the wolves, and retains a distinct recollection of the vigorous barking of these creatures as he would be out riding late at night, perhaps miles from any habitation.

ALFRED LAYMONS was born in Grayson county, Ky., September 23, 1808, and removed to Macon county in 1829, where he married Rhoda P. Shepherd, as his first wife, who was born in Virginia, December 28, 1813, and died September 27, 1836. Of their two children—

HENDERSON M. was born April 15, 1833; died June, 1867. W. W. was born March 14, 1835; died February, 1870.

Mr. Laymons' second wife was Jane Manly, who was born in Grayson county, Ky., August 10, 1815, and died December 31, 1858. Of their children—

MARGARET A. was born May 22, 1839; died December, 1839. SARAH E. was born Nov. 3, 1840; died May 1, 1871. JNO. A. was born October 5, 1842; died January, 1870. JACKSON M. was born January 9, 1847. MARY A. was born October 10, 1849. NANCY E. was born June 27, 1854; died July, 1854.

REV. ALONZO LAPHAM was born in New Hampshire, May 29, 1797. He moved to Vermont; afterwards to Indiana, where he became acquainted with, and in 1828 married, Margaret Anderson. He came to Macon county at a very early date, when there were but two houses in the city of Decatur, and soon afterwards engaged in farming. Mr. Lapham was an ordained minister in the Methodist church, and assisted a great deal in the organization of churches in Central Illinois. Of the children of Alonzo and Margaret—

MARY J. was born October 18, 1829; was married to David M. Thornby, February 22, 1849, and are now living near Salt Creek. JOHN W. was born December 18, 1832; was married to Maria Hammond. He is now engaged as a minister of the gospel, in the M. E. church. TRUMAN C. was born August 28, 1835; was married to Jennie Downs, of Shelbyville, Illinois, January 6, 1863. He is now engaged as a book and music merchant in Shelbyville, Illinois. WM. W. was born March 7, 1836; was married to Mary J. Crowder, of Springfield, Illinois, March 7, 1861. He is now engaged in the wholesale music store of Story and Camp, St. Louis, Mo. MARTIN A. was born January 2, 1841; was married to Frances Frazier, of Danville, Illinois, where he now resides. He was for a time vice-president of Quincy College, and receiving officer of the Port of New Orleans. A. MILTON was born August 11, 1843. He has been engaged as a photographer, real estate and insurance agent in Decatur, Illinois, where he now resides.

GEO. POWERS was born in Charleston, Saratoga county, N. Y., January 17, 1814; was married to Almira A. Giles, in Alabama, April 30, 1840, who was born in Franklin county, Mass. They removed to Macon county in 1839. He was admitted to the bar soon after his arrival, and was elected to the State Senate in 1844. He held other offices of trust and responsibility, and died in 1849, leaving three daughters: Emma, who married John K. Warren; Sarah A., who married Geo. S. Durfee, and Ada, who married E. D. Bartholomew.

ROBERT LAW was born in Wilson county, Tenn., in November 1807, and moved to Macon county in 1830—having been here the year previous to see the country. He was out with the rangers in the Black-Hawk war, under Captain Warnick. He built the old horse-mill at Whitehouse's, in Mt. Zion township, in 1836-7, near where Mr. L. now resides.

JAMES LAW, John Law and Rose Ann, all came here about the same time. They were brothers and sister of Robert; John is dead.

JOHN LOWRY was born in 1803, in Green county, Tenn.; was married to Elizabeth Drennan in 1825. They removed to Macon county in 1834. Of their children—

JAMES A. was born in 1826 or 7. WM. A. was born in 1828. JACKSON C. was born in 1830. CHARLES D. was born in 1832. MARY P. was born in 1837.

ELDRIDGE H. McDANIEL was born November 25, 1807, and married Mary Pope, September 5, 1826. They came to Macon county in 1827, and resided here until their death. Mr. M. died June 29, 1859, and Mrs. M. died August 26, 1871. They raised a large family of children, the ages of which we cannot give.

ELIZABETH married Aaron Widick; both dead. SALAMANDA married Thomas Lord. LEACY married Jeremiah Turpin; dead. WM. G., DEMPSEY, THOMAS, (dead,) and JOHN A. B.

CHRISTOPHER MILLER was born in South Carolina about 1789; moved with parents to Kentucky, where he married Elizabeth Hays in 1808. He removed thence to Macon county in 1829, where he died in 1855. Mrs. M. was born in North Carolina in 1791; removed thence to Grayson county Va., and thence to Grayson county, Ky., where she was married, and came with her husband to Macon, where she is still living. Of their 11 children, we can give ages of but three—

WILLIAM was born in Kentucky in 1809. MARY was born in Kentucky in 1811. JAMES was born in Kentucky in 1813.

JAMES MILLER was born in Grayson county, Kentucky, August 26, 1813; removed to Macon county in 1829 and married MARGARET HOSTETLER, of Moultrie county, who died in 1852; he married a second time, in 1853, to ELIZABETH MILLER. By his first wife there were born nine children—

A. J. was born July 24, 1836. W. G. was born August 20, 1839, (no record of others). By his second wife— Jane W. was born June 4, 1853; married J. A. Vangundy. Wm. H. was born Aug. 11, 1855; died September 30, 1856. George W. was born September 10, 1857; died December ———, 1862.

DAVID MILLER was born December 27, 1790, and married as his first wife MARY MUIRHEAD, who was born July 17, 1808. Mrs. M. died September 19, 1832. Of their children—

JAMES D. was born October 10, 1828. WILLIAM M. was born February 18, 1830; died March 20, 1831. THOMAS E. B. was born February 9, 1832; died February 10, 1844.

He was married a second time to MARY Y. WHEELER, widow of Henry Wheeler (See Wheeler) by whom the following children were born. Mr. M. died October 6, 1853.

MARGARET T. was born July 3, 1835. ELVIRA V. was born January 25, 1837; died February 29, 1844. MAY H. was born July 12, 1838. GEORGE S. was born July 26, 1840. JOHN H. was born August 8, 1841; died September, 1841. TRYPHOSA was born May 14, 1843; died September 17, 1844. LAVENIA M. was born July 28, 1844. LUCETTA and GENETT were born February

26, 1848; the latter died March 12, 1848. DANIEL was born March 30, 1849. HARRETT A. was born March 30, 1853.

WILLIAM MUIRHEAD was born in Rockingham county, Virginia, in ———; he came to this state in 1830 and settled at Wykles Place, 4 miles west of Decatur, where he died. He had 5 children, to-wit:

ELIZABETH, who married Thomas Strain and moved in the neighborhood of Clinton, Illinois, and died there. ANDREW S., who was born in 1804, and came here with his father. We are unable to give names and ages of the other children.

EDMUND McDANIEL was born February 13, 1800, in Oglethorpe county, Georgia, and removed to Robertson county, Tenn., thence to Vandalia, Ill., and thence to Macon county, in 1826. He was married in Kentucky, to Margaret Widick, who was born January 19, 1800, in Virginia, and died November 2, 1874. Mr. M. was upon the first grand jury in this county, and would make at the present, a very efficient foreman. Of their children—

JOSEPH, born in Tenn., June 25, 1821; married Kittie K. Wilson, who was born January 21, 1827, in Tennessee. Of their children—

Margaret J. was born September 12, 1844; married R. B. Wilson. David S. was born January 3, 1847. Enoch was born July 18, 1849; married C. Hammers. Mary E. was born July 28, 1854; married John L. Smith, January 10, 1877.

WILLIAM W. was born August 11, 1820, in Tennessee; married Asenith ———, who was born May 15, 1831. Of their children—

W. E. was born October 8, 1850. S. C. was born March 18, 1853. Joseph H. was born February 10, 1855. E. Y. was born June 23, 1857. M. F. was born September 18, 1859. A. A. was born December 23, 1862. H. D. and R. C. were born January 18, 1865. J. B. was born March 4, 1869.

EMANUEL was born in Macon county, May 27, 1827, and married Caroline Hill. Their children are Margaret, Benjamin, Albert and Adaline. FRANCIS M. and JOHN W. died when young.

HENRY was born Feb. 20, 1833, and married Elizabeth Layton.

THOMAS R. was born January, 1835; dead.

ELIZABETH was born in 1838; married Wm. Boardman.

JOHN McMENNAMY was born March 10, 1793, in Rutherford county, Tenn., and came to Macon county in October, 1826, with his brother-in-law, James Ward. He removed to Texas in 1839, and died there. Of his children—

JOHN H. was born in 1814, in Tennessee, and has been constable in Macon county for 20 years. His wife died some 25 years ago. He had two children—

GEORGE, who died a few years ago, and Dr. B. F. McMENNAMY, now of Moultrie county.

LUCINDA (now Martin), who resides in Harristown township.

SAMUEL McKINLEY was born December 23, 1816, in Ross county, Ohio, and moved to Macon county in the month of March, 1834. Was married September 24, 1840, to Anna Hanen, who was born January 10, 1822, in Morgan county, Ala. She came to Macon county in the month of March, 1830. Of their children—

WILLIAM A. was born September 3, 1841, and died in Memphis, Tenn., March 19, 1863. JOHN H. was born November 23, 1843; married to Catharine Ghear, December 30, 1869. EMMA was born April 11, 1846; was married to John Hammond, June 18, 1868. EUGENE was born January 27, 1849. AMANDA was born October 26, 1851; died September 24, 1852. ALICE was born August 8, 1853; married to Joseph Baxter, October 16, 1873. ELSIE was born March 27, 1856; died April 24, 1856. MARY E. was born May 22, 1858. JENNIE was born December 6, 1860. EDWARD S. was born February 18, 1864.

WILLIAM F. MONTGOMERY was born January 7, 1812, in the State of Virginia; was married to Amelia ———, May 26, 1836, who was born January 14, 1814, and came to Macon county in 1835. Of their children—

RACHAEL was born April 9, 1837; was married to John R. Hays, March 26, 1857. MARY C. was born May 11, 1839; was married to Grason Hanks, January 16, 1862. EMILY S. was born March 12, 1841. SAMUEL K. was born December 17, 1842. JOHN F. was born February 11, 1846; was married to Ollie Campbell, September 20, 1871. PATRICK H. was born September 29, 1848. MARTHA A. was born April 9, 1851; was married to Lafayette Gulick, September 20, 1870.

JAMES MYERS was born October 4, 1804, in Grayson county, Kentucky, and was married to Mary Meeks, who was born in December, 1811, in Hardin county, Kentucky. They came to

Macon county in 1828, and settled the farm now known as the Henry Davis nursery farm, in Long Creek township; Mr. M. died in July, 1872, and Mrs. M. died in 1859. Of their children—

JOHN H. was born October 12, 1830; was married in 1848, to Elizabeth A. Park, who was born in 1828, in Virginia, and died in December, 1851; married a second time to Emily J. Howell, who was born June 21, 1821, in Sangamon county. Mr. M. had two children by his first wife, both dead; by his last wife has had eleven children, of whom six are living, viz: James M., Charles B., Livinda, Joseph, Daniel and Martha. JAMES B. was born in 1849, now resides in Texas. SARAH J. was born in 1836; married to Andrew Shoemaker. ANGELINA was born in 1847; married to Thomas Atchison.

MICHAEL MYERS was born about 1779, in North Carolina, and married Louisa Atteberry, who was born about the same date in Kentucky; they removed to Macon county in 1827 or '8. Mr. M. died about 1856, and Mrs. M. about 1862. Of their children—

MOSES was born about 1805, and now resides in Missouri. ELIZABETH, born in 1807 (about); married to Wm. Lacy; both dead. DENNIS, born 1809 (about), and died about 1861. His widow is now the wife of J. D. C. Travis. MINERVA, born about 1811; married John Wallace, who is dead, and she is the present wife of Henry Rhodes. NANCY, born in 1813; married Andrew Allsman; both dead. JAMES was born in 1824; died in 1870 or '71; married Nancy Howell; also dead.

SARAH MYERS was born about 1800, in North Carolina; married in Kentucky to Joseph Davis. Came to Illinois in 1831, and died in 1875. Of their children—

MATILDA was born ——; married Claiburn Jones. LYDIA was born ——; married to John Kiger. JOHN was born ——; now in Kansas. HENRY was born ——. MARY was born ——; married A. Camp. LOUISA was born ——. (See Henry Davis.)

JACOB MYERS was born in 1802, in North Carolina; was married to Elizabeth Wood, who was born————. Mr. M. died November, 1854. Their children were—

Joseph B., born in 1842; John A., born in 1840; Mary A., James Wesley, Sarah C. and James.

Second marriage in 1849, to Malinda White.

Nancy L. was born in 1851, and married James M. Bell, October, 1871.

THOMAS NELMS came to Macon county in 1827, from Logan county, Ky., and settled where William C. Smith now resides; died from the effects of a tree falling upon him, perhaps about 1830. A remarkable incident is related in connection with the tree causing the death of Mr. N. After it was cut down, and before being split, there was one continuous tingling sound came from it, similar to that heard from the splinters when a tough stick of wood is being split. This continued long after the logs were made into rails and laid up in a fence. The attention of travelers was attracted by the peculiar noise, while they were passing along the road by the side of the fence. The fact of this singular and unexplainable circumstance was attested by many of the early settlers—some of whom are still living. That the strange freak had any connection with the killing of Nelms, as was strenuously insisted, is probably without foundation.

Hon. R. J. OGLESBY was born in Oldham county, Kentucky, July 25, 1824. His parents died when he was but eight years old, and he was placed in charge of an uncle, and in 1836 was brought to Decatur with the family of his uncle, Willis Oglesby. He had, while in Kentucky, worked a year and a half at the carpenter's trade, and after his removal to Decatur worked six months with Hon. E. O. Smith. In 1844 he commenced studying law at Springfield with Judge Silas Robins, and read with him one year, and was admitted to the bar in 1845, and commenced the practice at Sullivan, Illinois, and remained there until the spring of 1846. In June of that year he went as Lieutenant in Co. C, 4th regiment, to the Mexican war, and took part in the battles at Vera Cruz and Cerro Gordo. On his return he continued to study and practice law; but on the breaking out of the gold fever, in 1849, he crossed the plains to California, driving a six mule team *en route*, with a company of eight men, of which Henry Prather was the leading man. In 1852 he returned home to Macon county, and was a Scott elector. In 1856 he visited Europe, Asia and Africa, and was absent twenty months. On his return he resumed practice, as a member of the firm of Gallagher, Wait & Oglesby. In 1858 he ran as the Republican candidate for congress, and was defeated by Hon. J. C. Robinson. In 1860 he was elected to the State senate. On the evening the returns of this election were coming in, Mr. O. had a fisti-cuff encounter with "Cerro Gordo Williams," in which he came out victorious, and which was regarded as the first fight of the rebellion. During the extra session of the legislature in 1861, Mr. O. was elected colonel of the 8th Illinois infantry. He commanded a brigade at Fort Donelson, and was stationed on the right of Gen. Grant's army, and rendered valuable service in that famous battle, where so many Macon county soldiers fell. He was engaged in the battle of Corinth, and in a brave charge at this place, was shot with an ounce ball, which he still retains, and was borne from the field, as was supposed, mortally wounded. He had been promoted to brigadier-general in April previous. After his partial recovery he was promoted to major-general, as a merit for his valiant services, ranking from Nov. 1862, and in the spring of 1863 was assigned to the 16th army corps. Owing to inability from the effects of his wound, to perform the arduous duties of his position, he resigned his command in July, 1863; but Gen. Grant refused to accept his resignation, and he was detailed, in Dec. 1863, to court martial and try the surgeon-general of the army, at Washington, where he remained until May, 1864, when he returned to his home, and was nominated and elected as the republican candidate for governor of Illinois, and served four years. At the end of his term he returned home to Decatur, and was re-elected governor in 1872; but upon the meeting of the legislature, in January, 1873, he was elected to the senate of the United States, and resigned his office of governor.

Senator Oglesby is a man of no common native ability. Almost without education, and by the force of his own powers, he has arisen step by step to his present position as senator of one of the most important states in the Union. Macon county is proud of Senator Oglesby, and we doubt not he is proud of Macon county.

JOSHUA G. PURDEW was born in Montgomery county, Tennessee, March 1, 1811, and moved to Macon county in 1832; was married to Margaret Ward, who was born in Tennessee January 11, 1814; she died in 1862. Of their children—

MARY E., born May 1, 1835; married W. A. Wilson. PHERIBA A., born October 5, 1836. JOHN B., born March 27, 1838; married M. A. Frazee; died March 27, 1863. NANCY A., born October 30, 1841; married John Neyhard; died March 31, 1861. WILLIAM M., born October 30, 1841; married M. H. Pound. JOEL T., born December 12, 1843; died March, 1863. JAMES Y., born May 12, 1845. WILSON S., born February 3, 1847. AMERICA M., born November 21, 1848. JOSHUA L., born April 26, 1850. LEWIS M., born July 28, 1854.

Mr. P. married a second time, to Mrs. Lucinda P. Widick, who was born in Wayne county, Illinois, August 1, 1825. Her first husband was Daniel K. Pound. (See Pound.)

DANIEL K. POUND and LUCINDA R. DAVIDSON were married, November 22, 1842—(See Purdue). He died August 10, 1875. Of their children—

D. K., JR. was born January 12, 1845; married April 29, 1866. J. B. was born March 26, 1859; died March 15, 1850. M. H. was born July 10, 1850; married W. M. Purdue, March, 1868.

Mrs. P. married Aaron Widick, January 22, 1858. Of their children—

LARKIN W., born January 23, 1850. Aaron K., born August 7, 1860.

DEMPSEY POPE was born in North Carolina, and removed thence to Tennessee, and thence to this county, in 1827, and settled on Mosquito Creek. He married in North Carolina, Sarah Edwards, who was born in 1794 and died 1874. Mr. P. died in 1853 or '4. Their children were—

Martha, Mary, Tabitha, Elizabeth, William, Leacy J., Sarah, James, Willis Zachariah, Penelope and Matilda.

NINIAN PEDDECORD was born in Montgomery county, Maryland, and removed to Macon county in 1836, where he engaged as a clerk for Adamson & Prather. He afterwards formed a copartnership with Joseph Stickel. He was clerk of the circuit court from 1840 to 1847, after which he went to Missouri, and thence to Clinton, Iowa, where he died about 1870. He married a daughter of John Stickel.

JASPER J. PEDDICORD was born November 8, 1818, in Montgomery county, Maryland, and came to Macon county in

June, 1838. He married Ophelia W. Adamson, sister of Senator R. J. Oglesby, August 30, 1842. Her first husband was John S. Adamson, who died in 1840. Mr. P. for a number of years was engaged in merchandising, with Joseph Stickel, and afterwards with Hosea Armstrong. In 1852 he formed a copartnership with Lowber Burrows, in the banking business, besides engaging to a large extent in manufacturing.

CAPT. JOEL S. POST was born in the town of Ontario, in what is now Wayne county, New York, April 27, 1816. In 1828 his father removed to Washtinaw county, Michigan territory, where he remained until the subject of this sketch was 23 years old. In 1839 Mr. Post removed to Macon county; and commenced the study of law under the late Judge Emerson in 1840; was admitted to the bar in 1841, and entered into the practice at Decatur, where he has since remained, being now the oldest practitioner of the Macon county bar. In 1846 Mr. P. enlisted in the service for the Mexican war and was appointed quartermaster with the rank of captain. In 1856 he was elected to represent the senatorial district including Macon and other counties, in the State Senate, and served two sessions. During this term of service he was mainly instrumental in securing the passage of a law establishing the Normal University, at Normal, Illinois. Mr. Post married Sally Ann Bunn, the oldest daughter of Rev. D. P. Bunn, in November, 1853. She was born in Ross county, Ohio, in 1823. Of their children—

BUNN was born in 1856. HELLEN was born in 1859.

It is proper in this connection to say, that in the preparation of this work, we have been materially aided and assisted by Captain Post. He has taken more interest in this effort by which something might be placed in a permanent shape, of the early history of the county, than any other person.

GEN. ISAAC C. PUGH was born November 23, 1805, in Christian county, Ky. He came to Illinois in 1821, and settled with his father's family in Shelby county, where he remained until 1829, when he came to Macon county; resided here until his death, which occurred November 19, 1874. He was married to Elvira E. Gorin, August 2, 1831, who was born in Todd county, Ky., December 17, 1814, and came to Illinois in 1829, and to Macon county in 1831. Of their eleven children, five died in infancy—

MARIA M. was born June 4, 1832, and married to J. Milton Lowry, February 17, 1852. JOHN H. was born December 30, 1838, and married Sophia Wood, May 29, 1862. BARTLEY G. was born April 22, 1841; married Mary C. Rohrer, September 3, 1862. ISAAC R. was born January 28, 1843; married Nellie M. Upton, June 21, 1867. He died July 20, 1868. VENITIN ISABEL was born March 11, 1846; married Perry B. Gilham, September 26, 1865. ALMIRA H. was born March 23, 1851; married John C. Mark, June 20, 1874.

Gen. Pugh has been prominently connected with all the important affairs of the county, and took a lively interest in everything calculated to advance the interest of the city and county. He was in the Black Hawk war, and served as Captain at the time of Stillman's defeat. He was also Captain of Co. C, in the Mexican war, and took a prominent and active part in the late war. He was Colonel of the 41st regiment, in the late war, and was promoted to the grade of Brig.-General for meritorious conduct. In 1865 he was elected clerk of the county court, and served for four years, and held other positions of trust during his long residence in the county, and always, whether in office or as a private citizen, was where duty called him. He was kind hearted, affectionate, and in all respects upright and honorable.

THOMAS H. READ was born February 24, 1798, in Charlotte county, Virginia, and died on the first day of September, 1874, in the city of Decatur. His father moved from Virginia to Rutherford county, Tenn., when Thomas was quite young. In the spring of 1831 the Doctor moved from Tennessee to this county; was married on the 24th of August, 1836, to Elizabeth Allen, of Loudon county, Virginia, who was born on the 4th of August, 1812, and came to Macon county in 1835. Names of children—

JULIA E. was born September 8, 1837, and died October 21, 1837. JOHN N. was born August 11, 1839. MARY S. was born March 22, 1841. ANNIE H. was born February 2, 1843, and died August 24, 1864. JAMES A. was born May 26, 1846. EMMA F. was born August 31, 1848. SUSIE C. was born January 12, 1831.

JAMES REA was born February 9, 1799, in Green Briar county, Va., and married in 1817 to Hannah Hudsinpiller, and came to Macon county in 1839, and remained until April, 1854, when he removed to San Jose, Cal. Mrs. Rea died in 1871. Their only child—

WM. REA, was born October 4, 1823, in Gallio county, Ohio, and came to this county with his father, and was married July 19, 1841, to Mary Howell, who was born August 22, 1823, and died Feb. 28, 1872. Their children are—

Cyrene, (dead), Frank, Mary, David, Mellissa, (married to John Shrader,) John and William.

SAMUEL REA was born in Virginia, January 17, 1819, and came to Illinois in 1830; was married March 11, 1856, to Catharine Dennis, who was born in Pennsylvania, January 31, 1823.

Mr. R., during his long residence in Macon county, has been honored by his fellow citizens with a number of county offices, which he filled to the entire satisfaction of his constituents, and is everywhere respected. His honesty and integrity perhaps no man has ever questioned. His word was as good as his bond, and his enemies, if any, are few and far between.

JAMES RENSHAW was born November 21, 1794, in North Carolina, and moved to Kentucky, where he married Sarah Phipps, in 1819, who was born in the latter State.

BERRY ROSE was born January 14, 1806; was married to Martha Pope, November 23, 1826. He died March 12, 1835. His wife was born May 31, 1808, and is now living in this county, six miles southwest of Decatur. Of their children—

ALBERT was born January 24, 1828; was married to Louisa A. Sprouse, October 10, 1850; is now living in Missouri. MARY JANE was born September 21, 1829; was married to Andrew Armstrong, July 25, 1835. They are now living in Blue Mound. BENJAMIN W. was born July 28, 1831; was married to Mary J. Darmer, March 27, 1856, who died in Missouri. He has since married Mrs. Rebecca Carter, September 6, at six o'clock. He is now living in Blue Mound township. ELIJAH T. was born March 8, 1833; died in the army, January 23, 1863. BERRY J. was born May 20, 1835; died July 10, 1835. MARTHA ANN was born September 20, 1836; was married to William C. Darmer, April 30, 1857; now living in Champaign county. JOHN V. was born November 26, 1838; died in the army, May 26, 1864. WM. C. was born July 15, 1841; died in the army, May 6, 1862. NANCY E. was born July 14, 1843; married Thomas Armstrong, in the month of March, 1865; now living in this county. SARAH E. was born October 24, 1845; married John Jeter; now living in Champaign county. JAMES T. was born September 22, 1850; married to Lizzie Cook; is now living in Daviess county, Mo.

REBECCA ROBINSON was born February 19, 1822, in Putnam county, Ind., and came to Macon county in 1831; was married in 1847 to John Drake, who was born October 5, 1811, in Piqua county, Ohio; came to Macon county in 1834, and died March 12, 1855. Of their children—

SARAH ANN was born June 29, 1843; died October 26, 1843. MARY JANE was born October 26, 1844; died August 26, 1846. SYLVANUS was born August 30, 1849. ISAAC was born December 7, 1852; died February 5, 1872. JOHN LEWIS was born October 25, 1854. Mrs. Drake was married second time, to Lewis Camp, about the year 1857. Of their children—

Samuel W. was born October 14, 1859; died in 1861. Hattie May was born November 4, 1865.

JOHN RUCKER was born in South Carolina in 1800, and removed from that State when quite small, to McMinn county, Tenn.; he remained there until 1833, when he removed to Macon county, and resided here until he died, in the year 1872. He was a hard working man all his life, and by industry succeeded in amassing property sufficient to class him with the well-to-do men of the county. He was for fourteen years one of the county commissioners of Macon county, holding the position longer than any other man since the organization of the county. Mrs. Elizabeth Rucker, his wife, is still living with her son-in-law, E. R. Eldridge, in Decatur. Mr. R., was, in all his transactions, strict, and required all he dealt with to observe the same thing. When he came to the State, his worldly possessions were carried on two horses, and his success in life is a monument to honest and patient toil and industry.

JAMES SANDERS. There are but few old settlers of the county who do not remember "Uncle Jimmy Sanders." He was one of the noted men, and almost every one knew him, by reputation at least, for an area of a great many miles. He was born in

Spartanburg county, S. C., June 15, 1800, and was taken on a pack-pony when very small, to Rutherford county, Tenn., where he remained until he was grown. In 1823 he married Polly Wilson, who was born in North Carolina in 1797, and died in Christian county, Ill., in 1866. In the year 18 29, he removed with his family to Illinois, where he has remained ever since On his arrival in Illinois, he says he had a wife, five children and an "old plug of a wagon, three old plugs of horses, one good mare, $6\frac{1}{4}$ cents in money. The money he had in his pocket with his shot and bullets a short time after his arrival, which he accidentally lost, and was thereby "broken up." Mr. Sanders was a man of most powerful constitution, and his strength and endurance were probably not excelled by any man in Central Illinois. On the day of Uncle Joe Stevens' wedding, Mr. S., in a general trial of strength among those persons present, took a piece of lead, 75 pounds in weight, in each hand, and raised them on a level with his shoulders, and then passed them around straight in front until they touched each other. At one time he had been sick for some length of time, and when he had sufficiently recovered to walk to the blackberry patch, he gathered his hat full of blackberries, and then sat down and ate them all. He returned to the house and said, "Polly, I have eat a few blackberries and feel better."

He was known far and wide as a good rail-maker, and would go as far as 15 and 20 miles and make rails for parties at 25 cents per hundred, or $37\frac{1}{2}$ cents in trade, which he regarded as a very liberal price. He was a man that possessed a great many peculiarities, a particular mention of which, would extend this sketch quite too far. He relates to-day, with pride, as one of his greatest achievements, the fact that he at one time in a wrestling match, threw down *Abe Lincoln, who had thrown the bully of the county. Of Mr. Sanders' children—

---

* NOTE.—It will be remembered in this connection, that Mr. Lincoln, when he first came to Illinois, was a resident of Macon county, and he and Mr. Sanders were great cronies and friends. Uncle Jim says that they spent many Sundays together fishing in the Sangamon, and were often together at barn-raisings, house-raisings, fox-chases and wolf-hunts. At these early gatherings, when Mr. Lincoln was an awkward gangling boy, he was often called upon, when the work was through, for a Jackson speech, and he seldom failed to respond. Mr. L.'s father was a Jackson Democrat, and his son grew up in that faith, and has made a great many Jackson speeches in this county. He after-

ELLEN was born in 1823, and now resides in Kansas. JOHN, their second, died in the Mexican war. JAMES B. died in 1854. JANE, wife of Prestly Travis, resides in Christian county. PETER H., PEGGY, MATILDA, BETHANY and AMANDA, are dead. FRANK, the youngest child, was born in March, 1845, and married Annis Hollingsworth, with whom Uncle Jimmy now resides.

JOSEPH and BARBARA SPANGLER came to this county in the fall of 1835, from the county of York, in the State of Pennsylvania. They were among the first permanent settlers of this county. They had nine children born unto them, all of whom came to this county with their parents, with the exception of the oldest daughter, who married in Pennsylvania. Barbara Spangler died in March, 1847. Joseph Spangler died February, 17, 1862, leaving surviving him all of his children, except Felix, who had moved to California in 1852, and died while there.

wards changed his politics and became a Whig of the most pronounced type, which incensed his father no little. Mr. Lincoln commenced his law studies in this county under the following circumstances: He had gone to "Uncle Billy Warnick's" to see one of the girls; but in going, his shoes not being good, he got his feet frost-bitten, and was unable to return home. He remained there for a week or ten days under the medical treatment of old Mrs. Warnick, and while so doing became greatly interested in reading the statutes and a few other stray volumes of law-books, which, no doubt, afterwards materially determined his course in adopting his profession. It was reported in the newspapers during the campaign of 1860, that Mr. Lincoln in his early day was a great rail maker; but Mr. Sanders says that while it is true that "Abe" did make some rails, yet they were few in number. Mr. Sanders also relates the circumstance by which Mr. L. ceased to be a resident of this county, which is this: A man by the name of Offit purchased a few hundred hogs, and Mr. Lincoln and his step-brother, John Johnson, were employed to assist in driving the hogs to market at Beardstown. When they had disposed of the hogs they invested the money in groceries, which consisted, as Uncle Jim says, of "sod-corn," spun-cotton, sugar and coffee, powder and lead, etc., the greater part of which were brought back as far as Salem, where they started a grocery, and Mr. Lincoln was left in charge of the goods, to keep store. This was the last of Mr. Lincoln's personal history in connection with this county. Mr. Sanders' last interview with Lincoln was but a day or so before Lincoln's departure for Washington. As they were separating—which proved to be their last—Mr. Sanders said, "Now, Abe, don't do any wrong." Mr. Lincoln replied, "I will not, if I know it."

JACOB, JOSEPH and JOHN SPANGLER, and SUSAN and ELIZA, the sons and daughters of Joseph and Barbara Spangler, still reside in this county, each of whom have raised a family.

Their son, DANIEL SPANGLER, moved to California in 1852, where he still resides.

SUSAN SPANGLER was married to James D. Tait in 1842. James D. Tait came to this county from Lawrence county, Pennsylvania, in 1839. He opened the first saddle and harness shop ever opened in Decatur. He walked across the country from Naples, on the Illinois river, carrying his tools upon his back, frequently wading water up to his chin, which filled every slough and hollow during those days. He bought his stock of goods in Springfield, Illinois, after deciding to stop in Decatur, and had them hauled here by team. He followed his trade for several years, until he was obliged to discontinue on account of his health. Mr. and Mrs. Tait had born unto them five sons, to-wit: Joseph S. Tait was born March 28, 1843; was married to Martha E. Dillahunt, January 24, 1871. James H. Tait was born June 29, 1847, and died July 9, 1849. Felix B. Tait was born November 29, 1850. Daniel T. Tait was born February 25, 1853, and died October 8, 1873. Robert M. Tait was born December 10, 1856, and died November 17, 1873. Joseph S. Tait is one of the largest farmers of this county. Felix B. Tait graduated at the Illinois State Normal University, in June, 1873; was principal of the Woodstock Seminary, in McHenry county, Illinois, in 1874–75; was licensed to practice law in June, 1876.

JOHN SCOTT, SR., was born in North Carolina, in 1775, and married Mary Dodd, in Kentucky, who was born in South Carolina, in 1777. They removed from Tennessee to Indiana, in 1816, and thence to Illinois, in 1829. Mr. S. died December 20, 1830, and Mrs. S. died September 7, of the same year.

Of their two children, now residents of Macon county, see Francis and John, below.

FRANCIS D. SCOTT was born July 12, 1819, in Gibson county, Indiana, and removed to Illinois, with his father, in 1829, and settled in Macon county, in 1834, in Mt. Zion township. Mr. S. was married April 24, 1846, to Lucinda Fruit, who was born in Kentucky in August, 1824. Of their children—

Eli K. was born July 6, 1847. Albert was born October, 2, 1852. Charles was born September 22, 1858. Willie J. was born July 16, 1865.

JOHN SCOTT, JR., was born December 22, 1821, and came to Illinois with his father, as above stated. He married in March, 1852, Mary J. Davidson, who was born in 1830, in Macon county. Of their two children—

Oliver was born November 1, 1858. Rhoda was born April 22, 1862.

LEONARD STEVENS, SR. At this late day, and from the data at hand, it is absolutely impossible to give an accurate account of the ages, deaths, marriages, etc., of this family. It is also impossible to fix, with certainty, when Mr. Stevens came to what now constitutes Macon county. Joseph Stevens, now in his 68th year, and the 7th child of Leonard Stevens, fixes the date of his father's arrival at 1821; but his memory, I find, is quite treacherous, and his general health is very infirm. It is certain, however, that Leonard Stevens was the first settler of the county whose descendants yet remain among us. He was born in Connecticut, it is thought, about the year 1764; perhaps a few years earlier. His wife was Alice Gates, also born in Connecticut, about one year after her husband, and survived him about one year. They were married in Connecticut, and emigrated a short time afterwards to the state of New York, where most, if not all, of their children were born. They emigrated to Illinois, Randolph county, in 1818, and come from there to Macon about the year 1821, as above stated; certainly not later than 1823. Thomas Cowan, one of the commissioners who located the county seat of Macon county, was a member of Mr. Stevens' family, and removed to this county with them, from Randolph county.

BUELL STEVENS, the oldest son, was born in New York, about the year 1796, as he was but 22 when his father came to Illinois in 1818. He died about the year 1836. His first wife was a Manville, the date of whose death we have no means of ascertaining. His second wife was Polly Gray, who died about 1837. His children, by his first wife, were Leonard Stevens, Jr., who was the first white child born within the limits of Macon county; Ira Stevens, Clara Stevens, and Perry Stevens. Those by his second wife were, Dorus, James, Truman C., Hattie, Mary and Elizabeth. Leonard

Stevens, Jr., died in this county, and was buried by Col. E. D. Carter, as coroner; Ira was living in Stephenson county when last heard from; Clara is dead; James died during the late war; Perry was living, when last heard from, near Washington county, in this state; Truman C. lives near Taylorville, Christian county; Hattie married ———— Kelso, near Washington.

KEZIAH STEVENS, the second child of Leonard Stevens, Sr., married a man by the name of Lawrence, before the removal of her father to Macon county, and was never a resident of the county.

LEONARD STEVENS, JR., was born in New York, about the year 1800. He married Hannah Taylor, of Kaskaskia. He was not a resident of Macon county.

AUGUSTUS STEVENS was not a resident of the county. He married, and he and wife both died within about two years of each other; leaving no children. He was buried on Stevens' creek. He was born about 1802.

LUTHER STEVENS was born about 1804, in New York. He married Augusta Sprague, daughter of Abraham Sprague. He moved from Macon county to Missouri about 30 years ago. His children were, Augustus, Luther, John, Lewis, Alice and Elizabeth. He and his wife have been dead for a few years.

DORUS STEVENS was born about the year 1806, in New York, married Nancy Biglaw, as his first wife; then the widow Cooper, near Henkle's, in Sangamon county. The date of his death is not known. His widow is still living. His children were, Perry, Hattie and Mary.

JOSEPH STEVENS, to whom we are indebted for what meagre information we have of the Stevens' family, was born in New York, March 7, 1808. He came to this county with his father, when he was but 13 years old. He married in 1830 to Mary Warnick, daughter of Wm. Warnick, the first sheriff of Macon county. By his first wife he had three children, Francis M., now in Mo.; Wm. Henry, now in this county; and James M., in Kansas. By his last wife he had one child, Cyrus. His first wife died about 1848, and he then married Mrs. Cunningham, whose maiden name was Margaret Sentenay, who was born in Ky., and is still living; she was born about 1816. Mr. S. is now the oldest settler in the county.

HARRIET STEVENS married William Hollenback, and was, when last heard from, living in Stephenson county. Their children's names cannot be given.

JAMES STEVENS was born about 1812, in New York. His second wife's name was Fordice, who died about 1868. He died about three years ago, in Bloomington, Illinois.

ROBERT SMITH, SR., was born in Guilford county, North Carolina, September 11, 1782. His father removed to Tennessee, near Nashville, about the year 1803, and remained there about a year, and removed to Stones River, near Murphreysborough, where he remained until his death, in 1830. Mr. Smith removed to Illinois in 1828, and located in Sangamon county, where he remained until the spring of 1828, when he came to Macon county, where he settled about six miles south-west of Decatur, and died in 1855. His father whose name was also Robert, was engaged in the Revolutionary war, and was taken prisoner in North Carolina. Robert was with Jackson in the battle of New Orleans. His first wife was Elenor Wilson, who died in 1824; he afterwards married Jane Allen, who now lives in Mt. Pleasant, Iowa. His children were— Andrew W., Nancy, Robert, Wm. C. and Margaret; all by his first wife.

ANDREW W. SMITH was born in Rutherford county, Tennessee, November 25th, 1806. He married Elizabeth Blankenship, who died in 1831. He afterwards married Rebecca R. Smith, January 28, 1836; who died in November, 1875. He was a member of the old county commissioners court for several years, and was engaged in the Black Hawk war; he was with the company of rangers that went out from Macon county, towards the head of the Sangamon, in the vicinity of Cheney's Grove. He died in October, 1875, just one month previous to the death of his wife. Of their children—

ELIZABETH M. J. was born March 14, 1832; she married Jos. Trobaugh, and now lives in Texas. ALEXANDER A. was born November 25, 1838; was married to Laura Jacobs, October 7, 1869. He now resides in Wheatland township. ABIGAIL E. was born July, 30, 1840; was married to B. G. Henry; who now lives on the Lewis Ward place. MARGARET A. was born September 5, 1844; was married to Nelson Odor, October 6, 1868; now living in Wheatland township.

WM. C. SMITH was born in Rutherford county, Tennessee, July 5, 1819, moved to this county in 1828, from Sangamon county; married Leacy J. Pope, February 17, 1842, who was born in Wake county, North Carolina, October 25, 1819. Of their children—

JOHN W. was born February 9, 1843; married Mattie J. Weekly, September 1, 1868; now resides in Decatur.

GEORGE R. was born October 2, 1844; died November 17, 1845. WILLIAM B. was born January 5, 1847; married Elizabeth Goff, July 2, 1867; now lives in Wheatland township. ROBERT H. was born November 27, 1849; married Belle Wilson, September 23, 1875; now resides in Blue Mound township. SARAH E. was born February 5, 1852. JAMES M. was born March 20, 1854. DANIEL C. was born March 24, 1857; died September 23, 1857.

PARMENAS SMALLWOOD was born in Virginia, near Charleston, on the 27th of April, 1782; was married to Deborah Brown, in the same state, on the 23d of June, 1807. She was born near Charleston, May 12, 1792, and died November 7, 1873. Parmenas S. died in the month of December, 1851. Of their children—

YAMZEN B. was born May 9, 1808; married to John Murphy, August 1, 1832, who is now living on Salt Creek. Yamzen S. died August 27, 1835. GEORGE D. was born March 31, 1810. JOHN B. was born November 5, 1811; died September 15, 1868. SAMUEL A. was born April 27, 1813, and now lives north of Decatur. JAMES M. was born November 8, 1814; died June, 1852. DANIEL M. was born May 1, 1816; died July 17, 1839. AMELIA A. was born February 17, 1818; married William Bennett, and now resides on Salt Creek, in Dewitt county. ELIZABETH H. was born December 1, 1819; married Walter Roben, in Dewitt county. DOUGLAS B. was born July 6, 1821; died September 25, 1844. SUSAN C. V. was born February 14, 1828; married Emanuel Davis, and now lives near Decatur. PARMENAS A. was born Aug. 31, 1824; now lives in DeWitt county. SARAH J. was born July 27, 1827; died October 5, 1846. JOSEPH P. was born July 10, 1829, and now resides in Decatur. ASBARINAH was born November 27, 1827; died in October, 1831. GIDEON P. was born May 16, 1833; now resides in Dewitt county.

JOHN SMITH was born June 28, 1796, in Rutherford county, Tennessee; where he married Margaret Wilson, who was born at Guilford C. H., North Carolina, July 25, 1801. They removed to Illinois about 1829 or '30, and settled at Mt. Zion, where he died, a few years since, loved and respected by all who knew him. Of their children—

MARY J. was born November 10, 1822; died at 18. GEORGE A. was born April 6, 1825; died July 29, 1873; married Elizabeth Wilson and as second wife Martha Wilson. LOUISA C. was born May 2, 1829; married Rev. J. C. Smith. CANDOR R. was born November 17, 1832; died at 13. NANCY M. was born November 20, 1837; married W. S. Parr.

MRS. L. CATHARINE SMITH was born May 2, 1829, in Windsor county, Tennessee, and married Rev. J. C. Smith, July 22, 1845, who died January 4, 1872. Of their children—

M. R., born April 19, 1848; married Joseph Wood, September 19, 1872. Z. L., born August 16, 1851; died July 11, 1852. A. L. born August 29, 1853. F. A., born April 14, 1855; died June 28, 1858. L. L., born October 13, 1866.

WILLIS STALLINGS was born in October, 1807, in Smith county, Tenn., and came to Macon county in 1832; married in 1830 to Jane Law. Their children are—

JAMES M., who now resides in Atchison, Kansas, THOMAS B. and R. M. HILL, residing in Macon county.

DAVID SMICK was born in 1798, in Lincoln county, Ky.; came to this county from Kentucky in 1834, where he has ever since resided; was married November 5, 1829, to Eliza Ann Ferris, who was born in Kent county, Va., December 6, 1812. Of their children—

EMILY A. was born April 10, 1838; married to Dr. Carr, April 28, 1859, who was born May 13, 1832, in Sussex county, N. J. They are now living in Newburgh, this county. Of their children—

AURA was born May 25, 1860. DAVID E. was born March 22, 1863. CHAS. W. was born September 5, 1865. MARY E. was born November 25, 1867. ROBERT F. was born November 21, 1870. WALTER S. was born July 14, 1874.

MARTHA L. SMICK was born ———. Now living in Decatur. AARON was born December 7, 1840; married to Florence E. Hawkins, who was born in Clinton county, O. They now reside in the city of Decatur. Of their children—

Walter C. was born May 17, 1870. Mabel Clare was born February 12, 1874. ELMER was born October 22, 1876.

HENRY TRAUGHBER January 9, 1803, in Logan county, Ky.; came to Illinois in November, 1825; staid there until 1829; then came to Macon county, and was married to Nancy Smith, who was born in Tennessee, and died in August, 1863. Of their children—

ROBERT S., born September 2, 1830; died February 8, 1863; married Elizabeth Bell. DAVID, born September 2, 1832; died in infancy. A. C., born April 3, 1833; married V. C. Whitehouse. E. M. E., born about 1843; married Wm. Cox; dead. M. J. C. married D. P. During. M. R. died in 1868. CAROLINE married Kitt ———; died in 1874.

REV. DANIEL TRAUGHBER was born in Logan county, Ky., in May, 1800, and came to Illinois in 1837 or '8, and settled on Big Creek, in Mt. Zion township. He married Mary Banks, in Kentucky, by whom he had four children—

ELIZABETH married Robert Lansden, Wilson county, Kansas. GABRELLA married Robert Foster, Wilson county, Kansas. HENRY married in Wilson county, Kansas.

Mr. T. married a second time to Elizabeth Foster, by whom the following children were born—

CYRUS lives at Ottawa, Kansas.

Mr. T. married a third time to Eliza Smalley, by whom the following children were born—

Mary A. married John Edwards; lives in Wilson county, Kan. DANIEL B.; dead. HARRIS lives in Wilson county, Kan.

Mr. T. moved to Fredonia, Kan., in 1872, and now resides there.

JOHN TRAVIS was born in South Carolina in 1768, where he married Rebecca Travis, born in South Carolina in 1777. He died in Wayne county, Illinois, in 1824, and Mrs. T. in Macon county, in 1850. Their children were Allen, Thomas, Finis and Harvey, mentioned below.

ALLEN TRAVIS was born May 18, 1789, in York District, South Carolina. In 1805 his father removed with the family to Livingston county, Ky., where Allen was married, October 5, 1820, to Margaret Campbell, who was born March 5, 1801. They removed to Wayne county, Illinois, perhaps in the spring of 1821, and to Macon county in March, 1829, in company with his brothers Finis and Thomas, James D. Campbell, Andrew and John Davidson. Mrs. Travis died some five or six years ago. Of their children—

JOHN B. was born January 9, 1823, in Wayne county, Illinois. JAMES D. C. was born March 7, 1825, in Wayne county, Illinois. PRESLY A. was born April 24, 1827, in Wayne county, Illinois. REBECCA was born February 24, 1829, in Sangamon county, Ill. WM. H. was born March 30, 1831, in Macon county, Ill. ELIZABETH J. was born May 23, 1834, in Macon county, Ill.; died January 5, 1863. SAMUEL H. was born September 14, 1836, in Macon county, Ill.; died January 9, 1863. ULYSSES D. was born March 5, 1839, in Macon county, Ill.; died April 27, 1863. MARGARET Z. was born February 3, 1841, in Macon county, Illinois. THOMAS C. was born March 23, 1844, in Macon county, Ill.

THOMAS TRAVIS was born in South Carolina, and was married before removing to Illinois, to Sarah Davidson, and settled one and a half miles northwest of Mt. Zion.

FINIS TRAVIS was born in Kentucky, in 1810, in what is now Crittenden county, and was married in 1840 to Nancy J. Foster, who was then the widow of Wm. Foster, maiden name Bell. She died, and he married a second time to Nancy Mahollen. Both are now dead.

HARVEY TRAVIS was born in Wayne county, Illinois, in 1823, and removed with the family to Macon county in 1830. In 1851 he married Elizabeth Cox, who died in 1862, and he married a second time to Harriet M. F. Campbell; now resides in Decatur.

WM. TURPIN was born in Grayson county, Ky., in 1809, and came to Macon county in 1831, and settled on Big Creek.

MATTISON TURPIN was born in 1813, and came to Macon county with his brother William.

EDMUND TURPIN was born in 1811. The two latter brothers are still residents of the county.

JOHN WARD, the father of the Wards who were among the early settlers of Macon county, was born in England, in 1769. He emigrated, when a young, man, to South Carolina, where he married Mary Ward, who was born in Ireland in 1768. They removed thence to Tennessee, near Nashville, and remained a few years, and removed to Logan county, Ky., where Mr. W. died in 1811. Mrs. W. and the family remained in Logan county, Ky., until 1819, and left in October of that year, and removed to within 11 miles of Vandalia, Fayette county, Illinois, where they arrived November 11. They remained in the latter county until 1824, and then removed to what is now Macon county, and settled on the south side of the Sangamon river, and constituted what was known in early days as the "Ward settlement." Of their children—

JERRY WARD was born in South Carolina, January 27, 1788. His wife was Dolly Derrington, whom he married in Logan county, Ky. He removed from Macon county to Missouri, and thence to Texas in 1832, where he died.

JOHN WARD, Jr., was born in South Carolina, in 1790, and married Jane Madol, in Logan county, Ky. They had a very large family of children, 17, perhaps, in all. Mr. W. died in 1831, and is buried at Walnut Grove. Of such of their children as we can obtain the names of—

MARGARET (see Perdue.) MARY died in Fayette county. JOHN, JR., 2d, died in Fayette county. SARAH married Moses Turner; died in the poor house. AARON and JOSEPH, twins; Aaron died in Fayette county; Joseph, dead. LUCINDA married Isaac Miller, and has children living here. NANCY married Nat'l. Murphy; now resides in Missouri. MARTHA died of cholera in 1832.

JAMES WARD was born in South Carolina, in 1792, and was married in Logan county, Ky., to Elizabeth Freeman; removed from Illinois to Missouri, and thence to Texas, where both died. They had six children, none of whom now reside here.

SARAH WARD was born in South Carolina, in 1794. She married Wm. Gambrel, in Logan county, Ky.; removed to Illinois, thence back to Kentucky, thence to Missouri, thence to Texas, where she died.

MARGARET WARD was born in South Carolina, in 1796, and married in Kentucky to Elisha Freeman, who was one of the first county commissioners of this county. They raised a large family of children. Mr. F. died in 1858, and Mrs. F. in 1873. Their children were: Polly, William, James, John, Jerry, Andrew, Thomas, Albert and Henry.

POLLY WARD was born in South Carolina in 1798, and married Wm. Freeman, and now resides in Missouri.

LUCY WARD was born in South Carolina, and came to Illinois in 1819, and married Hiram Reavis. They removed to Missouri in 1832, and now reside in Vernon county.

WILLIAM WARD was born in South Carolina in 1802, and came to Illlinois in 1819, and lived here the remainder of his life. He died, and was the father of Franklin, Hiram and John Ward, who still reside here.

THOMAS WARD was born in 1804, and came to Illinois in 1818; married Elizabeth Widick, daughter of Jacob Widick. They had seven children, most of whom reside in Christian county, where Mr. and Mrs. W. died.

NANCY WARD was born in 1806, and married Lambert S. Bearden, at Vandalia, Illinois, and moved to Macon county in 1823, and removed to Missouri in 1832, where their children now reside.

LEWIS B. WARD was born in Logan county, Ky., January 17, 1809, and removed to Illinois in 1819, and to Macon county in 1824. On the 23d of December, 1830, he married Elizabeth Walker, who was born September 8, 1813, in Rutherford county, Tenn., and became a resident of Macon county in 1829; died June 7, 1852. Of their children—

ALFRED was born October 16, 1831. MARY J. was born November 18, 1833; married S. B. N. Vaughan. ELIZABETH was born March 13, 1836; married Woodson Parker. ROBERT was born June 13, 1838. CAROLINE was born November 14, 1840;

married J. B. Moore. HARRIET was born November 26, 1844. REBECCA was born November 29, 1846. LEWIS J. was born February 26, 1848. NANCY A. was born May 15, 1852; died September 28, 1853.

Mr. Ward was married a second time to Matilda Parker, who was born August 14, 1832. He sold his farm in Macon county in the fall of 1876, and removed to Girard, Kansas, prior to which he was the second settler, in point of arrival, residing in the county. From him we derived most of our information in reference to the Ward family and Ward settlement. He fixes the dates of the erection of the first houses in the county in the following order: 1st, William Downing's, south of Sangamon; 2d, Leonard Stevens', on Stevens' creek; 3d, Abraham Sprague's, just south of fair-ground; 4th, Hubble Sprague's, on the inside of the present fair-ground inclosure; 5th, William King's, a short distance south of the fair-grounds. Mr. Ward says the first mill in Macon county was on Stevens' creek, and was built by William King in 1826, which was afterwards owned by and known as Renshaw's mill; also, that the first house in the limits of the old town of Decatur was just north of Priest's Hotel, and was built by Reuben Miller, who sold out to James Renshaw, in which the first store was kept. He also states that the first school house in the county was on the old Widick place, now owned by P. M. Wickoff, three and a half miles southwest of Decatur, and was erected in 1825, and the first school teacher was "Frozen" Taylor; and that the second school house was on land now owned by W. C. Smith, erected in 1828, in which one Nelson, "a little Yankee," taught. At this school house Abraham Lincoln went to singings and spellings. In the spring of 1826 Mr. W. raised 1,800 pounds of cotton in Macon county.

HIRAM WARD was born in Macon county, Illinois, January 28, 1837; was married to Clara E. Odor, March 11, 1858, who was born in Garrard county, Kentucky, January 7, 1843, and came to this county in 1850. Of their children—

LAVENA E. was born June 20, 1860, and died July 24, 1861. HATTIE BELL was born March 10, 1863, and died July 30, 1864. LAURA A. was born December 27, 1864. EVA MAY was born May 17, 1867. FRANK NELSON was born February 7, 1869. MIR-tie LUELLA was born April 6, 1871; died August 30, 1872. Infant son was born December 29, 1872; died January 16, '73. SARAH ELIZABETH was born February 8, 1874.

ROBERT WILSON was born October 4, 1779, in Mecklenburg county, North Carolina, and moved to Murray county, Tenn., when about 18 years old. He moved thence to Wilson county, Tenn., where he married JANE DONALD, who died in 1829. Of their seven children—

THOMAS F. was born July 26, 1813; died August 29, '35. MARY B. was born June 14, 1815; died August 17, '39. NANCY E. was born September 28, 1817; died April 6, '34. SARAH G. was born November 1, 1819; died November 1, '52. WILLIAM A. was born August 22, 1822. MARTHA J. was born June 10, 1825; died ——, 1850. CYNTHA E, was born July 9, 1828; died ——, 1846.

Mr. Wilson's second wife was Mrs. Sallie Hodge, widow of Joseph H. Hodge, and who was born April 26, 1792, in Orange county, North Carolina. By her first husband the following children were born:—

Henry J. Hodge, born March 11, 1813; died August 30, 1838; married P. Traughber. Talitha J. Hodge, born December 9, 1814; married N. N. Baker. Arraanna H., born June 25, 1816; married J. M. Baker. Margaret C., born February 1, 1819; died —, 1864; married John Hanson. Joseph J., born February 10, 1822; died September 7, 1872; married M. A. Ferriss. Eli L., born October 24, 1824; died March 26, 1849.

After the marriage of Mr. Wilson and Mrs. Hodge, in 1829, they removed to Sangamon county, Illinois, and came to Macon county in 1830, where Mr. W. died, March 4, 1873, and Mrs. W. January 20, 1872. By the last marriage there were three children—

ROBERT D. was born October 18, 1830; married Mary Outten. SARAH A. was born January 5, 1833; married John H. Davidson. JAMES A. was born September 5, 1835; married Sarah Jones.

D. K. WILSON was born March 27, 1825, in Rutherford county, Tennessee; came to Macon county in 1835, and was married to Mary J. Dickey, February 25, 1845, who was born July 31, 1827, in Florence, Alabama, and came to Macon county in 1829. Of their children—

SAMUEL was born April 17, 1846; was married to Eveline Dresback in September, 1868, and died January, 1877. MARGARET C. was born December 17, 1847; was married to S. B. Betz in March, 1869. ELIZA J. was born October 8, 1849; died April 16, 1866. ANDREW was born September 1, 1851; was married to Ella Bundy April 13, 1875, who was born April 26, 1859, in Piqua county, Ohio; came to this county in 1875, and died December 15, 1876. SARAH A. was born October 25, 1852; was married to R. J. Ross December 9, 1874. MARY E. was born January 17, 1858; was married to Marian Ranabarger, February 27, 1876. ZARITHA M. was born December 3, 1859. WILLIAM A. was born December 8, 1862. JOHN W. was born April 27, 1865; died September 17, '67. GEORGE W. was born July 28, 1868.

BENJAMIN WILSON was among the early and prominent citizens of Macon county, and came here in 1827, and was one of the county commissioners who assisted in the county organization. He held the position for a great many years. He was born at Guilford Court House, in North Carolina, and removed thence to Tennessee, and afterwards to Illinois. He married JANE WARNICK in the state of Tennessee, who was a sister of "Uncle Billy" Warnick, the first sheriff of the county. Their children were, Polly, (see Sanders,) Rachel, (see Hill,) Peggy Smith, (see John Smith,) Robert, Nancy, Hannah, (see Blankenship,) and—

JOHN WILSON was born in Rutherford county, Tennessee, in 1813, came to Illinois in 1828, and was married to Nancy Wilson, March 1, 1832, who was born July 6, 1813, in Greene county, Tennessee, and became a resident of Macon county about 1830. Of their Children—

BENJAMIN T. was born August 19, 1836; died February 5, 1854. MARY A. was born October 23, 1833, and married JOSEPH M. DAWSON, who was born April 5, 1828. Of their children—

John A. was born July 8, 1853. Thomas M. was born April 6, 1855. Nancy A. was born January 19, 1857; died December 29, 1857. Luella B. was born August 4, 1859. C. E. was born January 18, 1863. Edwin P. was born December 17, 1864. Oscar W. was born April 26, 1867.

ANDREW WILSON was born March 3, 1785, and was married to MARY ANN WILSON, who was born January 30, 1788.

They removed from East Tennessee to Macon county about 1830. Mr. W. died August 10, '44, and Mrs. W. September 17, '72. Of their children—

THOMAS B. was born July 26, 1807; died July, '73. ALEXANDER M. was born May 6, 1809. ELIZA D. was born April 15, 1811; died September 13, '15. KATHARINE was born ―――― 21, 1816; died January 7, '55. JOHN A. was born January 9, 1819; died December 18, '21. JAMES J. was born November 12, 1822; died April 28, '54.

WILLIAM WHEELER, SR., was born in Virginia about 1790, and married ELIZABETH HAYS, who was born in the same State. Mrs. W. died about 1836, and Mr. W. in 1866. Their children were, James, Stacy, Henry, William, jr., Elizabeth, Raliegh, Burton, Larkin and Nathaniel. Mr. Wheeler and family removed to Illinois and settled in Macon county, in 1828.

JAMES WHEELER was born in South Carolina in 1799, and died in 1867. His wife was Margaret Mayberry.

STACY WHEELER was born about 1800, and married William Christopher, and died about 1831.

HENRY WHEELER was born in 1801, in Tennessee, and was married in Tennessee to Mary Y. Braden, who was born January 4, 1800. Of their five children—

Elizabeth E. was born May 7, 1826; married David Brett; died 1864. Samuel R. was born August 16, 1827; married Jamima Abrams, who was born in 1828, in Illinois. William E. was born October 23, 1828; married Ellen Frazee; he died 1875. Nancy J. was born January 9, 1830; married Samuel Woodward, first husband; Mason Packard, second husband; now resides in California. Andrew J. was born January 16, 1832; married N. E. Cox, who was born in Scott county, Illinois, 1837.

WILLIAM WHEELER, JR., was born on the 28th of Dec., 1809, in Rutherford county, Tennessee; was married Oct 27, 1831, to Sarah A. Ward, (daughter of Jerry Ward,) who died in August, 1869. Mr. Wheeler has been prominently connected with the affairs of the county, and has been repeatedly elected sheriff, assessor and collector. Of their 10 children, but two are living, viz:—

Mary E., who married Thomas Inscho, now resides in San Jose, California; and Lewis Cass. Andrew M. died in '69; Calvin R.

died in '61; Lucinda K. died in '63; William L. died in '66; Henrietta died in '62; James C. died in '51; Thomas B. died in infancy, and Alice died in 1874.

ELIZABETH WHEELER was born in 1811, and married William Ward, the father of Franklin and Hiram Ward, well known in the county.

RALEIGH WHEELER was born in 1813, and died in 1834; his first wife was Rebecca Travis, and second Mary Fields.

BURTON WHEELER was born in 1815, and resides in Moultrie county, Illinois.

LARKIN WHEELER was born in 1817; died in 1838.

NATHANIEL WHEELER was born in 1819; died when young.

IRA WARNICK was born in Tennessee, August 7, 1823; he moved to this county in 1825, and settled at the place afterwards known as the William Warnick place, and has ever since resided in this county; was married to Julietta Priscila Burke, April 17, 1843, who was born in Kentucky, June 30, 1822, and came to this county in 1840. Of their nine children all of which are now living—

JAMES W. was born April 11, 1844, and married Ann E. Stevens, September 14, 1869. ELIZABETH E. was born May 10, 1846; and married Edward Hill. ARTHUSA D. was born August 6, 1848. THOMAS T. was born December 30, 1851, and was married to Mary E. Lynch, in February, 1874. NANCY C. was born February 18, 1853, and married S. P. Falconer, September 18, 1873. MAJOR M. was born March 13, 1855. HENRIETTE L. was born December 10, 1857. JULIETTA A. was born September 27, 1860. IRA G. was born March 7, 1864.

WM. WARNICK, was born in 1784, in North Carolina, and married ———, who was born the same year. He removed from North Carolina to Rutherford county, Tennessee, and thence to this county, in 1825. He was the first sheriff of Macon county after its organization, and held the office from 1829 to 1835, and was also re-elected again for two years, in 1840. He was in the Black Hawk war, and participated in the famous Stillman's defeat, where he received a slight flesh wound. He was also captain of the rangers, during the same difficulty. It was Mr. W.

who, as sheriff of the county, whipped Redmon and Wyatt, by order of the court, giving them 39 lashes apiece. This was the only punishment of the kind ever inflicted in the county. Mr. W's father, James Warnick, was from Ireland, landing in New Castle, August 15, 1758. Their children were—
JOHN, MARGARET, POLLY (first wife of Joseph Stevens), JAS., LUCINDA, BETSY (married John Taylor), CLARK, IRA, ROBERT, SARAH (married Benj. Taylor; now dead.) Mr. W. died February 12, 1855.

LAVINA WILLIAMS, daughter of J. D. Long, was born December 26, 1826, and married JACKSON WILLIAMS, who was born December 4, 1826. Of their children—
LAFAYETTE was born July 17, 1852; died 1873. JEROME was born August 21, 1854; died 1856. WALTER L. was born February 26, 1856. LAURA M. was born September 12, 1857. JOSEPH W. was born November 6, 1859. MARY C. was born May 11, 1861. EDWARD was born August 25, 1864. JASPER was born January 2, 1867. EFFIE was born March 12, 1869.

EMANUEL WIDICK was born February 2, 1806, in Tennessee, and came to Illinois and settled in Macon county, in 1826. He married Sarah A. Cox, who was born May 23, 1811. Mr. W. died March 4, 1863, and Mrs. W. died December 10, 1863. Of their children—
ALBERT was born September 3, 1835. WILLIAM was born August 8, 1837; died March 1, 1845. MARGARET C. was born May 5, 1838; died November 2, 1853. JOHN was born February 2, 1840. ANDREW was born March 27, 1842. EPHRIAM was born ———, 1844. MARY A. E. was born May 6. 1847. ELIZA J. and AARON were born April 21, 1850.

JOHN WIDICK was born in Rockingham county, Virginia, and removed to Macon county, in 1826. He married Cohorine Traughber; but what was the date of the births and deaths of each we cannot ascertain. Mrs. W. died perhaps, about November 1, 1832. Their children were—
WILLIAM, MARGARET (See McDaniel), EMANUEL (dead), MICHAEL, ELIZABETH (married Lemuel Walker), RIAL (of Homer, Iowa), AARON (dead), ELI (Saxton Station, Mo.), EDMUND (Moultrie county), HENRY and JOSIAH.

HENRY WIDICK was born September 30, 1828, in Macon county, and was married to Elizabeth Mathews, October 30, 1850, who was born May 2, 1833. Of their children—
Wm. H., born July 14, 1852. Sarah E., born June 8, 1854. Laura E., born August 9, 1856. Arminda E., born August 4, 1859. Lavena A., born October 12, 1863. Ida M., born July 29, 1867. George C., born August 23, 1872; died September 7, 1874.

SAMUEL, JACOB, GEORGE and JOSEPH WIDICK were all brothers of John Widick, above mentioned, and removed to this county in 1825, at least the former and latter did. Joseph settled at the old Caulk place, recently purchased by P. M. Wykoff, Samuel on the old Wm. Young place and Jacob the place where Robert H. Smith now resides. Joseph was accidentally killed by falling on a pitchfork, and Samuel died at Jefferson Barracks, during the late war.

NOTE.—The following were omitted in their proper places in this chapter.

HENRY PRATHER was born November 26, 1802, in Montgomery county, Maryland, and removed to this state in 1836, and settled in Macoupin county. His first wife was a Miss Ratcliff, whom he married before leaving Maryland, who died in Macoupin county. He came to Macon county in 1837, and in 1838 married *Amanda Oglesby, who still resides in Decatur. He was killed accidently by being thrown from a buggy in 1869. He was an honest, upright citizen, prominently connected with all the public enterprises tending to advance the interests of Macon county and the city of Decatur. He was public spirited, and nothing calculated to advance the material prosperity of the city or county escaped his earnest solicitation and support in both means and influence. He was a member of the legislature in 1852. He left no children. A fond recollection in the hearts of the people with whom he associated will last during their lives.

DAVID FLORY was born in 1803, in Virginia. Came to Illinois in 1825, and settled in what is now Macon county. Came

* See Oglesby.

with Draper, P. D. Williams and Epperson. Was married to ISABELLA WRIGHT, who was born in Virginia. One child was born of this marriage—JEROME, who was born in 1838, now resides in Macon county. Was married a second time to RACHAEL RITTENHOUSE, who was born in 1826. Of their children— J. W. was born in 1850. MELLISSA J. was born in 1858. FRANKLIN was born in 1862.

ERRATA.

On page 26, line 6, read 12 for " 8."
" " 26, read Leonard for " Buel " Stevens.
" " 31, Note, read 46 for " 36."
" " 50, last line but one, read 1834 *to* '40.
" " 57, 2d line, read 1863 for " 1853."
" " 92, for " Sam'l A. McDonald, deserted," read, discharged on account of sickness.
" " 171, for " which they have all accomplished," read, what they have all accomplished.
" " 182, for " Old School or Presbyterian," read, Old School or Predestinarian.
" " 240, read, these for " them," and them for " these," in the line following.
" " 241, for " set " at these desks, read, sit, &c.
" " 244, for S. P. " Mickey," read, S. P. Nickey.
" " 285 ¶ 3, for James " M," read, James W.

INDEX.

A
	PAGE.
Austin, B. R.	55-246
Austin, Wm. A.	246
Austin, Jesse	247
Allen, S. C.	55-248
Agriculture	211
Argenta	232
Abrams, Josiah	247
Allen, D. L.	247

B
Board of Supervisors	37
Biographies of County officers	49
Benedict, K.	49-50-250
Bear, John W.	53
Boyd, Wm. M.	55
Buckingham	56
Bunn, D. L	56
Barnes, W. A.	57
Brown, J. A.	57
Black Hawk	58
Black Hawk War	38
Black Hawk War, Enlistments in	59
Baker, E. D	61
Baptist Church	181
Baptist, Separate	181
Baptist, Predestinarian	182
Boyd, Haskell & Co.	199
Blue Mound	231
Boody	232
Bell, Alexander	248
Braden, Samuel	248
Braden, J. T.	249
Blankenship, John L.	249
Baker, Newton	249
Baker, Wm. D.	250
Baker, James M	250
Brett, Richard	251
Barnwell, David	251
Burke, Micajah	252

C
Crozat, M.	13
Company of West	13
Company Royal of I.	13
Crittenden, John and Wm	14
Columbia's Review	16
County Seat	22

	PAGE.
Clinton	29
County Officers	35
County Commissioners' Court	35-36
County Court	36
County Clerks	45-52
County Treasurers	45
Circuit Judges	43
Circuit Clerks	45-50
Circuit Courts	47
Court Days,	166
Cantrall, Wm	55-252
Curtis, Ira B	55-254
Cavalry, 7th Ill	64
Cavalry, 7th Ill., Enlistments in	67
Characteristics of Early Settlers.	154
Churches	171
Circuit Rider	174
Cumberland P. Church	178
Christian Church	179
Church of God	182
Catholic Church	183
Chambers, Behring & Co	198
Cox, Ephraim	252
Cox, Wm	254
Crissey, W. S	253
Carter, E. D.	253
Campbell, J. D	253
Caulk, Jacob	254

D

Decatur laid out	23
Decatur, County Seat	22
Decatur, first sale of lots	23
Decatur Public Library	187
Decatur Furniture Company	191
Decatur Bagging Company	193
Decatur, City of	216
Decatur, Stephen	216
Decatur, first Buildings in	220
Decatur, Trustees of	221
Decatur City Council	222
Davis, D.	55-255
Deep Snow	144
Deer Huntings	165
DeWitt County, Settlement of	28
Dickey, Wm., Sr	255
Dickey, John	256
Dickey, William, Jr.	256
Dickey, Alexander	256
Dickey, Harvey	256
Dickey, David	256
Davidson, Samuel	257

E

Emmerson, Charles	49-50-258
Elwood & Co.	203
Edward, James	257

INDEX.

F
	PAGE.
Forstmeyer, M	54
Fox Hunting	165
Ferris & Emmons	203
Fire Department	226
Forsyth	232
Falconer	261
Flory	297

G
Grand Jury, 1st, 2d	47
Green, S. L.	50
Gorin, H. M.	50
Goodman, George	53
Good Templars	187
Greenfield, Bell & Co	202
Gorin	261

H
Hennepin	12
Hammer, W. L.	51
Hale, E. B.	52
Hostetler, Joseph	55
High Water	153
Hard Trials	157
House-Raisings	166
Haworth & Sons	195
Hill, H. W. & Co	197
Harpstrite & Schlandeman	202
Harristown	232
Hostetler	261
Herrell, James	262
Hanks, John	262
Howell	262
Hefton	263
Hamilton, Andrew	264
Huston, W.	264
Hornback	265

I
Illinois, Discovery of	11
Illinois, Government of	13
Illinois, Settlement of	12
Infantry, 8 Ill	71
Infantry, 8 Ill, Roster	72, 73
Infantry, 8 Ill., Enlistments in	74
Infantry, 8 Ill	Co. A. 74, Co. B. 76
Infantry, 21 Ill., Roster	80
Infantry, 21 Ill., Enlistments	Co. A 82, Co. K 84
Infantry, 35 Ill.,	84, Co. A 86
Infantry. 41 Ill.,	Roster 87, Co. A 88, Co. B 92, Co. E 93, Co. F 96, Co. H 97, Co. I 67
Infantry, 68 Ill	Roster 99, Co. H 100
Infantry, 115 Ill	103, Roster 105, Co. A 106, Co. E 106, Co. F 108, Co. H 109, Co. K 110
Infantry, 116 Ill	110, Roster 113, Co. A 114, Co. B 118, Co. C 121, Co. D 125, Co. E 129
Infantry, 116 Ill	Co. F 133, Co. G 133, Co. H 136, Co. I 137, Co. K 140
Indians	10

J

Joliett, M. ...11
Judge of Circuit Court ...43
Judge of County Court ...43, 49
Judge Probate Court ...43
Jones, John E ...54
Jennings, J. D. ...54
Johnson, James ...55
Johnson, John ...265

K

Kramer & McClelland ...250
King, Dr. ...265

L

Laswell ...12
License ...24
Loeb, Peter ...200
Laymons ...266
Lapham ...266
Law ...267
Lowry ...267
Lincoln ...279

M

Memorial Lines ...8
Marquette ...11, 13
Macon, Nath ...17
Masters in Chancery ...43
McCall, D ...49
McClellan, E ...52, 53
McMennamy, Jno ...53, 269
Murray, A. A ...
Miller, John ...55
McComas, C. C ...56
Mexican War ...61
Mexican War, Enlistments in ...61
Meteorological ...147
M. E. Church ...175
Masonic Organizations ...184
Manufactories ...189
Macon County, Organization ...17
Macon County, Act to Establish ...18
Macon County, Boundaries ...21
Macon County—General Remarks ...24
Macon County, Its Settlement ...26
Mails ...167
Mueller, H. & Co. ...200
Maroa ...227
Macon, City of ...229
Mt. Zion ...232
Morris, Cornelius ...253
McDaniel ...276-269
Miller ...268
Muirhead ...269
McKinley ...270
Montgomery ...270
Myers ...270

INDEX.

N
Navigation of Sangamon..164
Niantic...231
Nelms...272

O
Odor, J. Q. A...51
Oglesby, W. W...52
Oglesby, R. J..272
Odd Fellows Organizations..185
Oreana...232
Oakley...

P
Piatt County, Settlement of...27
Prather, Wm..50-51
Prather, Henry...297
Peddicord, N. W..51-274
Peddicord, J. J...274
Powers, Geo..55-267
Pugh, I. C..55, 35, 57, 59, 275
Parks, R. H..56
Pioneer Preacher..172
Pioneer Circuit Rider...172
Presbyterian Church..176
Presbyterian Cumberland Church..178
Protestant Episcopal...183
Priest & Co. Geo..202
Purdeu..273
Pound..274
Pope..274
Post...275

R
Read, T. H..50-55-276
Ricketts, John..50
Rea, Samuel...52-53-277
Rea, James...277
Renshaw, James..55-277
Retrospect, a..161
Roberts, Lyttle & Co...146
Railroads, 204; Wabash, 206; Illinois Central, 207; D. & E. St. Louis, 209; D. & St. L., 209;
    P., Q. & D., 209; D. M. C., 210; D., S. & M., 210; Q. M., 210; I., D. & S, 210
Rose...277
Robinson..278
Rucker..278

S
Slavery in Illinois..13
St. Clair, A..14
Settlements of County, When Made..29
Settlements of County, How Retarded................................30-31-32
Supervisors' Courts...37
State's Attorney..43
Sheriffs...45
Spear, John G...50
Stevens, Jas..53
Stevens, Jos..55

	PAGE.
Snyder, H	55
Sudden Freeze and Change	146
Sangamon Navigation	164
Stages	169
Sawyer, W. & B	198
Shellaboyer, D. S. & Co	201
Sangamon	232
Schools	233
School Teacher, Ye Olde	234
School Houses	240
School Statistics	244
Sanders	278
Spangler	280
Scott	281
Stevens	282
Smith	284–286
Smallwood	285
Stallings	286
Smick	286

T

Tonti, M	13
Todd, John	14
Taxation, Rate of in 1829	24
Tavern Rates in 1829	24
Travis, Jas	54–287
Thompson, M. B	56
Tait	281
Traughber	287
Turpin	288

U

United Bretheren Church	180
Universalist Church	182
Union Iron Works	192

W

Waggoner, W. W	53
Warnick, Wm	53–295
Wheeler, Wm	63–294
Whitehouse, S. M	53
Wood, G. M	54
War, Black Hawk	58
War, Mexican	61
War, Late	64
Water, High	153
Wayne Bros	201
Water Works	225
Warrensburg	232
Wheatland	232
Ward	289-290-291
Wilson	292–293
Williams	296
Widick	296–297

www.ingramcontent.com/pod-product-compliance
Lightning Source LLC
Chambersburg PA
CBHW050432240426
43661CB00055B/2351